UNDERSTANDING SUICIDE

Lucy Costigan & Anthony E. Walsh

Understanding Suicide

EXPOSING THE WORLD OF PAIN
WITHIN THE SUICIDE BOX

CURRACH
PRESS

www.thesuicidebox.com

First published in 2015 by
CURRACH PRESS
55A Spruce Avenue,
Stillorgan Industrial Park,
Blackrock, Co. Dublin

Cover design by Helene Pertl/Currach Press
Cover images from the Biodiversity Heritage Library. Digitised by Smithsonian
Libraries and Cornell University Library | www.biodiversitylibrary.org; William
C. Hewitson, *Illustrations of New Species of Exotic Butterflies Vol 01*; Jan Sepp,
Surinaamsche Vlinders; William Lewin, *The Papilios of Great Britain*.
Origination by Currach Press
Printed in Ireland by SPRINT-Print Ltd

ISBN 978 1 78218 842 1

To those who live and grapple with the emotional pain of feeling pressured and inauthentic because of life experiences that caused trauma or a loss of self-love. To all families who suffered the overwhelming loss of a loved one who died by suicide. To those who could no longer withstand the pain and mistakenly saw the world as being better off without them. To you, the reader, that you will embrace and empathise with what this book espouses and join us on this road less travelled. May you all find some understanding, comfort and hope within these pages.

Foreword

I welcome this publication, which contributes to the debate about suicide. This debate is important to obtain an understanding of the complexities around suicide and the complexity of the decision to take one's life.

The journey to suicide is multifaceted. It is influenced by several interacting factors – social, personal, psychological, cultural, biological, environmental and spiritual. The World Health Organisation (2014) in its recent report 'Preventing Suicide: A Global Imperative' highlights the need to have strategies to target vulnerable groups. These groups include refugees, and migrants, persons bereaved by suicide, the homeless, prisoners, lesbian, gay, bisexual and transgender people, etc. Those who are victims of sexual violence and child sexual abuse are especially vulnerable. What causes suicide? Is it because of poverty, unemployment, breakdown of relationships, or depression or other mental disorders, an impulsive act or is it due to the disinhibiting effects of alcohol or drugs? I feel that this book may help us all develop a broader understanding of what causes suicide.

Stigma surrounding mental disorders and suicide means many people are prevented from seeking help. Stigma is one of the most pervasive barriers to seeking help for mental health problems and suicide ideation. It leads to people avoiding living, socialising, working, renting or obtaining employment. It causes low self-esteem, a sense of isolation and hopelessness.

The stigma that surrounds mental, psychological and emotional ill-health must be removed. Raising community awareness and breaking down taboos and stigma are important means of making efforts to prevent suicide.

There are many misconceptions surrounding incidents of suicide. One of the harshest realities for the bereaved family left behind is the admission that their loved one found life too painful and came to the conclusion that suicide was the only way out. But there should be no denying the fact of the death. We need to call it what it is: suicide. Yet in this current publication, suicide is viewed as the extremity of human pain, and we are reminded that we are all united in experiencing pain.

Those who die by suicide do not want to die, but they just cannot bear to live in the incredible pain that they feel. It is very important for people to hear this message. People who die by suicide want to live as much as anyone else, but living becomes too painful.

Who is responsible for suicide prevention? While the responsibility for leadership lies with the state, civil society organisations and the general population can play a key role in reducing suicide and deliberate self-harm. Community organisations and other local services like the police, citizens information personnel, addiction counsellors, clergy, representatives of sporting organisations, teachers, parents, the suicide bereaved and members of the public all have a key role to play in reducing suicide. I sincerely welcome this book and congratulate Anthony Walsh and Lucy Costigan on their contribution to this important social health issue.

Dan Neville TD
President, Irish Association of Suicidology

Preface

Anthony's Story

Directly and indirectly I have been involved in twenty-eight suicides. I have spoken with many people who were contemplating suicide or had attempted suicide. One event in particular stands out. It was during the time I worked in the prison service. It was night-time and for some inexplicable reason I was drawn to look in on one particular inmate. I walked up the landing and peered into Martin's cell. I witnessed what appeared to be Martin's last movements. I unlocked the door and rushed into the cell, encircled Martin's legs and lifted him upwards while shouting for help. I later heard that it had been touch and go but that Martin had pulled through. Many years later as I was strolling along a street in Dublin I met Martin as he walked beside his partner who was wheeling their lovely young daughter. He asked if I'd have coffee with him while his wife went shopping. We chatted about many things, including his work that he really seemed to enjoy and his family that he obviously adored. One thing I'll always remember that he said: 'If you hadn't found me that night, none of this would have ever happened. Even my little daughter wouldn't be here now.' His little girl sat happily playing with her toy completely oblivious of her miraculous existence.

My work with Living Links has brought me into direct contact with many families who have been bereaved by suicide. In every single situation, the families bereaved by suicide are devastated by their loss. In contrast to the distorted belief of those who attempt or complete suicide, there is always desolation, confusion and complicated grieving following a suicide. These and many other life experiences have raised my awareness of suicide and has brought me to try to contribute, at least, to reducing the unnecessary human pain that we consciously or unconsciously facilitate.

Lucy's Story
The single event that brought the reality of suicide to my front door happened when I was seventeen. My best friend tried to kill himself one autumn night. Such was the stigma around suicide that his parents told no one, not even his older siblings. He was hospitalised for a few days without visitors. Everyone thought he'd had a car accident. It was only later that he confided in me what he'd attempted that night, and the stranger who had saved his life by happening upon his car in the middle of a forest and driving him to hospital. I felt devastated and shocked to the core; guilt and anger mingled with the sheer relief that he was still here, still sitting beside me. I couldn't understand why he'd attempted such an extreme act. To me he was a hero, super intelligent, original, incredibly talented, witty and utterly lovable. Yet in his eyes he was a failure, not having reached his potential, feeling rudderless and not belonging anywhere. He confided that he felt numb inside. He'd never been allowed to express his true feelings so he'd tried to bury everything. In school he had been ruthlessly criticised and physically punished for his defiant and rebellious spirit. At that time I had little understanding of how the mind or emotions work. During the weeks and months following my friend's suicide attempt I fretted that he might try to take his life again. I worried that I couldn't stop him if he really chose to end his life. I was one of the lucky ones because I did get to see my friend grow and flourish, to discover

ways of dealing with the world when storms battered his bow and bent his sails, as they inevitably do in all our lives.

It was this event more than any other that set me on a lifelong quest to understand our rich yet complex emotional lives, the nature of the mind that seems to drive our behaviours, and that wise, intelligent core that can offer great clarity around problems and situations if only we can access it. I volunteered for a few years with the Samaritans and became immersed in their open and non-judgemental ethos, learning to listen to those who were depressed, lonely or suicidal. Later I became a counsellor and psychotherapist. It was then that I met deeply courageous men and women who felt suicidal or who had already tried to take their own lives but had chosen to burrow deeply within themselves, to discover the roots of their deep pain, anguish and lack of self-value, and to begin to build a new foundation based on inquiry, awareness and self-care.

Why Write this Book?
This book has been written for the general reader and is filled with stories and insights by real people about many aspects of society's dysfunction. Throughout the book we use the concept of the Suicide Box to represent society's warped and limited view of the full spectrum of human pain that includes suicide. This view, that also curtails individual expression, has been fostered throughout history by various social institutions including politics, religions, the law, education, work, mental health, the family and the media.

Suicide is the most extreme manifestation of pain that a human being can ever express. But what is the underlying motivation for such an act? Although there may be as many reasons as there are suicides, many causes lie deep within society's beliefs and practices that are reflected and personified within the Suicide Box. The source of much personal pain and alienation can be found by posing the following questions: How can I really be true to myself and still be accepted by society? When can I speak openly about who I am and the way I really want to live – as long as I intend no harm to anyone, and only desire the chance to explore my uniqueness? When individuals feel that they have to hide their true identity because of a personal fear or a belief that they don't fit into society, suicide may become an option to take away the pain of social exclusion or isolation.

This book is divided into four parts. Part One: Making the Suicide Box Visible describes the Suicide Box that is fear-based, steeped in myths and stigma. It explores why explanations for suicide almost exclusively focus on the individual while society's flaws and failings remain largely hidden. Part Two: Understanding Its Construction examines how social structures have contributed to suicide over time, through damaging practices and a gross lack of awareness. Part Three: Dismantling Its Structure highlights crucial elements within the Suicide Box that need to be dismantled and transformed in order for positive social change to take place. Part Four: Towards a New Perspective outlines a blueprint for education, familial and social interactions, where the importance of emotional expression and the embracing of human diversity in all its forms is championed.

It is our sincere wish that this book will shine a new light and bring a real shift in the understanding, prevention and treatment of a wide spectrum of self-harming behaviours, including suicide. Most of all, we want this book to awaken society's institutions to the enormous part that each plays in the formation and development of the human heart, mind and soul. We also hope to demystify and dilute the phenomenon of suicide so that all of us can adopt a more courageous and informed perspective around it. As participants in society, our friends, family and the wider community sustain each of us. It is the responsibility of every person to free themselves from the stereotypes, stigmas and intolerance that block and hamper true expression, that so often prevent us from loving and living fully and gloriously. More than anything, we wish that each one of us can push up the lid and step outside of the Suicide Box, to watch it fall away and dissolve, to feel that sense of freedom and innate power that is our inheritance.

Lucy Costigan and Anthony E. Walsh
24 February 2015

Acknowledgements

An enormous thank you to the Costigan, Cullen and Walsh families for all your love and support during the writing of this book, and for the many discussions we had that were so helpful and inspiring. Thanks also to Michael Cullen for his wonderful work on the accompanying website to this book: www.thesuicidebox.com. A very special thank you to all our contributors. This book could not have been written without you, as the sharing of your stories and experiences has added depth and life to all other aspects of the text. We believe the pain you shared and the resilience you showed will give hope and empower others who are suffering on their journey. A heartfelt thank you to Dr Fergus Heffernan, Dan Neville TD, Mayor of Wexford George Lawlor, Kay Quinn, Denise Hewitt and Rose Tully for the informative and thought-provoking interviews that really got to the core of what real change in our thinking and awareness can mean for society and for each individual.

Contents

Part Three: Dismantling Its Structure

Part Four: Towards a New Perspective

PART ONE

Making the Suicide Box Visible

CHAPTER ONE

Introduction

You may be holding this book in your hands for many reasons. You may have lost a loved one through suicide. You may be depressed; you may be in despair, feeling hopeless and alone. You may be a carer, a volunteer or a professional who supports those in deep emotional pain. You may be at a loss to understand why a person ends his or her life. Whatever the reason, this book is in your hands, and the whole world of suicide and unnecessary human pain is about to be laid bare. All that has previously been hidden is coming into sharp focus. The Suicide Box – the cause of so much pain – is about to be revealed.

Seán's Story: Four Versions
To illustrate the whole meaning of the Suicide Box concept, let's take a look at the life story of one fictitious male named Seán. Seán may be a fictional character but the features of his story are of real people who died by suicide. The story is told from four different perspectives. Three of these are stories that come from life within the Suicide Box. The first is society's version of events. The second is from the perspective of family, friends and colleagues. The third is Sean's private experience of his own life. The fourth is a version of the story from outside the Suicide Box. It is based on the New Perspective proposed in this book, adopting features that emerge following the dismantling of the social structures identified that facilitate suicide.

1) Society's version of Seán's life from within the Suicide Box
To be fair to children it is necessary to channel their lives in directions that will maximise their potential in what society has to offer them. Boys and girls have very different needs. As girls are more emotional and not as strong physically, it is clearly better if they are guided in ways that prepare them for life experiences appropriate to their biology and abilities to become worthwhile citizens. Similarly, boys need to be prepared for the male experience. These strong societal values are reflected in our families and throughout our media. Seán's father believed that children, especially boys, need to be toughened up and part of this process is the rough and tumble play all children partake in with their siblings and other children. Seán had heard him say this often. His mother had lovingly told him that 'big boys don't cry'. Like all other children in the state Seán was given the necessary educational requirements to become a productive member of society. All school reports indicated that he was a happy and well-behaved student throughout his school years. All indications were that he achieved only average results in his exams which is a great indicator for teachers and schools that a student needs to work harder. Seán, over time, did excel in sports and achieved many accolades for his school. Seán became apprenticed to an electrical firm. He was receiving an adequate salary and he had good prospects for becoming a qualified electrician. His family were well respected in the locality. The mystery of suicide has struck again. His former school and his workplace have expressed great shock on hearing of his death.

2) The version that is told by his family, friends and colleagues
Seán was always a happy child. He loved sports and had plenty of friends. He got on well with his sister and older brother. He was particularly close to his mother and seemed to get on fine with his father. He was average in school and passed his exams. He was an

outdoor lad and loved training, playing football with his mates, going for a pint after games and at the weekends. He had a great sense of humour and he was well liked by everyone who knew him. After leaving school he became an apprenticed electrician. It was a job and a way of earning money. He mentioned problems he was having with one of his bosses who he nicknamed 'Hitler'. He had a few girlfriends but when he met Jenny he didn't want to look any further. His family and his mates really liked Jenny. Seán did well with the electrical firm he was working with. Life seemed to be going just fine. About a week before it happened, his mother did think he was looking a bit pale. She asked him why he'd lost his appetite. She wondered if he was coming down with something. He said he was a bit tired, that was all. Two days later she noticed he was particularly quiet. She asked if things were ok at work. He said things were hectic and he was working flat out. She said she'd get him some vitamins, as maybe he was overdoing the training and he needed to get more rest. The following day she asked Jenny if she'd noticed anything wrong with Seán. Jenny said that he had seemed withdrawn for about a week but reassured her that he was just training very hard for a marathon and that afterwards he'd be fine again. That Friday Seán kissed his mother before going out to play football as usual. He seemed happier, which pleased his mother. That evening he went out with a few mates to the local pub. By all accounts he seemed in good form. It was a terrible shock to everyone when it was discovered the following day that Seán had taken his life. Even those closest to him were surprised to find the excellent sketches he'd done that were found in his room.

3) Seán's private experience within the Suicide Box
This story takes us below the surface into Sean's inner world. In childhood, Seán had many happy times with his family but it was the 'bad' moments that he had difficulty dealing with. Seán was a

very sensitive child who often spent time alone. Fights with his siblings caused him a lot of hurt. The persistent name-calling, such as 'the sprat', seemed to hurt him most. He was often compared with his sister, with people often saying he was more of a girl than she was. At school, comparisons made by the teachers with other children or his older brother were difficult for him to take. He loved to draw and paint pictures but was told a few times that he seemed to like girly things and that instead he should be outside playing football or hurling like his brother. His drawing and sketching over the years were mainly done in private. Few knew of his creativity. He loved his family and he was especially close to his mother. He was often worried though when he heard his father shouting at her when he came in late. Seán sometimes lay in bed listening to the shouting and his mother's sobs, yet he felt he couldn't do anything. School days were a constant strain for Seán. He liked parts of some subjects, but he found it very difficult to remember lots of information that he didn't understand. His ability to draw and paint were utilised when posters were needed for fundraising or sports day but outside of that, nobody ever encouraged him. In fifth class in primary school, the bullying got really bad and he was constantly jeered about being small and thin. He became withdrawn then and felt that there must be something wrong with him. Even at this stage of life he remembered wanting to be dead. This feeling of not being 'right' persisted into adulthood.

In order to fit in, Seán played football and hurling at school. He noticed that the more fiery and aggressive he became on the field, the more praise he got from his father and his teacher, and the more respect he got from other players. He never really got to grips with secondary school. He found it difficult to understand most subjects and hated doing homework. He barely scraped through in his exams. He was very relieved to finish school. He had always felt out of place in school and never even thought about going to college, as that was a hallowed place for the intelligent ones. He was satisfied to become an apprenticed electrician and got on well with his co-workers, though he hated his boss, who had a nasty streak and criticised everything he did and put him down. This reminded him of being jeered as a young boy in school. At times he would be boiling with frustration, anger and humiliation after having to listen to his boss nitpick over every minute mistake. He started to drink more to get rid of these feelings. Many times he wished he could leave the job but then he'd have nothing to offer Jenny, and his mother would start worrying about him. Sometimes he wished he didn't feel anything because there was so much pain about never being good enough.

There were a few things in life he loved, his mother, Jenny and sketching. He'd known Jenny for two years and he was very much in love with her. There was one incident that really shook him. He was at a party when a friend of Jenny's came up to him. She obviously had a lot of drink taken so he shouldn't have listened to anything she said. But it did affect him so much when she said that Jenny had told her she liked him, but he wasn't as good in bed as her former boyfriend. That one thought really consumed him. He had never fitted in anywhere, in school or in work, and now he wasn't good enough to be with Jenny. The thoughts just continued rolling around inside. He told no one about any of this because he would have been too embarrassed. Finally all other ways forward became futile and he was left with only one option; ending the pain and no longer being a burden on his family or Jenny was all he could think of. He felt that the world would be better off without him. Seán felt he did not belong here. He began planning to take his own life. One evening when he had taken enough alcohol he carried out his plan and exited this life.

*4) How his life could have been so different from the New Perspective,
   outside of the Suicide Box*

The educational system is geared to discovering the innate intelligences and learning styles that a child possesses to flourish and to find happiness and well-being. A caring, nurturing teacher and adequate resources were made available to Seán to facilitate his exploration of his talents. It quickly became apparent that Seán's great ability lay in creative areas. He spent many happy hours at school and at home working on projects that aided his development in art and related areas. There were a few incidents of name-calling at school but these were dealt with by their proactive all-school/community programme to deal with antisocial behaviours. As a result Seán actually ended up feeling positive about himself. In one case, the boy who had called him names became a good friend and this friendship has lasted into adulthood. He also learned at school that everyone is unique and how important it is to allow this uniqueness to blossom, as to limit a child's potential would cause much unhappiness and pain in later life. Seán especially enjoyed the mindfulness moments that they practised in class several times a day. Even outside of class it made him feel calm and at peace when he focused on being alive in the moment, and not worrying about the past or the future.

At home and in school Seán was encouraged to say what he thought and to express what he felt. His parents learned through an all-school/community programme the importance of being patient and calm, and truly listening. They also learned to empower their children to solve their own problems by helping them to work through various options. This was mainly the effect of developing a family plan to design agreed ways of handling difficult situations that may arise for the family. Learning to be observant for those gifts and talents that facilitate a child's happiness and development was a great tool to cultivate family relationships. As a result, Seán developed a good sense of what was right for him. As he became older, he was allowed to work out his own problems and to make decisions that affected him, with the support of his parents. They had mellowed a lot and seemed to have a better relationship since attending seminars on parenting that were offered in community programmes funded by the government. Seán knew his particular gifts were in the artistic areas so he understood that it was ok for him to have difficulty with academic work. He was happy to spend time on projects in all subjects and this helped him to get good overall marks through continuous assessment, though he always excelled at art. This was the area he was determined to study and to eventually find work in. He enjoyed the discussions and seminars in secondary schools, about relationships, sexuality and how to take care of himself, especially how to keep thoughts and feelings from becoming unbalanced and out of control. He enjoyed chatting with his parents and siblings about many aspects of life. He had good discussions with Jenny too. They were both aware that respect and mutuality in relationships, especially in sexual relations, was very important. He loved Jenny and enjoyed many aspects of his life. He was also aware that life wasn't always going to be perfect and there would be ordinary problems along the way.

In school, he attended many powerful seminars. He learned that his life was worthwhile, that he was a person of worth and value, no matter what happened to him in life. Seán and Jenny married. They continue to enjoy exploring and respecting all dimensions of each other including physical, spiritual, sexual, emotional, intellectual, creative and social. Negative external influences and judgements had no impact on their relationship as they became the best friends and lovers they could possibly be to each other. Seán got a worrying illness in his thirties that kept him from his much-loved art studio and shop for six months, but natural pain was understood as part of life and he learned much from this experience. Their three children are learning the importance of emotional expression, resolving personal issues as they arise and caring for all dimensions of themselves. Seán lives a happy life, free from unnecessary pain. The society he lives in presents opportunities that nurture his natural talents, supports his natural right to be true to himself and celebrates his uniqueness.

Different Versions of One Life
The different versions of Seán's story give us a better understanding of why he chose certain behaviours when surrounded by particular sets of societal values and beliefs. In the first version, several social structures, namely education, work, the media and the family, are blind to the damage that is often done by curtailing the emotional and creative expression of our youth. In the second version of Sean's story, those who inhabited his world, namely his family and friends, were unaware of his experiences and the ways in which these affected him emotionally. Therefore they were deeply shocked by his suicide and were left with the sense that nothing could explain his decision. In the Suicide Box this is the common reaction to suicide.

In the third version, Seán lived within the Suicide Box where he was oblivious to the social structures that shaped him and forced him to deny his natural attributes and preferred choices. This ultimately brought about feelings of alienation and pain that led to his decision to take his own life. Almost from birth there was a tension for Seán between complying with life as it was laid out for him within the Suicide Box, fulfilling the requirements of society, and expressing the uniqueness of his own individuality. This story was used to identify the type of elements that contribute to an increase in unnecessary human pain, and how we may learn to become free from the worst effects of the Suicide Box that keep us locked into negative thinking, lost in fear, stigma, shame and unawareness. Most of all, this entire book offers a New Perspective – a fresh way to view your own life, to clearly see the social structures that surround you, not to aggressively oppose it but to rise above it. Then we can embrace human diversity in all its complexity, and collectively move towards a more compassionate, expressive and enlightened vision of emotional health and well-being.

Thus, the fourth version of Seán's story takes the same life, and many of the same situations, but views this from the New Perspective as outlined in Part Four of the book. Within this more enlightened society individuals are encouraged to discover their unique gifts, to facilitate their strengths and to create a truly nurturing environment for all. Children then have the opportunity to become adults who value their own lives, and become empowered to care for all aspects of themselves. There may be situations where people choose to take their own lives and we can still help by being there as they weather their temporary private hell, guiding them towards a life of hope and meaning. However, it is the unnecessary human pain that arises from external forces that is within our power to ameliorate for ourselves and for each other. It is this societal transformation that will have the greatest impact on reducing the numbers who suffer unnecessary human pain or who are driven to take their own lives. Are you ready and willing to smash through the Suicide Box and embark on this crucial journey together?

Trapped within the Suicide Box: A Modern-day Parable
To her friends, Jennifer is cool, smart and attractive. On the cusp of sixteen, Jennifer should be on top of the world but from her perspective life is spiralling downwards fast. She believes that the constant pain she feels is because she's really not good enough, her

grades aren't high enough and her latest worry is that she's so abnormal that no one will ever love her. There are so many things very wrong in her world. When she compares herself to the glamourous models in glossy magazines she feels ugly. She's scared that very soon she will destroy her parent's image of her as a confident, happy teenager who is going places. She loves art and fashion and would dearly love to design beautiful clothes but her Dad insists that she follow in his footsteps and become an accountant. Then there's her boyfriend, Jack. He's been pressurising her for weeks to have sex but she doesn't feel ready. She likes him a lot but lately she's confused because he keeps saying maybe she's not normal. He showed her examples of girls around her age on social media who appear to be having sex and he said that's what every girl wants. This is supported by many of her peers who accept this view. Everyone tells Jennifer the world is her oyster but she feels upset and overwhelmed by so much anxiety. Her greatest fear is that she'll let everyone down and end up a failure. She's been waking early for the past few weeks with feelings of dread and doom. Thoughts of suicide as a way out have become more frequent.

Jennifer, like all of us, is caught within the Suicide Box. This is a metaphor for the constructed society we live in where various institutions stifle individual expression, rearing and educating us to serve a flawed society. Within the Suicide Box our unique gifts and natural talents are measured on a sliding scale of value, and those traits that are considered important to the controlling elements of society, such as industry, are cultivated. The consequence of this system however is that individual gifts and talents are too often crushed; opportunities for personal fulfilment are limited; the psychological objective of being true to oneself becomes unachievable (Maslow, 1943), leaving individuals feeling like square pegs when society only offers round holes. This societal structure is anything but conducive to promoting mental and emotional health. Instead it facilitates human pain that often culminates in suicide.

The premise of this book is that, far from being an individual choice, suicide is a final response to an accumulation of forces that fail to create a healthy environment where all people can thrive and flourish: social dysfunction, political error, economic ineptitude and a spiritual void. We are socialised within our families and our schools. We learn what is acceptable to say, to think and what is off limits. We discover that emotion, particularly pain, needs to be hidden. Then we are saturated by media images as to the way we should look, what we should aspire to be, to do and to have. Social media sites bombard us with all kinds of crazy notions about what is 'normal', what is acceptable, all with the sole purpose of propagating conformity, and most especially controlling vulnerable young people. Our socio-economic position in life largely determines our dreams, our friends, our work or lack of it. The policies established by our political system determine our access to education and the quality of that experience, the mental health services available and their effectiveness in healing our inner wounds. Global economics largely determine the quality of our lives in terms of employment, housing, and financial sustainability.

With only a tiny shift in our understanding we may begin to courageously listen to those whose voices cry out to be heard above the din of ignorance, fear, stigma and myth that have accumulated over centuries. For Jennifer, there are so many voices around her demanding that she follow their needs and expectations while her own sweet voice is blocked out and forced into silence. This book is for Seán, Jennifer – and the whole human race – to speak your own words and live your own dreams, beyond the Suicide Box.

What is the Suicide Box?

Suicide, the act of taking one's life, is a highly complex, emotive and difficult subject to understand. For many, suicide is almost impossible to come to terms with. No one set out to create the Suicide Box.

In this book, the Suicide Box symbolises a collective way of thinking about suicide and mental illness that has emerged over time. It is society's unhelpful and unconscious response to dealing with the extremities of human pain that it neither understands nor seeks to embrace. The structure of the Suicide Box is usually invisible to us. We have become accepting of the forces that weaken us to such an extent that we fail to question or consider alternatives. While there are positive elements in socialisation that maintain beneficial social structures, there are some features that profoundly hinder our most basic need to express our truths and reach our optimum potential. The core theme of this section is to bring all parts of the Suicide Box into the light, to make the box visible in order to analyse its construction.

The Suicide Box is generally fear based and has been developed throughout history. It has been energised by many elements within society, such as religious, educational, industrial, familial, cultural, political, economic, legal and psychiatric beliefs and practices. In spite of society's taboos and laws that forbid and repudiate the taking of one's own life, the existence of suicide as a phenomenon continues unabated. The ways in which society has depicted suicide have been particularly damaging. We have separated out the extremities of human pain, perpetuated myths, stigma and falsehoods, created a Suicide Box that lies somewhere within society's larger container, then tightly closed the lid to keep it from spreading its destructive and contaminated contents. The simple truth is that the Suicide Box exerts tremendous fear: for as long as suicide remains cloaked in myth, shrouded in secrecy, and veiled in deep misunderstanding, we will all remain captive within its walls.

Explanations for Suicide
Most explanations for suicide focus on the individual. Following a suicide the individual's life is scrutinised in an attempt to gain some

understanding of how this seemingly inexplicable event took place. It is common to refer to the deceased as having been 'the life and soul of the party' or 'young, beautiful and talented'. Therefore, people are mystified as to the reasons for the suicide. Rarely are the broader local, cultural or social levels explored, in search of a greater understanding of why a suicide has occurred. An analysis of cultural and social beliefs and practices globally reveal that:

+ Suicide is present in all societies.

+ Differences between countries, societies and even regions within countries appear to support the premise that social, cultural and local factors profoundly influence the reasons why people take their lives.

According to the Organisation for Economic Co-operation and Development (OECD, 2012), 'the intentional killing of oneself can be seen as evidence not only of personal breakdown, but also of a deterioration of the social context in which an individual lives'. The individual is largely a product of the society into which he or she was born and reared. Therefore, in the case of a suicide, it is important to shift the focus from individual explanations to local, social and cultural ones.

Within the Suicide Box reasons why people kill themselves are presented as being clear, even among the highly qualified. They confidently assert reasons, such as those outlined by Lickerman (2010): 'they're depressed … they're psychotic … they're impulsive … they're crying out for help … they have a philosophical desire to die … they've made a mistake.' However, the burning question on the minds of those who have lost a loved one to suicide is never answered by these surface reasons. This is because these explanations fall flat when trying to apply their empty logic to the beautiful person they loved, with all the multifaceted elements to their character and so many life stories. A mother remembers

15

holding her beautiful baby and wonders what went wrong between then and now. A sister remembers her fun-loving brother, pondering how it all got too much for him, and beats herself up for not noticing when this happened. A father wishes he could switch places with his dead child so she could have a chance to live out her life.

The main assumption in the reasons given is that society is stable and a natural progression but that the individual is flawed and unable to contend with the demands of life. Of course, this is a very warped and painfully narrow view, and one that could only come from the cosseted few who have no idea what it feels like to be marginalised by society's unfair structures and biased attitudes. Since 'expert' opinions are given immense value within the Suicide Box, they are effectively the most powerful source of myth and stigma for a phenomenon like suicide. It is only when we peel back the thickly laid cover that keeps us blinded that we can discover an awful reality that conceals the truth and explains why, deep down, the surface reasons never help answer our questions. The awful reality is the realisation that we have been born into a world that is pre-ordered, where our place is determined by general, rigid rules. Our carers have already been moulded into the process through socialisation. The most successful individuals then will be those whose skill set dovetails with society's requirements. If your unique make up is favourable then society embraces you, if not, then you have to move to the periphery of society, a social pariah, while you are replaced with a 'useful' member.

All too often a person who is not a great match for some or many aspects of society feels alienated and a failure. This is how Jennifer feels in our example above. This is the Suicide Box in action, where society's flaws and failings remain invisible while the individual suffers, placing all responsibility on the self for not fitting in with social requirements, no matter how unfair or absurd.

Personal Responsibility

From the outset we want to state clearly that this book does not advocate that individuals shirk personal responsibility in their lives. An important element of the book emphasises that our social structures have great power and scope to influence an individual life. It is essential that every person sees through the workings of each structure. Take Jennifer for example. If Jennifer could only realise that her father favours a safe, economically viable career because he has been socialised to believe that it's not important to follow your dreams, then this may give her the chance to view life from a different perspective. Although Jennifer attends a school where academic achievement is espoused, there is little taught in the area of emotional intelligence, sexuality or relationships and hence Jennifer does not receive the guidance and support she needs to make choices that are valid and necessary for her own well-being. This realisation would give Jennifer vital information to show that the system is loaded against her. But far from advocating that Jennifer should spend her life bemoaning her situation, we focus on her responsibility for self-care, for discovering nurturing support, for respecting herself and others, for expressing herself and exploring her unique talents, for being true to herself if that is possible in her life situation, continuing to live the best life possible while allowing others to live according to their unique aspirations, despite society's flaws and failings.

CHAPTER TWO

Embracing Suicide

We may believe that there will be fewer suicides if we never mention the word and avoid all references to the act. Then suicide remains 'the big S', cloaked in shame and stigma. This approach has so far failed to achieve anything except further pain as individuals and families struggle in isolation to deal with their problems and grief. If we can develop a much greater understanding and acceptance of suicide then we may become more compassionate in our whole approach when discussing suicide, when coming face to face with the act of suicide, when remembering those who have died by suicide, and when working with families who are grieving for the death of a loved one who has taken his or her own life.

When we develop greater compassion we may begin to open up the channels of communication as we discuss how society needs to change, how each one of us needs to grow in awareness, to contribute to a more loving and humane society. We need to listen to those who are suffering most, to those who are in deepest pain, to learn how we can offer empathy and guidance, to be of greatest service.

Falling into the Suicide Box
Throughout recorded history, suicide has been an option for ending overwhelming personal pain and for escaping from an ill-fitting world. The individual's mental and emotional states have largely been shaped by many social elements. Society has separated out the

extremities of human pain and labelled those who are suicidal as mentally ill, unable to cope with life's pressures, somehow weaker and more fragile than most. Suicide is thus most commonly presented as a personal tragedy rather than a collective cataclysm, exposing the false values and beliefs that spread and prosper in our largely unconscious society.

The individual does not live in a vacuum but is always reacting to and interacting with social elements that shape his or her identity. Just like a shrub whose needs are fulfilled with adequate water, sunlight and nutrients, a person when nurtured with essential life needs, be they physical, social, emotional or spiritual will similarly blossom. Most people are well-meaning and aim to do the best they can for themselves and their loved ones, yet many suffer from negative thoughts, overwhelming feelings and a lack of awareness to navigate through life from a more loving, holistic and rational perspective.

The Spectrum of Human Pain

All individuals feel pain. At times this pain can be excruciating, as when a person experiences deep trauma or loss. Intense inner pain may continue unhealed for decades. The effects of this stored-up pain can manifest as depression, health problems, the need to self-medicate with alcohol or drugs, or the compulsion to self-harm. The following table shows the Spectrum of Human Pain, comprised of official figures for those who die by suicide in Ireland on the far right.

Table 1: The Spectrum of Human Pain

Pain & coping alone	Pain and coping with support	Pain in Private	Pain & Self-Harm Unreported	Pain & Self-Harm Presenting	Pain & Suicide
Remainder of Society	Those who know when to reach out	One in five people develop a depressive episode (WHO, 2003). There are also those who attempt suicide, turn to drugs or alcohol, or develop eating disorders.	The 60,000 in Ireland estimated to self-harm without reporting (www.3Ts.ie)	The 9,483 in Ireland who Presented at A&E in 2012 who self-harm (NERF, 2013, 1)	The 554 in Ireland who died by suicide in 2011 (CSO, 2014)
Resilient	◄─────────────────────────────────►				Vulnerable
Tolerable	◄─────────────────────────────────►				Over-whelming

Suicide is the extreme manifestation of human pain. This is followed by those who present at accident and emergency hospital departments after self-harming – a further demonstration of extreme levels of pain. Also present are those who self-harm but do not report the episode. Next come people's private pain that may cause bouts of debilitating mental illness, such as attempted suicide, depression, overindulgence in drugs or alcohol, or the development of eating disorders. Then there are those who are in pain and reach out for help, such as those who attend counselling or contact their GPs. Finally there is the remainder of society: those who deal with their pain alone by developing coping skills.

To illustrate this spectrum further, imagine a sliding scale that measures complete mental well-being at one extremity and suicide at the other, with many gradations of self-care and self-harm in between. Complete mental well-being would comprise of positive thoughts, feelings of contentment, peace, self-love, self-respect, a strong sense of one's intrinsic value, and a well-developed system of relating to others based on deep compassion, empathy, love, care and respect. But somewhere along the scale the positive, loving feelings and thoughts would begin to lessen and fade. Other darker feelings and thoughts would gradually appear, coupled with destructive behaviours that people use to cope with a myriad of feelings and issues, including drinking alcohol to access, becoming dependent on prescribed or illegal drugs, becoming addicted to activities such as gambling, the practice of self-harming, such as cutting or causing pain to oneself, and other potentially dangerous behaviours that are diametrically opposed to taking good care of oneself. To begin to understand suicide, it is vital to view it as the final act at the end of a scale that spans from those who are resilient and content at one end, to those who find themselves vulnerable and overwhelmed at the other. Suicide, therefore, cannot be seen as a behaviour onto itself that has no relation to other destructive ways that people try to cope with life's difficulties, momentarily suppressing their mounting feelings of pain, anxiety and despair. However, no individual can be rigidly pinpointed on any part of the spectrum as it is vital that the human being is seen as resilient and always capable of returning to full health in spite of any life setback.

For many, the Suicide Box remains at least partially hidden, concealing an incomprehensible act that exists in a vacuum separated from other human experiences. In spite of society's taboos and laws that forbid and repudiate the taking of one's own life, the existence of suicide as a phenomenon continues unabated.

Myths About Suicide
Myths include misconceptions, fables and falsehoods that have become rooted in people's minds as to the nature and causes of suicide. Myths permeate the whole of society; even statistics about suicide are often used to isolate suicide as a phenomenon, thereby perpetuating mythical thinking. An example is the frequently quoted statistic that men are much more likely to take their own lives, yet the statistic that many more women attempt suicide than men is rarely noted (McIntosh, 1993; National Center for Health Statistics, 1994). A study by Corcoran et al (2004) found that women had 19 per cent higher suicide attempts when the entire population was considered and 17 per cent higher for those over fifteen years of age. These statistics indicate that if women chose more lethal methods, a far more serious phenomenon of completed suicides would prevail. This feeds into the myth that men are more likely to suicide than women. The truth however is that men often choose more lethal methods than women. It follows also that because women choose less lethal methods and are more likely to survive their attempt that their intent is misinterpreted as a cry for help. Since all the emphasis is placed on death by suicide and that men are statistically more likely to die from attempted suicide, the degree of pain experienced by women that is reflected in self-harm and suicide attempts is given little credence and attention. The fact that women are at greater risk of suicide in the first year after childbirth is also rarely quoted (Appleby et al, 1998).

An example of myths that permeate society and inhabit our thinking once we are inside the Suicide Box include:

✦ A person who is suicidal won't tell anyone.

✦ Every person who takes his or her own life is mentally ill.

✦ Suicide is hereditary.

✦ Keeping silent and never mentioning suicide at home, in school or among friends is a way of keeping young people safe so they won't ever have suicidal thoughts.

✦ A person who has become suicidal will always be suicidal.

✦ More men than women attempt suicide.

✦ Taking one's life is a selfish act that is carried out to punish loved ones.

The Non-Existence of Those who Die by Suicide

Through various epochs there has been the extraordinary view that taking one's own life is glamorous. From Shakespeare's *Romeo and Juliet* to the pre-Raphaelite artist, Millais's depiction of *Ophelia*, a sordid link has somehow developed between youth, glamour and suicide. In a recent report on suicide, the *Irish Examiner* (8 October 2013) printed comments from students after a suicide had occurred in their school saying 'What a great way to go' and 'I'd like to have the courage to do the same'. The stark reality, however, for the families of those who die by suicide, is one of devastation and a deep enduring heartache. The misperception of viewing suicide as glamorous could only be perceived by those who are inexperienced or unacquainted with the true nature of suicide. Far from becoming celebrated or immortalised, the lives and deaths of many who die by suicide become unspeakable, their very existence shrouded in mystery, their names never spoken and their memories often eradicated. All of these elements: the false and deceptive depiction of suicide as glamorous, the actual silence and eradication of the memory of those who have died by suicide, and the stigma attached to the act of suicide are all deeply embedded features of the Suicide Box.

Tanya's Story of Losing her Mother and Aunt to Suicide
Tanya told us of events that took place around 1973/4.

> I was taken from my mother when I was three weeks old and put into an industrial school. I was a mixed race child. I discovered that my mother kept in touch with me. It wasn't until I got the records under the Freedom of Information Act that I realised that she'd been trying to get me back. That's one of the reasons I think that she killed herself, because she couldn't get me back. Later my mother married – I think she felt if she got married she'd be able to get me back. But because I was mixed race she was told she couldn't. My aunt also married and had a family. I was about ten when my mother came to visit me. I also spent a week once with my aunt.
> When I tried to get information later on from my family or from state records I couldn't get any. There's no birth cert or death cert that I can find for either my mother or my aunt. I did find out that they both died by suicide. I was devastated when I first found this out. My mother was quite bohemian. She was living in London when she died. My aunt died in her bedroom. When I began to look for information about them there was nothing. I don't even know if there are graves for them anywhere. I'm not sure of their birth dates or the year of their deaths. I have tried everything.
> It's hard to take that I can't find any records, especially when I look at that program *Who Do You Think You Are?* There are people tracing

their families over hundreds of years, even back to the Jamaican plantations. I think my grandparents felt shame around my mother and my aunt and they probably wanted to cover things up. My aunt was suffering from clinical depression. My mother seemed to have been quite fearless but she must have been excluded by society, as well as excluding herself. It was all very sensitive. I have searched for my mother's and aunt's records using many variations of their maiden names and married names, and using different dates of birth and death, but all my searching has turned up a blank. Their existence has been wiped away.

CHAPTER THREE
Extent of Suicide

The uniqueness of each suicide is always lost in statistics. The often complex, interlocking reasons why one person needs to choose death to end his or her pain are rarely understood. Through working with individuals and family members that have been touched by suicide over decades, we have gained some insight into common thoughts and feelings that consume a person who is suicidal: 'I'm in the middle of a black tunnel and there's only one way out. I have to end this pain. I don't want to die. Everyone will be better off without me. Then it'll all be over. I'm a failure. I've tried everything else. It's like ticking off a shopping list – now there's only one item left. I can't tell anyone. No one else can help.'

Studies most frequently used to determine a person's psychological profile after dying from suicide are psychological autopsies. This method offers the most direct technique available for examining the relationship between particular experiences and suicide. An example of such a study is from the National Suicide Research Foundation (2013) on the risk factors for 190 suicides completed in Cork during the period September 2008 to March 2011 (Arensman et al, 2012). The problem with these studies is that the true cumulative factors that contributed to a person's decision to suicide may never be known, as the deceased may not have confided these to anyone, or may not have been consciously aware that a particular experience had such a devastating impact. While the most comprehensive findings come from a combination of both quantitative and qualitative studies, these psychological autopsy findings are useful for giving an indication of risk factors in suicides. In many ways these studies mirror and uphold society's version of an individual's life, as outlined in society's version of Seán's life from within the Suicide Box, described in Chapter One.

Some people who have attempted suicide and have survived have told us how they felt when they tried to take their lives. Without exception they wanted to end the pain. They felt alone in their world. There was a final, personal driving force for their decision. The desire to self-destruct was present. Quite often the decision to suicide was a relief. Sometimes people who are suicidal may seem happier; they may begin to give away their possessions. Humiliation and shame are often powerful motivators. A person's self-esteem may be severely damaged by bullying, character assassination or by an inability to cope with some aspect of life, including problems at work, sexuality, relationships, or managing finances. A person is particularly vulnerable when charged with a crime or imprisoned. There may be a secret that the person feels they cannot share with anyone: it may be very difficult to face family, friends and the wider society, for fear that affection and support might be withdrawn or that their life would be ruined if their secret was discovered.

From those who did not complete the act of suicide, a common thought expressed in their distorted thinking processes at the time, is that their decision to die was based on freeing their families and the world from the burden that they had become. The lack of knowledge around suicide draws ill-informed assumptions as common facts, such as, that suicide is selfish; attention-seeking behaviour or a thoughtless act. People say these things and feed into these myths because they are trying to apply logic and reason to an action that was completed by someone who was totally overwhelmed and confused. Emotions such as fear, inadequacy, loneliness or feeling a burden, have become part of the perception of those who are contemplating suicide. They have reached a point of aloneness where there is no one else in the world at that moment in time that they feel connected to. While this thought might hurt families and friends who have lost loved ones through suicide, it is important that they do not apply normal reasoning to this fact. The person who is suicidal is cut off from such feelings and he or she is not functioning at a reasonable level. The person's thoughts have become fixated on one option and his or her awareness outside of this is very limited.

Prevalence of Suicide

According to the International Association of Suicide Prevention (www.iasp.info):

- One million people worldwide die by suicide each year. That's one suicide every forty seconds.

- More people die by suicide each year than by murder and war combined.

- It is estimated that approximately 5 per cent of people attempt suicide at least once in their life.

- Between 10 per cent and 14 per cent of the general population experience suicidal thinking.

- Suicide is the second leading cause of death worldwide among 15–19 year olds.

- 100,000 adolescents die by suicide every year.

- Suicide is estimated to be under-reported for reasons of stigma, religion and social attitudes. Many suicides are hidden among other causes of death.

Suicide in the United States

According to the Organisation for Economic Co-operation and Development (OECD, 2013), an average of 12.5 deaths was recorded per 100,000 of the United States' population during 2010. Statistics for suicide in the United States reveal that (Centres for Disease Control and Prevention, 2012):

⁂ Suicide is the tenth leading cause of death among Americans.

⁂ More than 38,000 people died by suicide in 2010.

⁂ More than 1 million people reported making a suicide attempt in the past year.

⁂ More than 2 million adults reported thinking about suicide in the past year.

Suicide in Asia

Asian countries account for approximately 60 per cent of the world's suicides (Chen et al, 2011). If commonly used estimates are applied to Asia, then approximately ten to twenty times as many suicide attempts as other deaths occur, and five to six people are affected by each suicide death, implying that more than 60 million people may be affected by suicide annually (Pirkis et al, 2006, cited in Chen et al, 2011). There may, however, be even higher suicide rates in some Asian countries, as it is suspected that there is substantial under-reporting of suicides in China, India, Thailand, and Sri Lanka (Hendin et al, 2008). Social, cultural, and religious factors affect the reporting of suicide and are compounded by poor population estimates (Chen et al, 2011). According to the OECD (2013) report into suicide, the two Asian countries with the highest recorded suicide rates for 2010 were Korea (33.5 per 100,000) and Japan (21.2 per 100,000).

Suicide in Europe

Suicide is a significant cause of death in many European countries. In the European Union member states 60,000 suicides were recorded in 2010 (OECD, 2012). A breakdown of these is outlined below:

⁑ The rates of suicide were recorded as low in southern European countries: Cyprus, Greece, Italy, Malta, Portugal and Spain; as well as in the United Kingdom, with eight deaths or less recorded per 100,000 of the population.

⁑ Suicides were reported to be highest in the Baltic States and Central Europe. Hungary recorded the highest suicide rate of all European countries during 2011: 22.8 per 100,000 (OECD, 2013). In Estonia, Latvia, Lithuania and Slovenia there were more than seventeen deaths recorded per 100,000 of the population (OECD, 2012).

⁑ Despite the high standard of living and social freedom experienced in Scandinavia, 11.7 deaths per 100,000 were recorded during 2010 (OECD, 2013) in Sweden. Norway recorded 12.1 deaths from suicide per 100,000 in 2011 (OECD, 2013) and Denmark reported 10.1 deaths per 100,000. Finland recorded a particularly high rate of suicides, with 16.4 deaths per 100,000 during 2011 (OECD, 2013).

Suicide in Ireland

A modern system of recording deaths by suicide began in Ireland in 1968. A comparison of deaths attributed to suicide in 1987 and 1998 showed that suicides had almost doubled, from 245 to 478 (Corcoran et al, 2006). Recorded suicides between 2000 and 2011 total 5,979. Due to the time lag between a suicide and the registration of the death, final statistics may not be compiled by the CSO for up to four years. There were 507 deaths by suicide registered in Ireland during

2012 (CSO, 2013a). However, these figures may increase with inquest verdicts recorded at a later date. The most complete recent statistics for suicides in Ireland show that 554 people took their lives during 2011 (CSO, 2014). The 2011 number of suicides – 554 – is the highest rate of suicide ever recorded in Ireland. There were 458 male suicides (or almost 83 per cent of the total) compared with 96 female suicides in 2011 (CSO, 2014). However, the true rate of suicide in Ireland, as in many countries, is questionable. According to the Irish charity Console, Ireland's true suicide rate may be significantly higher. The charity suggests that official levels of suicides may be wrongly classified during inquests (Ó Cionnaith, 2013). In 2010 for example, the cause of death in 123 cases remained undetermined.

A recent report published by the European Child Safety Alliance (2014, 18–20) found that the highest suicide rates for males, for those aged up to nineteen years, occur in Lithuania (6.58 per 100,000), Ireland (5.12 per 100,000) and Estonia (3.99 per 100,000). The report also found that the highest rates for female suicides, aged up to nineteen years, occur in Ireland (2.09), Lithuania (1.94) and Finland (1.39). Data for the report was collected from government departments and national organisations in the twenty-eight EU countries, plus Norway. The report highlighted the worrying trend in young suicides for both males and females in Ireland that places it second on the European chart for the highest rates of child suicides. Of those countries surveyed, nine governments, including Ireland, had no national strategy to prevent suicide or self-directed violence (European Child Safety Alliance, 2014, p. 76). The report also stated that the recession and economic downturn were having serious effects on the income levels of families in some countries and that there was a direct link between poverty and an increase in child maltreatment, neglect, abuse and suicide (European Child Safety Alliance, 2014, p. 76).

CHAPTER FOUR
Risk Factors

Many studies have highlighted risk factors that are deemed to be closely associated with suicide. It is important that we regard these with caution as they are products of the Suicide Box. Statistics are all too often used to simplify highly complex problems. They suit the human desire to pigeon-hole complex issues so generalisations can be made. Statistics are routinely interpreted to focus on individual characteristics while excluding vital social factors that greatly influence people's lives. The truth is that every suicide has a complex story to tell. Alan ended his own life at nineteen by drug overdose. Statistics and all records place Alan in the drug overdose category. Nowhere in the statistics is there a mention of Alan's abuse by his father, his abandonment on the streets to fend for himself as a child, or the sexual abuse he suffered at the hands of a trusted neighbour. So, keeping the limitation of statistics in mind, let us look at some of the risk factors suggested by studies that have been conducted within the Suicide Box.

Individual Characteristics
According to many studies, certain individual characteristics and conditions are associated with suicide. These include personality traits and ways of thinking, including self-criticism, negative thinking, impaired social skills and poor peer relationships (Wiley et al, 2012; Task Force into Suicide Prevention in Victoria, Australia, 1997). Studies have also indicated that a past history of attempted

suicide (Kessler et al, 1999; Brent and Perper, 1995; Johnsson-Fridell et al, 1996), self-harming (NERF, 2013; Owens and Horrocks, 2002) and mental illness (European Union Report, 2011; O'Neill and Corry, 2013) are risk factors for suicide. Many international studies have also found a direct link between drugs and/or alcohol, and suicide (Arensman et al, 2012, p. 8; Silins et al, 2014; Wilcox et al, 2004).

Every person is highly influenced by how they interpret events. When a person experiences trauma or abuse, the impact of this may be lost in well-meaning reports such as those offered above. To produce meaningful change, risk factors must include social elements that contribute to the incidence of suicide, such as unskilled carers, bullying individuals and organisations, the misuse of alcohol, or alienation in a prejudiced educational system that can lead to great upheaval in individual lives. In the case of prior suicide attempts being a predisposition for suicide, a series of suicide attempts may simply indicate the intensity of the pain felt and the inability of the individual to rationalise the imposing factors particular to their lives. The lesson for society here might be to look at the early need to develop self-care, coping strategies, assertiveness, and ways to limit and identify powerful risk factors, such as emotionally deficient educational environments and syllabuses.

In the case of a diagnosis of mental illness, clinicians may be inclined to opt for convenient but erroneous biological explanations. Within the Suicide Box, the causes of mental health problems are most often attributed to chemical imbalances, genetics, or an individual's failure to cope with particular life stressors. Thus, a simplistic blinkered view and solution, such as medication, may be proffered for complex phenomena. This is tantamount to society washing its hands of any responsibility, such as the extent to which institutions have contributed to the individual's distress and the onset of mental illness.

When alcohol or drugs are indicated as a risk factor, it is often an ideal opportunity for society to deflect from its hypocritical position by blaming the individual. There is a grave reticence to highlight the fact that misuse of alcohol is embedded in the Irish culture. The reality of alcohol misuse is even more devastating, with its significant contribution to street violence, domestic abuse, and millions of work hours lost annually. The social and political denial becomes even more glaring when a respectable image is portrayed, especially at budget time, to justify increases in revenue from alcohol sales. Little thought is given to findings that more than 50 per cent of all suicides have alcohol as a factor, rising considerably for eighteen to thirty year olds (Bedford et al, 2004; National Suicide Research Foundation, 2013). Within the Suicide Box this is considered the fault of the individual.

Cultural Factors
Differences in culture appear to influence the rates of suicide. Cultures that are oppressive, where governments are frequently in violation of human rights, have significantly higher suicide rates than cultures that advocate more individual freedom (Joiner, 2005, p. 154). Cultures that espouse and highly value strict codes of honour also tend to have higher suicide rates, such as Japan (Duignan, 2013). Scandinavian countries are among the happiest in the world (Helliwell et al, 2012) but they also have very high suicide rates. In contrast, in times of war, when a nation's citizens pull together with a shared purpose, suicide rates decrease (Thomas and Gunnell, 2010). The closest that social analysts have come to explain this phenomena is based on research conducted in the US, where the richer states with the highest levels of satisfaction had the highest suicide rates (Daly et al, 2011). Thus a theory has developed that the pressure to be successful and happy has had an adverse effect on the

most vulnerable people in that society, thereby increasing suicidal tendencies.

As the wealth/poverty spectrum widens, the inequalities become more visible, making harsh realities more intolerable for the less fortunate. Ireland, for example, has been ranked in the top ten happiest nations in the world (Helliwell et al, 2012), yet it has the second highest suicide rates in Europe for males up to nineteen years, and the highest rate for female suicides in the same age group (European Child Safety Alliance, 2014).

Social Factors
Recent research has yielded several important findings as to the link between social factors and the risk of suicide. The major social risk factors identified can be summarised thus: social exclusion (Jehoel-Gijsbers and Vrooman, 2007; Arensman et al, 2012; Walker, 2008), childhood abuse and sexual assault (Arensman et al, 2012) and problems at school (National Suicide Research Foundation, 2013; Arensman et al, 2012).

Economic Factors
A recent international study suggests that the 2008 global economic crisis may be responsible for the surge in suicide rates in twenty-seven European countries and eighteen American countries due to high rates of unemployment (Chang et al, 2013, cited by Hawton and Haw, 2013). International trends in suicide showed that there were more than five thousand male suicides in all countries studied during 2009, an increase of 3.3 per cent. These studies found that men experience shame because of unemployment, are less likely to seek support and as a result may suffer from social isolation. Although the studies inferred that women are less affected in terms

of vulnerability to suicide than men, completion of suicide by men is largely due to the lethality of the methods they choose and not the frequency of attempts (Crosby et al, 2011; suicide.org, 2005). In Ireland, results of research into suicide rates from 2008 to 2012 found a significant link between increased rates of suicide and self-harm during times of recession, in part due to unemployment (O'Riordan, 2014; Arensman et al, 2012). A report by Arensman (2013) highlighted the impact of suicide on the most vulnerable sectors of society.

Vulnerable Groups

Studies have found that people are more vulnerable to suicide when they are marginalised or disrespected by society. Examples of such groups are lesbian, gay, bisexual and transgender people; offenders and those charged with a crime; members of the travelling community, and the elderly. The plight of each group is discussed in this section. Finally, there is the group that is most often referred to as being at risk of suicide: young people. The various pressures that impinge on this group in particular are also discussed below.

Lesbian, Gay, Bisexual and Transgender People

It is estimated that one-third of young people who attempt suicide or take their own lives are homosexual (Berkovitz, 1985). Routine stressors and lack of support that non-heterosexuals have to deal with due to their orientation include verbal and physical abuse from peers, difficulties with or exclusion from family, and lack of institutional support (Gonsiorek, 1993, p. 470). Being marginalised and socially excluded can bring about 'internalised homophobia', whereby negative societal reactions to homosexuality are incorporated into a person's self-image (Gonsiorek, 1993, p. 475). The negative stereotyping of lesbian, gay, bisexual and transgender people in the media creates further difficulties for their acceptance within society (Gross, 1989, p. 135). Within many religions there is the teaching that any sexual practice other than heterosexual is unnatural. This may result in non-heterosexual religious members feeling guilty, alienated or rejected by their church, families and the wider society (Grollman and Malikow, 1999, p. 69).

Transgender people face enormous alienation and discrimination. According to Amnesty International (2012) there may be as many as 1.5 million transgender individuals living in the European Union. At a political level, transgender people have been campaigning for years to have the right to change their birth certificates to reflect their new gender. Since gender is such a fundamental part of a person's identity, the pain of not being accepted by one's family, society and government when a change of gender occurs is devastating. The following insights by Denise poignantly depicts the difficulties suffered by a child and later an adult who is cast within the wrong body, craving to experience life as the opposite gender but frequently feeling suicidal.

Denise's Heartfelt Account of being Marginalised in Ireland

I just want to live and work and be an ordinary functioning member of society. However, nature has been very cruel to me. From my earliest memories I knew something was wrong. I felt that I was a girl in every sense but I had been placed in the body of a boy. I felt so confused growing up in Ireland. I shared a bedroom with three brothers. I resisted being a girl but it was just happening to me. For society, there are just two boxes to tick for sex differences, but gender is not so black and white. External genitals don't always determine sex or gender. Terrible assumptions are made at birth even when babies are born with both male and female genitals.

37

For me there seemed to be no box that I could tick. I wanted to conform to the female box but I felt society wanted me to act as a male so I did as well as I could. Making my communion was terrifying for me. While in the line of boys and girls as we approached the altar where the boys were to bow and the girls genuflect, I genuflected. A teacher pulled me aside and admonished me for making such an error. I felt my life was a lie so I treasured those moments that allowed me to be faithful to my true nature. On Saturdays growing up I was usually alone at home so l could dress up and feel pretty and feminine.

I think I felt suicidal all my life. It was always an option to deal with the confusion. This was so difficult to deal with as a child. It seemed I was never going to fit in. What society considers normal is so rigid and restricting and this is not only reflected in the structures and laws that most take for granted every day but is evident in the faces, words and behaviour of people I meet. I have become expert in reading the subtle disgust, shock, revulsion and even the contempt on faces no matter how hard they try to hide it.

I finally had an operation to remove those parts of my body that suggested maleness and I now dress and live openly as a complete woman. It amazed my medical team that it only took the smallest dose of oestrogen to trigger the transition. It seemed my body was poised for change. Many people try to be accepting but they seem to be in the minority. But even they are looking out from their 'normal' world, trying to make space for people like me. My father does not want me calling around as he sees me as an embarrassment. My sister introduces me as a friend since she has difficulty explaining that her brother is now her sister. Even the therapists I visited seemed to find my 'problems' to be entirely connected to my conflicting body/mind sexuality. The questions they asked were stupid and obnoxious. I need support and understanding to get through another day and I get asked 'Did you have sex with another man?' I want to scream at them, 'I am not gay, I am not transsexual. I am a woman in here.'

Offenders and Those Charged with a Crime
People who are charged with a crime, and those imprisoned after being convicted of a crime, are particularly vulnerable to suicide (Department of Health, Australia, 1997; Suto and Arnaut, 2010). The report by the National Suicide Research Foundation (2013) found that 24.2 per cent of people they studied who had died by suicide had experienced legal trouble with the Gardaí in the month prior to suicide (Arensman et al, 2012). The social stigma associated with a conviction, the personal anguish and trauma of being separated from families, the guilt, loneliness and loss of freedom that many experience in prison can bring about feelings of hopelessness, leading in some cases to suicide (Humphreys, 2013). A number of issues that have adversely affected prisoners leading up to their suicides or suicide attempts include: mental health; relationship and prison issues, such as moves within the prison; employment and activity-related difficulties and placement in the Disciplinary Segregation Unit as a form of punishment (Suto and Arnaut, 2010). The poor conditions in prisons are also contributory factors to suicide, including overcrowding and the degrading practice of slopping out cells. Altercations with other prisoners, feelings of fear and lack of safety have also been identified as causes of self-harm or suicide in prisons (Liebling, 2007). Staff-offender interactions are also a dominant factor as power differentials and ways of managing this are rarely explored or included in staff training (Liebling, 2001).

A study by the National Suicide Research Foundation estimated that a rate of attempted suicide in the prison population is 3,438 per 100,000, while the rate in the general population is 202 per 100,000 (Humphreys, 2013). Studies suggest that change needs to take place in attitudes and assumptions relating to punishment and long-term labelling that facilitate suicide in society's handling of crime. Instead, attitudes that foster restoration and rehabilitation would likely reverse the endemic trend of suicide in prisons. The way of dealing with crime in society is unfair and is based on skewed societal values and partisan basic assumptions. White-collar crime involving huge sums of money rarely results in convictions whereas the non-payment of a television licence may result in a prison term. Being of lower socio-economic status usually means reduced access to the best lawyers, socially acceptable mitigating circumstances or resources to avoid imprisonment. Hence, our prisons fill up with an imbalance of society's marginalised people thereby providing scaffolding for the warped stereotypes that pervade social thinking.

The Traveller Community

The traveller community has traditionally been rooted in its own cultural and social traditions (Walker, 2008) and has always had a strong allegiance to family. Today, however, young travellers have more in common with the settled community than they do with their parents' generation. As travellers begin to take on the values of mainstream society, there is a loss of cultural traditions that sustained their ancestors for centuries. There is also enormous stereotyping to deal with, where travellers are largely rejected by society.

Traveller men are particularly vulnerable to suicide as unemployment is rife (Walker, 2008). To alleviate boredom they may drink, take drugs, joyride and engage in other forms of anti-social behaviour. All of these risk-taking behaviours are associated with suicide. Recent studies have found that the suicide rate for traveller men is over six times higher than the general population (Walker, 2008; The All Ireland Health Study, 2010). Walker (2008) found that some traveller suicides revealed a very troubled existence for the deceased that involved alcohol or substance abuse, violent behaviour, and a history of self-harm or suicide attempts.

The Elderly as High Risk Group for Suicide

Elders once occupied an exalted position in the community. As family structures have changed, the position of elderly relatives has perhaps suffered the greatest shift of all. Nowadays it is common for frail or sick relatives to end their days away from their family home. Studies report that elderly people account for one-fifth of all suicides (Salvatore, 2011) and that the suicide rate among elders is three times higher than in younger age groups (European Commission, 2011). The number of suicides rises significantly with age among men (The European Commission, 2011). Men aged seventy years or older die by suicide up to five times more often than women in the same age group. This may be due to a range of factors including men's retirement, being single, the lethality of the suicide method chosen, being widowed or suffering from poor health (Djernes, 2006). Depression also remains largely untreated in the elderly (Conwell, 2001).

The suffering of abuse may also be a factor in some suicides. In Ireland, more than 2,400 complaints of elder abuse were received by health chiefs during 2013 (Carty, 2014). The HSE report found that older people are most likely to suffer psychological abuse, with 33 per cent of all complaints related to emotional bullying, intimidation or harassment. In 80 per cent of cases abuse is most likely to be perpetrated by a direct family member or by relatives. Over a quarter of complaints related to financial abuse, 21 per cent were due to neglect and 14 per cent to physical abuse. Within the Suicide Box, the abuse of the elderly highlights the lack of respect and declining values that permeates society, particularly for the most vulnerable.

According to Turner (1992), admission to a nursing home is also fraught with difficulties. When people feel helpless and hopeless due to lack of independence and control over their environment, illness and depression may occur (Fry, 1986; Blazer, 1982). Risk factors for suicides in nursing homes were found to include loss of hope and

41

the will to live, loss of a loved one or a pet, the loss of one's faculties, such as eyesight, hospitalisation due to a major illness, and loss of one's possessions (Osgood and Brandt, 1988). The following story told by Mags highlights the need for training, particularly in empathy skills for staff that are caring for the elderly, and for policies in care homes to cater for resident's emotional needs, to enable them to feel they have purpose and autonomy in their lives.

Mag's Insights into Life in a Nursing Home

I've been in the nursing home for five years. I really miss my independence. The staff are very kind but I often feel smothered as I have no other purpose but to wait to die. In the beginning, I used to move a chair or a table to see how long it would be until someone moved it back to its original position. It usually didn't take long. If someone brings me in a plant, it's put on a shelf out of my reach so I can't tend it myself. I don't bother anymore.

My daughter and I never saw eye to eye. She doesn't come to see me much but her two children are just treasures. They run and hug me the minute they arrive. One night I had all the little things that my grandchildren brought me, like shells and coloured stones from a beach they visited, all laid out on the dressing table when a nurse came in to settle me for the night. She looked at these precious little items and said, 'What do you want me to do with these bits and bobs, I can dump them for you if you like?' I began to cry uncontrollably and couldn't tell her why. She tried to console me but then said that she would put me down to see a counsellor. If she only knew how happy those 'bits and bobs' made me. I never did get a visit from the counsellor.

I had a friend, Kathleen, who died a few months ago. That upset me a lot. Such a lovely gentle soul she was who loved to sing. Her job, as she was so proud of telling everyone, was to set the tables in the dining room. When she was told that she could no longer do this due to health and safety concerns she was devastated. I watched her deteriorate. She wouldn't even sing for me. The light died in her eyes that day and she was never the same again. I believe it killed her as she only lasted five months after that.

Young People

Ireland has the fourth highest rate of youth suicide in Europe, and suicide is among the top five causes of mortality in the fifteen to nineteen years age group (CSO, 2012). Self-harm is also of major concern in Ireland. The *My World Survey, National Study of Youth Mental Health in Ireland* (Headstrong, 2012) revealed that over 20 per cent of young adults surveyed had engaged in self-harm and 7 per cent reported a suicide attempt. The National Registry of Deliberate Self-harm (NERF, 2013, p. 1) reported that 9,483 individuals presented to hospital emergency departments as a result of deliberate self-harm in 2012. A European study (Brunel University, 2008) found that self-harm is rife amongst teenagers: 3 in 10 girls and 1 in 10 boys had either self-harmed or considered doing so in the previous year. Turn the Tide of Suicide (3Ts) estimate that 60,000 incidents of self-harming in Ireland remain unreported each year.

Pressures on young people are complex and manifold. The pressure to excel at school is incalculable, coupled with the stress of choosing a career that may shape one's life for decades. Other stressors include the common experience of being bullied at school, the all-pervasive nature of social media where teenagers dare, challenge and taunt each other, all too often with a lack of sensitivity and an agenda of conformity. Sexuality and relationships bring fun, excitement and delight to many, but also confusion, feelings of inadequacy and heartbreak. Young people's lack of experience in handling intense emotions and disappointments may also trigger pessimism and feelings of failure. In a culture where binge-drinking is socially acceptable the danger of young people becoming addicted to alcohol and drugs is considerable and puts their mental health at risk. Individuals with either a diagnosis of abuse or dependence on alcohol or drugs were found to be almost six times more likely to report a lifetime suicide attempt than those without a substance use disorder (Kessler et al, 1999).

PART TWO

Understanding Its Construction

CHAPTER FIVE

How the Suicide Box is Constructed

In the previous section we met Jennifer who was struggling with several issues that were causing her confusion and pain. The options open to Jennifer are sadly limited by important social structures that hold power, status and state recognition, keeping her enmeshed within the Suicide Box. In Part Two, we continue our analysis of the Suicide Box and explore how it is constructed. Above all else, the Suicide Box is a social construction. It is driven by fears around suicide, self-harm, human pain and mental health. It is steeped in misunderstandings, misinterpretations and ignorance that are established as truth and reality. These are the walls of the box. These beliefs are reflected in our wider social structures, including education, work, the family, legal, political and economic systems, and the media.

These powerful institutions inform the family and the individual, spreading myths and stigma about suicide and mental health. These institutions largely fail to educate individuals to understand how the emotional and cognitive system actually works, and to develop ways of taking good care of our mental, emotional, and spiritual selves. Young people like Jennifer need to learn what the mind requires in order to function in a healthy way, as well as understanding how the human mind can become unbalanced. Apparently, it is not a normal or natural instinct to care for the self, particularly in the area of mental and emotional health, considering there is so much self-harm in one form or another in society.

Focus on the Individual

While these powerful social structures have created the conditions that enable suicide and construct common views about suicide, the almost exclusive focus is on the individual for both causes and solutions. This results in well-meaning individuals and organisations pouring all their efforts and resources into working at a level that is more likely to maintain a status quo than to radically alter suicide trends. It is evident from available statistics that we are treating a festering wound with only a surface dressing. As long as we spend our time running along the clifftops, awaiting the arrival of those opting to die because of their unbearable pain, the less likely we are to examine and challenge the powerful influences that helped them come to make this deadly decision. Getting back to Jennifer, if she attended her local doctor and confided in him as to the nature of her problems, she would more than likely be given tablets to ease her 'depression'. The systemic factors, that facilitate needless collateral pain, routinely go unnoticed.

How did the Suicide Box become a Collection of Agreed Perspectives?

Gradually over time, the Suicide Box has become packed with myths, stigmas, half-truths and falsehoods that are now largely accepted as fact. This occurred through lack of awareness and understanding as to the complex causes of suicide. Each individual act of suicide is considered isolated from society, from the mountain of human pain that is part of the human condition. It is interesting to compare society's response to suicide with its incredibly enlightened response to road deaths. In Ireland, the recent policy with regard to road-traffic deaths has been to introduce a national campaign based on advertising, stricter penalties for speeding and other offences, and a greater police presence on our roads. This has had the effect of drastically reducing road deaths throughout

Ireland. While the logistics and mechanisms required to deal with a national suicide campaign would differ greatly from the effective road deaths one, the question must be posed: Why has a similar energy or will for a national policy to reduce death by suicide not been shown?

The institutions that greatly influence our social and public lives are politics and economics, religion, the law, mental health and psychiatry, education, work, the media, and the family. These are the cornerstones of our society and each has contributed to the content of the Suicide Box, either by propagating myths; being unaware of the true nature and causes of suicide; making judgements that suicide is not important enough as a social problem to invest in its prevention; neglecting the education and guidance of young people towards well-being, emotional health and positive self-esteem; adding to the stigma and pain around suicide through ignorance, lack of empathy or compassion; the overriding desire for power and control over others. Each of these social structures is examined in detail below. Social exclusion is the fate that some citizens may experience due to poverty, but it is also a penalty that is imposed on citizens who are perceived as different, or whose culture or lifestyles are considered unfavourable by current social dictates.

CHAPTER SIX

Politics and Economics

The political system of every nation is responsible for setting its policies in line with its citizens' deepest aspirations. Economically, there are always great demands on the allocation of funds to various projects and services. Government spending falls into three categories: transfer payments that are mainly social welfare payments; current government spending, such as salaries, pensions, health and education; and capital spending, to finance the maintenance and upkeep of a country's infrastructure, including roads, hospitals and schools. A nation's priorities can be quickly assessed by a review of its economic policies, its allocation of funds and the degree of severity of its social problems.

Henry Giroux (2012), professor of English and Cultural Studies at McMaster University, has savagely critiqued the state of American society, including its political system: 'As social protections are dismantled, public servants denigrated and public goods such as schools, bridges, health care services and public transportation deteriorate, the current neo-liberal social order embraces the ruthless and punishing values of economic Darwinism and a survival-of-the-fittest ethic.' Giroux refers to America as 'the Suicidal State' (Virilio, 1998), where political parties reward huge corporations, banks and financial institutions and the defence establishment, while its most vulnerable citizens are left to perish in abject poverty, surviving on food stamps and without adequate health care.

Unlike the United States' philosophy of liberal individualism, the basis of the European Union is the welfare state, and the implementation of welfare economics. The welfare state is supposedly dedicated to the well-being of its citizens, to their health, education and the fulfilment of basic economic, social and humanitarian needs (Pestieau, 2006, p. 4). The ideals proposed by the welfare state, however, often fall short in the implementation of policy. It is only when we see government programmes in action that we realise the underlying assumptions that drive policy. For example, concepts such as the provision of social protection, assistance and services, or what is considered to be in 'the national interest' ring hollow when we see that the most vulnerable are failed by society.

A pluralist and democratic society is meant to hear and respond to the voices of its people. When we consider the large numbers of people who are deeply distressed, as revealed by global statistics on mental illness, self-harm, attempted suicide and completed suicides, can we infer that many of our citizens are being marginalised by a system that is oblivious to the provision of health care and education that nurtures emotional health? The political lack of empathy has become all the more stark when policymakers, who claim to possess a social conscience, accept grotesque salaries, dictate and erode the income of the unemployed, the elderly, the disabled and the sick. The vulnerability and financial stress that is experienced by many due to long-term unemployment, and the financial difficulties experienced by the elderly who are living on state pensions needs to be addressed at a political level.

In Ireland, while a large percentage of overall funding is spent on health, the amount spent on mental health is disproportionate to the number of people requiring treatment, while the amount allocated to suicide prevention is miniscule. The total budget for mental health in the majority of nations tends to be less than 1 per cent of total health expenditure (World Health Organisation, 2001a; Kemp, 2007, p. 102). The poor allocation of funding to suicide prevention places politics and economics as central components within the Suicide Box, as the message being sent out loud and clear is that escalating suicide rates are not important enough for the allocation of sufficient resources. Thus vital funding could be used for research, for campaigns, for education, for individual services, for social transformation in the ways we treat each other, judge ourselves, become lost in negative thoughts and fail to express our emotions in healthy ways. In particular, resources could be used to assess the extent of unnecessary human pain facilitated by social institutions.

State Abdication of Citizen's Welfare

A state's political ideology seeps into every facet of an individual's life. Where state ideologies are deeply oppressive there are significantly higher suicide rates than states that advocate more individual freedom (Joiner, 2005, p. 154). Ireland's recent political history is worthy of mention. The Irish state won partial independence from Britain in 1922, and gained full sovereignty in 1949. The years of suppression and colonisation, however, continued to take its toll on Irish citizens who now found themselves subject to laws drafted by one of the most conservative governments in Europe. The government gave enormous power to religious orders of the Catholic Church to administer education and run children's residential homes. This resulted in a litany of abuse that was finally revealed by the Commission to Inquire into Child Abuse Report (2009).

The report outlined in harrowing detail the emotional, physical and sexual abuse inflicted on children who attended schools and institutions from 1940 onwards. More than a hundred institutions and religious orders, including the Sisters of Mercy, the Christian Brothers and the Presentation Brothers, were investigated over the last decade. The key findings of the report concluded that physical and emotional abuse were features of the institutions and that sexual abuse, neglect and malnourishment occurred in many of them; the submissive attitude of the Department of Education towards the orders running the institutions compromised its ability to carry out its duty of inspection and monitoring in institutions and schools (McCarthy, 2009).

Religious institutions were also allowed to run private homes for profit, such as the Magdalene Laundries, where young women who had given birth outside of marriage suffered a form of enforced slavery and abuse. The Irish Human Rights Commission Assessment (2010), published in November 2010, concluded that there was significant evidence that the state failed to protect women and young girls from 'arbitrary detention, forced and compulsory labour, and servitude'.

Joe's Story

I'm telling this for my Dad who's no longer with us, and for his brothers and sister who had their lives destroyed by the nuns and the Irish state. My Dad's parents died within a year of each other. That left Dad and his siblings without parents. The state put the boys into an industrial school and put their young sister into a home run by nuns. My Dad hated talking about what happened to him there. One of his brothers was put into a mental institution because he couldn't cope with the tough regime. Another brother was sexually abused and that destroyed him. He ended up emigrating to get away from everything, but he turned to the drink and finally killed himself. There's only one of my uncles alive now and he's very bitter about what happened to them all. He hadn't heard from his sister in over fifty years but she finally contacted him out of the blue. She had been trying to trace our family for decades. She had been sold by the nuns to a very rich American family and had been brought up in a privileged home. She was the lucky one as she'd been well treated and had a good life in America. She got married and had her own family, though her daughter sadly killed herself. It's sad how that whole family was destroyed because of bad laws that had no care whatsoever how children were treated when placed under the authority of depraved priests and nuns.

The Aftermath of Abuse

It is impossible to calculate the damage and destruction that has been caused to individuals, their families, their communities and the wider society where institutional abuse was allowed to manifest and prosper. The last two decades in Ireland have revealed unprecedented neglect, abuse, corruption and gross mismanagement within the former cornerstones of society: the Catholic Church, the Irish state and our financial institutions. Our confidence and faith in those who hold power and authority has never been more dented and sullied. In a time of such social uncertainty and near chaos, perhaps it should be no great surprise that Ireland's suicide rate for young men and women is a close second for the highest suicide rate out of twenty-nine European countries (European Child Safety Alliance, 2014). The state, the Church and the entire economic system has failed its citizens. It is indeed time for rebuilding, for enormous change to take place in our social institutions, but most of all it is time to accept responsibility for looking on silently while the most vulnerable among us were trampled underfoot. The price we are paying as a society for neglect, for prejudice, and for gross inequalities is an increase in mental illness, in emotional collapse, in substance abuse, in attempted suicide, in self-harm, in completed suicides, and in an escalation of unnecessary human pain.

Global Economic System

Capitalism as a global economic system is a very attractive one for those who possess the resources to exploit it. It is an economic system where trade, industry and the means of production are privately owned and operated for the sole purpose of profit. The protectors of the system have shown a propensity to succumb to pressures in order to ensure that the status quo is preserved. Governments accomplish this by exploiting the energy that capitalism generates and present the spoils as appeasements to the people who elect them. Nevertheless, due to the power of the capitalist system, a government's ultimate inclination is to lean on the side of capital as it is dependent on it. There are immense inequalities inherent within such a system. The elements that are seriously lacking in this system are: human compassion, equality and fairness. These have to be fought for. Capitalism plays on and depends on segregation, and, much like a sociopath, is devoid of empathy. It needs us to focus exclusively on the self. This is the principal of its 'free enterprise' maxim; every person for him or herself. While Ireland claims to be a democratic and welfare state it has been ineffective in altering levels of fairness or equality while a feigned compassion presents only to placate. What government efforts can take credit for, though, is the embedding of learned helplessness and hopelessness into the lives of many.

All compassion, equality and fairness to date had to be fought hard for under this and other systems. Collective social blindness is a desired goal of the drivers of capitalism to aid profit maximisation. Therefore, it is vital that we begin to turn attention on the general human needs of all, and strive to reduce the unnecessary human pain inherent within systems like capitalism. Otherwise, we can learn to accept suicide as an unfortunate by-product of a system that serves to fulfil the needs and comforts of a privileged minority. The problem is that we are not looking at low levels of collateral damage here. Those who die by suicide are not the only ones who suffer unnecessary pain from the coldness of the system, which includes many of the 1 million people who die by suicide globally every year. The true estimate of those who suffer unnecessary human pain due to systems like capitalism and rigid socialisation is incalculable.

Political Priorities in Allocation of Funds

Much has been written on the banking crisis and the collapse in property prices that occurred in Ireland in 2008. The Irish economy suffered an immediate drop in output and employment, exacerbated by the onset of a world recession. Most economists agree that the catastrophe occurred due to a number of factors. Healy (2013, p. 2), director of the NERI Economic Research Institute, attributes the debacle to: 'Bad corporate governance, excessive and inappropriate lending with the consequence that bank balance sheets became bloated and potentially unstable in many private financial institutions. These failures were facilitated by grossly inadequate public regulation and oversight.'

The total cost of bailing out the banks by the Irish taxpayer is estimated to have been €64 billion. Since the beginning of the crisis, Irish governments have introduced austerity measures that have directly impacted the lives of millions of Irish citizens, including cuts to social welfare payments, placing an embargo on the hiring of health care staff, and imposing extra taxes and levies. The debt incurred through borrowing to bail out the banks is estimated to have cost €14,000 for every Irish man, woman and child (McCabe, 2014). This amount continues to multiply every second due to interest added. To date (16.30, 14 June 2015) the debt per head of population now stands at €45,480 (http://www.nationaldebt clocks.org/debtclock/ireland). The constricted economic situation is relevant to the lack of funding allocated by the Irish government for suicide prevention. Ireland has the fourth highest rate of youth suicide in Europe (*The Irish Examiner*, 31 January 2013): this makes it imperative that all sectors of society, most particularly our political system, will prioritise funding for a new, multi-tiered approach that will foster a reduction in suicide. However, if all the funding possible were poured into the Suicide Box as it exists with its distorted perspectives, it will merely continue the practice of putting bandages on gaping wounds, ignoring the poison beneath.

The Role of Economics in Suicide

The findings of a report carried out by a number of organisations in cooperation with Senator John Gilroy, revealed that from 2008–2012, there was a noticeable increase in suicides and self-harming which the senator believes was directly linked to the economic downturn (O'Riordan, 2014). During recessions, increases in suicide mainly occur in men, with particular rises in the 15–24 age group. This is seen as a consequence of the larger rates of job loss and un-employment in this group, especially in the construction industry. It is estimated that between 305 and 560 people who came under increased pressure because of the recession took their lives. The number of self-harm cases also noticeably increased. It is estimated that there were 6,200–8,600 more cases than usual over the same five-year period. In 2008 when unemployment stood at 6.1 per cent, suicide rates increased to 11.4 per 100,000 of the population. There was a rise in unemployment in 2009 and suicide increased to 12.4 per 100,000.

The causes of suicide are usually viewed at an individual level, such as having a mental illness or self-harming, rather than in the context of social, economic and cultural norms that may be causing the individual great distress and pain (Wylie et al, 2012). Social factors also impinge on people finding work in their middle and later years, as age discrimination and employer prejudice make it very difficult to obtain employment (Thomas and Pemberton, 2011). Being reliant on welfare payments may also lead to a very low standard of living and further limit opportunities for basic social interaction.

Evictions and House Foreclosures linked to Suicides

The need for adequate housing as a physical, psychological and emotional requirement, and the level of distress engendered by the enforced loss of a person's home was highlighted by a recent study in the United States. The study links severe stress around housing problems to suicide. Researchers linked with the Division of Violence Prevention, Centers for Disease Control and Prevention in Atlanta analysed suicides in sixteen states and found that suicides spurred by severe housing stress doubled between 2005 and 2010 (Fowler et al, 2015). The researchers identified 929 suicides related to housing stress: 51 per cent were eviction related and 49 per cent foreclosure related. A large number of deaths (37 per cent) occurred within two weeks of a particular housing crisis, such as an eviction notice or court hearing. The overwhelming majority of these suicides (79 per cent) took place before the renters or owners actually lost their housing.

The study recommended that training of professionals, including bank officials, may be helpful to recognise suicidal stressors and tendencies before they emerge (Fowler et al, 2015). However, the main social causes of people losing their homes, namely a fall in income and unemployment, and the failure of banks to negotiate fair mortgage repayment schemes based on a person's ability to pay, need to be addressed politically for the overall well-being of individuals, families and society. Suicides directly linked to evictions have also recently been reported in Ireland (Naughton, 2015) and Spain (Press Association, 2013).

Mental Illness, Self-harm and Economics
A growing body of research supports the view that mental illness and behavioural disorders are the result of both genetics and environment (Rochefort, 1997; Kemp, 2007, p. 103). Social factors such as poverty and urbanisation can play a role in the development of mental disorders (World Health Organisation, 2001a). Research from a cross-national survey in Brazil, Chile, India and Zimbabwe show that mental disorders are twice as commonly found among the

poor as the rich (Patel et al, 1999). Modern urbanisation may have negative consequences for mental health through increased stress and adverse life events, including reduced social support, overcrowding, poverty, pollution and violence (Desjarlais et al, 1995).

According to the World Health Organisation (2003), 'mental health is a most important, maybe the most important, public health issue, which even the poorest society must afford to promote, to protect and to invest in'. Although Ireland's adjusted total health expenditure for 2011 was the third highest out of the thirty-four OECD countries (publicpolicy.ie, 2012), its budget for suicide prevention for the same year was less than €5 million (Muldoon, 2011). Despite the importance of routing finance into mental health and suicide prevention, the provision of these services by the government was delayed in December 2012, so that funds could be used to reduce the overspending of the Health Service Executive (O'Brien, 2012). Plans to invest €25 million in modernising mental health services during 2012, including the recruitment of staff that specialise in suicide prevention was postponed.

The Economics of Reducing Tragedies

Suicide and road accidents account for the largest number of deaths of young people in Ireland. Throughout the 1990s, the carnage and death on Ireland's roads was appalling. In 1997, the number of deaths reached an all-time high when 472 people lost their lives. The Irish government was slow to act, but in September 2006, it established the Road Safety Authority. The Authority was given the task of improving safety and reducing the number of road deaths through the promotion of road safety, conducting research on accidents, overhauling driver testing and licensing, as well as establishing vehicle-related and other safe driving standards. A national campaign ensued, led by TV personality Gay Byrne. The government's road safety target of achieving no more than 252 deaths per annum by the end of 2012 was achieved three years ahead of schedule. This acknowledged society's role in the prevention of deaths on Irish roads.

In Ireland, a call for the establishment of a national suicide authority to apply the same energy given to the Road Safety Authority for actions appropriate to suicide prevention, has been made by all sectors of the community. While it is clear that great differences exist between dealing with road safety and dealing with suicide, it is the dynamism that has been applied to road safety that is urgently required. The closest that Ireland has come to a national body specifically dedicated to reducing suicide is the National Office for Suicide Prevention that was allocated a budget of €8.8 million in 2014. However, this is merely a coordinating body for suicide prevention organisations within the Suicide Box.

It is a tragedy for society that even one life is lost through suicide, notwithstanding the subsequent pain and grief caused to the family and friends of the suicide bereaved. For governments that are primarily driven by economics, the cost of even one suicide demonstrates the economic sense of putting a suicide authority in place to tackle the many social issues that exacerbate self-harm and suicide. Suicide costs include direct expenses, such as funeral, emergency services and medical; indirect costs and intangible human costs (Kennelly, 2007; Zechmeister et al, 2008). In the United States, suicide costs society approximately $34.6 billion a year in combined medical and work loss costs, based on 2005 figures. One suicide is estimated to cost $1,061,170 (Centers for Disease Control and Prevention, 2012). In Ireland, estimates for the cost for each individual suicide in 2002 was €835,663 (Arensman, 2012).

Government Reports Fail to Consult Suicide Bereaved

Many experts in the area of research, sociology, psychology and mental health have contributed greatly to our understanding of the causes and effects of suicide by producing balanced, statistically accurate and thought-provoking reports. An essential ingredient, however, that needs to be present in all reporting or discussion of suicide, particularly reports published by the government, is the consideration of the opinions, feelings and experiences of those who have been bereaved by suicide. The exclusion of these 'expert' views are evident in documents and reports commissioned by the government, where the more acceptable type of academic 'experts', who write with proficiency from within the Suicide Box but without the life experience of being bereaved by suicide or at least listening to those who have been, show the tendency to be influenced by the myths and stigma that impact society's thinking.

Insights from Sharon

My beautiful son died by suicide. He chose to die by hanging. It was devastating for us as a family. He really had everything to live for. We have such a hard time coping with his death and the fact that he choose to remove himself from us and the world. In 2011, I read the government document called *Suicide Prevention in the Community: A Practical Guide*. At the beginning I was delighted with this initiative but as I read through I got the feeling that the authors were coming from a place of fear where they seemed to lose sight of the human behind the act of suicide and through their fear of suicide made recommendations that only defined people who suicide by their death. What really upset me was when they recommended that trees used in a suicide should be cut down to prevent them becoming a memorial tree. My son chose that tree because he loved sitting under that tree with his friends as he grew up. It was a place of peace for him and as the turmoil in his mind grew he was obviously drawn to end his life there. No one has ever suggested making that a memorial tree to my son and I have never heard or seen a tree used in this way. Should we also consider knocking buildings or bridges used in suicides? Surely this recommendation has to have been the imagination of someone who had already false assumptions and fears around suicide. If someone tried to cut down the tree my son used to die I would defend it with my own life not because of my son's connection with it but because I don't see what the tree had to do with it. I wish someone had asked my opinion before they wrote this document.

The Role of the State in Reducing Suicide

The state will do little to reduce suicide as long as it sees suicide as being a problem that affects a small minority of individuals. It distances itself further from the problem because it fails to see a role for itself in influencing individual decisions such as whether or not a person chooses to take his or her own life. The state's basic underlying assumption is that any person who cannot survive effectively within its system is somehow flawed. This is why any state funding is focused on supporting organisations that work at the level of the individual. This, of course, exonerates the system that includes education, justice, health, etc. from having to look at its many flaws or take responsibility for the part it plays in suicide. This may also account for the state's small allocation of funding, particularly in Ireland, for working towards reducing suicide and for the almost total exclusion of emotional intelligence in the school curriculum. The state's ultimate failure is in not recognising the causes of unnecessary human pain. By seeing the individual as failing to 'fit' within society and being 'the problem', society restricts the individual from becoming his or her true self. This alienation from the self, causes great emotional pain that is manifest in social problems such as alcoholism, drug addiction, self-harm and the ultimate manifestation of human pain – suicide.

CHAPTER SEVEN

Religion

It is clear from earliest cave paintings and megalithic artworks that people have always believed in a divine force, a god or goddess, a magnificent being or higher power, to soothe their woes, give meaning to their earthly toil, and provide instruction as to how to obtain eternal salvation. Western culture has been dominated by allegiance to the Jewish and Christian religions, whereas the philosophy of Buddhism and the Hindu religion prevail in the East, with Islam being the primary religion in the Middle East. The act of suicide has experienced centuries of retribution at the hands of all global religions and this more than any other factor has contributed to the Suicide Box, to the continuance of myths, fears, taboos and stigma, each mingled and blended with emotions of powerlessness and shame for many who have attempted suicide or for those who have been bereaved by suicide.

In relation to mental health, stigma has been defined as (See Change Campaign, 2004), 'A cluster of negative attitudes and beliefs that motivate the general public to fear, reject, avoid and discriminate against people with mental ill health.' Stigma is a result of ignorance, fear and misunderstanding. The stigma around suicide that derives from the teachings of the world religions on the subject are even more menacing to eradicate than those that originate from fears around mental illness. They have been constructed over thousands of years, packaged as church doctrines that require blind belief. They are lodged so deeply within the individual mind and social structures that we can hardly recognise their existence or the damage that is done through their perpetuation.

Religious Stigmatisation of Suicide

Punitive practices following a suicide have been recorded since the Middle Ages and have very close roots with institutionalised religion's condemnation of those who have died by suicide (Feigelman, Gorman, and Jordan, 2009). Suicide corpses were mutilated to ensure that evil spirits were kept at bay. Suicides were also denied burials in consecrated ground and their families were punished by having their lands confiscated and by being excommunicated from the community (Cvinar, 2005). Families also had to endure the payment of heavy tithes demanded by the Church after the death of a loved one through suicide (Dunne-Maxim, 2007). This practice often resulted in the family's destitution or emigration. These barbaric and occult-like practices, carried out in the name of God and the Catholic Church, made an indelible mark on the human psyche and ensured that the act of suicide, as well as the families bereaved, were highly stigmatised throughout the centuries (Cvinar, 2005). This stigmatisation of those who have died by suicide, who have attempted suicide or those who have been bereaved by suicide, continues today.

Teachings of Major Religions on Suicide

The roots of this insidious stigmatisation are found in the beliefs of the world's main religions. Although suicide is not prohibited in the Hebrew Bible nor in the New Testament (Evans, Farberow, and Kennedy Associates, 2003, p. 138), the condemnation of suicide was professed by leaders of Judaism and Catholicism so that the act was viewed as a sin (Frankel and Kranz, 1994, p. 18). In Judaism today, suicide is still considered a crime against God, but in some cases the person may be forgiven (Evans, Farberow, and Kennedy Associates, 2003, p. 139).

The Quran (Koran), the book of Holy Scriptures of Islam, forbids suicide as a grievous sin. Muslims believe that each person has a destiny or kismet that is preordained by God, so interfering with this is a serious crime that leads to eternal punishment (Evans, Farberow, and Kennedy Associates, 2003, p. 135; Blom, Bracaille and Martinez: 2007, p. 6). In Hinduism, suicide and murder are considered equally sinful. Hindu scriptures state that suicides become part of the spirit world but they are bound to wander the earth until their preordained time to die naturally arrives (Evans, Farberow, and Kennedy Associates, 2003, p. 20). Buddhists believe that suicide occurs due to a person's lack of tolerance or patience towards life's stressors (Evans, Farberow, and Kennedy Associates, 2003, p. 29). Generally, Buddhists are sympathetic and show mercy for those who have killed themselves and for their loved ones. Their fundamental belief is that life is difficult and those who do not achieve enlightenment in this life will reincarnate again. The Buddhist view of suicide is that the act postpones the inevitable task of learning about the nature of illusion and eventually becoming enlightened (Evans, Farberow and Kennedy Associates, 2003, p. 197).

The greatest stigmatisation of suicide in Christianity occurred at the hands of St Augustine, and later St Thomas Aquinas. St Augustine stated categorically that suicide was equivalent to self-murder and, therefore, a sin (Evans, Farberow, and Kennedy Associates, 2003, p. 45). He took the sixth commandment literally: 'Thou shalt not kill' as applicable to all human situations. In 563, the Fifteenth Canon of the Council of Bragan denied those who killed themselves the funeral rites of the Eucharist. In 673, the Council of Hereford withheld burial rites from those who killed themselves. In 1284, the Synod of Nimes refused suicide burial in holy ground.

Catholic Doctrine and Philosophical Theories on Suicide
The influence of the Catholic Church has extended to most of Western civilisation in terms of culture, philosophy and legislation. For centuries the dogma of the Church became the basis for state laws in Catholic countries, including Spain and Italy. This has been the situation until quite recently in Ireland, where 84.2 per cent of the population are Catholic according to the national census (Healy, 2012).

The Catechism of the Catholic Church (1993) states that human beings do not have the right to end their own lives (Rosen, 2012, p. 121). Thus, God remains the sovereign master of life and it is the responsibility of every person to preserve one's life for God's honour and for the salvation of the soul. Philosophers, such as Immanuel Kant, have argued this point for centuries. In contrast, other philosophers such as Christine Korsgaard argue that people have the right to end their own lives if they want to because of self-ownership (Rosen, 2012, p. 149).

The Church's reaction to suicide, though somewhat diluted now, has been to blame those who have taken their own lives, to deny any responsibility for their action and their feelings of hopelessness, and to publicly expel them from the Church by refusing burial in consecrated ground. The arrogant assumption was that God would concur with this unloving, earthly decision and resulting actions. The Church's teaching that intentional suicide is a mortal sin has set the moral compass and influenced state legislation, so that for centuries suicide was deemed to be a criminal offence, and attempted suicide was punishable by incarceration in many Western countries.

The Power of Religion for Good or Ill

In many Western countries, attendance at religious devotions that once united whole communities has dropped significantly (The Pew Forum, 2010; World Values Survey, 2000). However, the power that religious beliefs exert continues to be significant. It has been proffered that a strong religious faith may act as a prohibition against suicide (Dervic et al, 2004; Evans, Farberow, and Kennedy Associates, 2003, p. 135). The loss of religious practice, especially in rural areas where the Church is often the centre of communities where people meet friends and neighbours, may be a risk factor in suicide (O'Sullivan et al, 2011). A belief in a grand plan, in a God and an afterlife may offer reassurance, guidance and comfort when there is great suffering, pain or confusion (Guglielmi, 2008). Also, the perceived consequences of perpetrating the act of suicide for someone who is deeply religious, such as breaking a sacred law or commandment, may persuade a suicidal person not to act on the impulses.

Dr Phipps (1985), Professor of Religion and Philosophy at Davis and Elkins College, West Virginia, appears somewhat perplexed at the absence of discourse on suicide in Christian services. Dr Phipps states that 'even though suicide occurs with frequency and in virtually every community, I have never heard or read a sermon on the subject. No mention is made of suicide in several books I possess that deal with Christian morality.' Since suicide has reached crisis point in many countries worldwide, it is indeed confounding that the Catholic Church appears to have been struck silent after centuries of publishing dogmas about the sinful nature of suicide. A most welcome and humane position has been voiced by Fr Saunders (Saunders, 1995), priest and author, who states that although suicide is regarded as a mortal sin by the Catholic Church, 'we do offer the Mass for the repose of the soul of a suicide victim, invoking God's tender love and mercy, and His healing grace for the grieving loved ones'.

Religion and Sexuality

Religions offer moral guidance to their members, laying the foundations for a fruitful life and the hope of another existence to come after death. Many religions, however, promote a negative view of sexuality that often causes feelings of deep guilt, confusion and frustration for members. The Catholic Church in Ireland is an example of a religion that emphasises the procreative aspect of sex, even going so far until recent times as to demand the 'churching' of all mothers following the birth of a baby. This involved the priest blessing the mother after her 'proof' of being unclean. Also the sacrament of communion is denied to a person whose marriage has broken down and who has entered into a new relationship. In a church that stipulates that its clergy remain celibate, virtually all sexual acts have become tinged with sinfulness. The Church continues to uphold the sanctity of marriage, despite depraved abuses that occur within some unions, completely removing all possible hope of happiness for those who wish to end a failed marriage as divorce is outlawed. All sexual relationships outside of marriage, no matter how mutually loving, are considered sinful.

Sexuality is a powerful force and instinct that needs to develop in a loving and holistic way. When viewed as a highly pleasurable means of expression between two mutually consenting and responsible adults, it can be a source of great joy and emotional fulfilment. However, when teenagers are raised in a religion where sexuality is viewed as immoral, a dangerous impulse to be denied and even feared, they may have great difficulties in experiencing loving and sexually fulfilling relationships. For homosexual adolescents who are raised in a family of a religious tradition that teaches that homosexuality is a sinful practice, there may be an enormous struggle to accept their sexual orientation. Religion may instil guilt, self-loathing and confusion in a young person who is gay or lesbian, and feels rejected by his or her church, family and wider society (Grollman and Malikow, 1999, p. 69). This rejection does little to improve the well-being or self-esteem of a homosexual teenager. This is all the more serious when faced with the estimate that one-third of young people who attempt suicide or take their own lives are homosexual (Berkovitz, 1985).

The Stigmatisation of the Suicide Bereaved

The depth of pain experienced by the families and friends of those who have died by suicide is often unbearable. A study by Crosby and Sacks (2002) found that, for every death that occurs by suicide, 7 per cent of the general population is affected over a one year period, including friends, acquaintances and family members. It is, therefore, a particularly cruel reality for many that shame, caused by stigma linked to cultural and religious beliefs about suicide, is also visited on the bereaved (Reed, 1998; Silverman et al, 1994–5). The deeply rooted stigmas that permeate every facet of society may cause survivors to feel humiliated, believing that suicide has brought dishonour and disgrace to the family (Seguin, 1995a) and has spoiled each family member's identity (Goffman, 1968). It is more than understandable, then, that families would rather keep the truth about the death of their loved one a secret, rather than exposing themselves to society's censure. Today, that censure does not involve the seizure of their property or assets, or excommunication from any church. It does, however, involve examination in a coroner's court which is usually open to the full glare of the public's curiosity. There is also censure from the insurance industry where policies are generally not paid if the insured has died by suicide (Bleed, 2007).

In a study conducted on the impact of stigma on the grief process of suicide survivors, religion was mentioned by all participants as contributing and perpetuating the negative judgements about suicide (Guglielmi, 2008, p. 33). Susan, who lost her sister through suicide stated that: 'I believe that the group that has the highest responsibility for the social stigma is the Church.' Alyssa reported that her Catholic upbringing had been very difficult to cope with since her dad died by suicide (Guglielmi, 2008, p. 34). The Church took away any hope that her dad was in heaven. It was very disturbing for the young Alyssa to be told that her dad was suffering in purgatory for all eternity. Dan, even as an adult, found it difficult to think of his sister who had killed herself, because of his church's teaching that suicide is a sin and that all suicides go to hell. This degree of ignorance, intolerance and insensitivity is difficult to contemplate, more especially when religious institutions that profess to believe in a loving and magnanimous deity propagate it.

The fears around celebrating the life of a loved one who has died through suicide during a religious service or in the erection of a memorial, due to the possibility of cluster or copycat suicides, is expressed in *Suicide Prevention in the Community: A Practical Guide* (2011). The booklet states that it is imperative that suicide is not made to sound 'glamorous' or 'normal', and that 'it is important that people speaking at the funeral do not glamorise the "state of peace" the deceased may have found through death'. It is a responsible practice to adopt, that no religious service should glamorise suicide. Yet the need for bereaved families to feel that their loved one has found peace must be overwhelming at such a traumatic and devastating time. The psyche must surely crave this solace; that those who were in darkest pain have now found serenity. Surely any religious institution or organisation that seeks to prevent suicide must feel deep empathy and compassion for anyone who finds themselves in such a predicament, grieving the death of a loved one through suicide, in desperate need of reassurance and the belief that their child, sibling or spouse has at last found peace.

The Halton Suicide Prevention Coalition, based in Canada aims to remove the stigma, shame and guilt that are associated with suicide in order to prevent more deaths by suicide. On their website they state that 'suicide stigma has deep roots in religion and the law ... Stigma is one of the biggest barriers in the grief process for survivors of suicide. Most importantly, stigma around suicide often keeps people who are suicidal from openly talking about their thoughts with family and friends and from seeking help, treatment and support. This means suicide stigma can actually cause suicide (www.suicidepreventionhalton.ca/suicidefacts/stigma1.php).'

It seems, on reflection, that the human handling of suicide throughout the ages has been more about human fears, ignorance and control than reflecting the word of a loving and compassionate God that is central to all known religions. There is surely no better time in human experience to practice 'loving your neighbour' than at a time of suicide when a person has chosen to die due to intolerable pain, often believing in their irrational state that this decision is best for the world, not themselves. It follows without saying that this same simple God-given commandment of love extends to the distraught family and friends.

CHAPTER EIGHT

The Law

The legal system purports to administer justice based on the premise of equality. The law has developed over centuries and, in each epoch, has mirrored the social mores and customs in vogue. The overseers of the law most usually come from society's privileged, in terms of wealth and education. The practice of the law, medicine and religion have traditionally bestowed great status and power on officials through the use of Latin, a language that is synonymous with privilege and high academic achievement. The code of dress and archaic customs also create deep inequalities between those who make judgements and those who are at their mercy. Inherent within the system, therefore, is the reality that those of lower income or status experience the harshest and most unfair outcomes, such as being brought to court or imprisoned for the non-payment of a television licence, or not having access to the best legal representation. Heavy-handedness and public humiliation is often the experience of the poorer class while the well-off are more likely to receive respectful and negotiated treatment.

While the law claims to be fair and just, societal biases are often reflected in judgements and sentencing practices. Examples of these include, race (Sweeney and Haney, 2006), gender (Graycar, 1998; Mahony, 1993), status and income (Nagel and Hagan, 1982), and first impression/looks (Porter et al, 2010). One of the noted characteristics of the legal system within the Suicide Box is its use of punitive responses to all perceived offences against society. The resultant inequalities have become so ingrained that the gross unfairness has become part of society's mindset and are rarely questioned.

The law within the Suicide Box is hierarchical and archaic. It is set up to be uncomfortable and fear based. The ordinary person is at a huge disadvantage where access to fewer resources increases the potential for penalty. While much talk is made of rehabilitation and restoring an offender to model citizenship, the irony is that the punitive process stacks the deck against this outcome. One of society's greatest stigmas is to have been charged with a crime or imprisoned as it seriously affects future career, livelihood and social inclusion. Furthermore, the media supports this process by spreading the perspective and facilitating the punitive mentality at the broadest public levels. Within the Suicide Box societies create their own monsters.

With regard to suicide, the act was punishable as a crime from medieval times. Suicide was finally decriminalised in many nations during the twentieth century. The main emphasis in this section is the description of the inquest process that is conducted as a legal requirement in most countries when a case of suicide is reported. This is presented as an example of the lack of social empathy that exists in our society, when twenty years after the decriminalisation of suicide in Ireland, inquests are still being carried out in courtroom settings that possess all the hallmarks that a crime has taken place.

Punitive Responses

Punishment in various forms is the penalty for breaking the law. Many countries aim to impose punishments that are in line with human rights legislation, though some countries, notably the United States, inflict the barbaric death penalty for certain crimes. The adoption of punitive responses that are so central to legal systems have become mirrored in all other areas of society, such as prisons, workplaces and schools. Society's approach to unacceptable behaviour is largely punitive. Responses to bullying in schools have been met with unhelpful punitive approaches for the purpose of immediate impact, even if it means ostracising and labelling a child. Perhaps a good example of the embeddedness of the punitive social mindset is found in our prisons. When a person is sentenced to imprisonment, the punishment under the law is deprivation of freedom for the crime committed. However, society's false assumptions and practices determine that the punishment should extend to demeaning the prisoner even when the person's time has been served. Evidence of the social support for this is echoed by empty and senseless phrases such as 'lock them up and throw away the key' or, to emphasise the punitive, 'they should be made split rocks all day and be deprived of any concessions'. Often it takes the incarceration of a close relative or friend to alter this unhelpful mindset.

Within the Suicide Box the punitive approach works like this. When an offence is committed a person is deemed by law to have offended against society. The offender and the victim of a crime are therefore separated and the management of the aftermath is taken over by the state. Little by way of healing or restoration is possible within this process. Absurdly, offenders are made victims of the legal process and have now to enter defence mode where protection of the self becomes a vital part of the process. They have to minimise the harm done and attribute blame to others, while essentially being excluded from the process of healing for their behaviour, just as victims of crimes are deprived of being freed from all blame by their exclusion. The process then produces its biggest impact by labelling and marginalising offenders for the rest of their lives, fuelling anger, hate and revenge. It is this punitive approach that enhances risk factors for the vulnerable, adding much unnecessary human pain that so often ends in suicide.

Suicide as a Crime

State laws that deemed suicide to be a crime largely followed the moral laws that vilified the act in organised religions. For centuries, the body of a suicide was desecrated with the approval of the state, and the property of those who had died by suicide, as well as the lands and belongings of their family, were confiscated and forfeited to the crown. In Western societies today, suicide is no longer punishable as a crime, although it is still fraught with the stigmas of shame and retribution that have long been associated with legal punishment. The roots of this negative and punitive association between the law and suicide have done much to contribute to the Suicide Box, to the spread of fear and the need for secrecy that many grieving families experience after the death of a loved one through suicide. Even the phrase that is still commonly used to describe the act of suicide: 'to commit suicide' is derived from the archaic legal view of suicide as a crime.

Throughout Europe from medieval times, the corpse of a suicide was degraded, mutilated or given to schools of anatomy for dissection (Alvarez, 2013, p. 64–5). In Danzig, the corpse was not allowed to be removed through the door but had to be lowered by pulleys from a window. Such was the level of stigma, superstition and revulsion around suicide, that the window frame on which the corpse was briefly placed was immediately burnt. As previously outlined, a similar degree of fear and stigma remains today where an Irish document promoting the prevention of suicide in the community recommends 'that trees used in a suicide such as a hanging are cut down to avoid them becoming a memorial' (O'Sullivan, Rainsford, and Sihera, 2011).

In seventeenth-century France, Louis XIV enacted a law to destroy the castle or property of any nobleman who killed himself (Alvarez, 2013, p. 65). In England and in many parts of Europe, the property and lands of a suicide could be confiscated and forfeited to the crown. This law continued until 1870. A person who attempted suicide in England could also be imprisoned or fined until 1961 (Holt, 2011; Alvarex, 2013, p. 65–6). As recently as February 1959, William Morgan, a 31-year-old Londoner who tried to take his life, was sentenced to one month in prison. As late as 1969, a teenager on the Isle of Man was birched as a punishment for attempting suicide (Gardner and Rosenberg, 1969). Attempted suicide is still a criminal offence in some countries, including India (Vijayakuman, 2003, p. 89). Section 309 of the Indian Penal Code states that: 'Whoever attempts to commit suicide and does any act towards the commission of such an offence shall be punished with simple imprisonment for a term which may extend to one year, or with fine, or both.'

The Decriminalisation of Suicide

In the mid to late twentieth century, all European countries decriminalised suicide. Ireland was the last European country to follow suit in 1993 (Hawton and Van Heeringen, 2000). The Suicide Act of 1961 decriminalised suicide in England and Wales. According to Dr Wright, author and professor of history at Canada's McGill University (Holt, 2011), 'From the middle of the 18th Century to the mid-20th Century there was growing tolerance and a softening of public attitudes towards suicide which was a reflection of, among other things, the secularisation of society and the emergence of the medical profession.' In 1958 the British Medical Association and the Magistrates' Association also advocated 'a more compassionate and merciful outlook', and a year later the Church of England agreed that it was time to change the antiquated law (Holt, 2011). Suicide was decriminalised in Canada in 1972 (www.thecanadian encyclopedia.com/articles/suicide). In Australia, the law relating to suicide varies between states and territories, but suicide is no longer

a crime in any jurisdiction (www.psychology.org.au/Content.aspx?
ID=5048).

The Inquest

An inquest is an inquiry that is conducted in public by a coroner,
with or without a jury. A coroner is an independent official with
responsibility under law for the medical and legal investigations of
deaths. It is a legal requirement to investigate unnatural deaths,
including suicide, by holding an inquest. A post-mortem may also
be required. In Ireland, the Gardaí act as coroner officers, reporting
the facts surrounding the death. It is intended to hold inquests
between six weeks and twelve months following the death but in
reality it can take several years for many grieving families to get past
this ordeal. The inquest establishes when, where and how the death
occurred. The inquest is open to the public. It does not investigate
why a person died by suicide. The coroner may require witnesses to
be called and to give evidence. Family members may be present at
the inquest. They may obtain legal representation to advise them or
they may ask questions themselves during the inquest. The existence
of suicide notes are acknowledged but are not read out. The death
is registered by means of a coroner's certificate when the inquest is
concluded. A verdict of accidental death, misadventure, suicide,
natural causes or an open verdict may be recorded.

The Irish state's position is one where the Minister for Justice,
Equality and Law Reform and his/her department denies any
involvement in the process of conducting inquests in Ireland, as per
correspondence from the minister's office that was forwarded to us.
Yet they stipulate that every reportable death be fully investigated
by a coroner and, if necessary, that an inquest be held. They also
demand that inquests are held in public. They point out that a local
courthouse is the preferable venue for this purpose, which is why

coroners mainly choose this setting as it has the necessary facilities to perform inquests. These facilities include a specific jury box and a jury room, an anteroom and meeting rooms where bereaved families can wait in private with Garda liaison officers, and the availability of equipment to show CCTV footage and photographs. If this is the cold administrative approach that our politicians and civil servants adopt, then possibilities for positive human change or the raising of our social consciousness is going to be a difficult task indeed.

Research studies attest to the distress and the negative impact on the grieving process when relatives are compelled to attend an inquest into the death of a loved one following suicide (Biddle, 2003). An inquest can interfere with the resolution of grief by exacerbating common grief reactions associated with suicide such as shame, guilt and anger (Arensman et al, 2012). Although most coroners seek to ensure that the inquest is conducted with as little distress or intrusion to families as possible, there are several factors inherent in the inquest system in Ireland that require immediate reform. In many counties, the inquest is held in a county courthouse that is generally used to try criminal cases. For the vast majority of families who have to attend an inquest into the death of their loved one, the court feels stark and intimidating, confounding feelings of being stigmatised and judged. Since most inquests are held periodically, relatives usually have to sit through a number of cases, listening to the traumatic and grief-filled details about the loved one of other families, before having their own case heard. This does not reflect well on our social empathy for members of our community who are in deep pain and grief. Suicide is a problem for the whole of society and should not be borne by any one family in isolation. Restrictive and archaic laws need to be brought up to date to allow healthy social progress to occur. The inquest deals with forensic examination focused solely on the facts surrounding the individual's death. This firmly keeps the *why* questions shrouded in mystery and any blame squarely on the shoulders of the deceased, the very issues that make grief following suicide so complicated. Of course, this process is useful for society to maintain a blameless position, especially with the absence of the star witness, to avoid having to look at the social journey that brought the person to their cliff edge to end their life.

In some Irish counties, inquests, particularly those investigating suicide, are held in hotels. The intention behind this reform is to try to make families feel more at ease in comfortable and familiar surroundings. The reality for many families, however, is that the aroma of food, the casual banter and laughter they hear on entering the premises, as well as memories of happier times in similar venues exacerbates their feelings of sadness and alienation.

Miriam's Experience Attending the Inquest into her Son Matthew's Suicide
Following Matthew's death by suicide, we, as a family, felt isolation by the circumstances of his death and separated from each other by the complications of our own individual grieving for him. The looming inquest, seemed to affirm that something sinister and illegal had happened. The implication was that a crime had taken place and that the facts would determine something awful, or paint Matthew in a very negative way because he took his own life. Now, I know it doesn't have to be like this, and much needs to be done to reduce the trauma for families who are already suffering severely.

After more than a year of waiting for the inquest to take place, which had been postponed for many reasons, mainly awaiting reports or the involved Garda being on annual leave, our day of reckoning had arrived. I can't imagine what it would have been like if the inquest had been held in a courtroom, but Matthew's inquest was held in a hotel. To someone who has never experienced a suicide of a close family member a hotel probably sounds like a great idea.

As the day of Matthew's inquest loomed we did not know what to expect. Nothing could have prepared us for the coldness and starkness of the event. At the time it felt like the inquest was a punishment we, as Matthew's family, had to suffer because he took his own life. Because of how the inquest was conducted (inappropriateness of the venue, lack of information, coldness of the process, no water available, etc.) it felt like everything was being made as hard and isolating as possible, as if it was a necessary follow-up to a suicide.

The hotel lobby (on entering) gave an atmosphere of relaxation, entertainment and comfort. Hotel noises and smells were disconcerting creating a surreal environment with background music, food aromas, glasses clinking, laughter, etc. The relaxing, calm atmosphere made the feelings of confusion, shock and emptiness even more apparent.

Walking into the function room (where the inquests were taking place), the atmosphere was tense and the people seated there appeared anxious. It was set up just like I had seen courtrooms on television with a position for a judge, seating for a jury to the side, uniformed police seated along the other side, an area for witnesses to give evidence, with a bible on the bench nearby, and the public facing all this.

The sheer volume of people seated was shocking. The singular large function room was an invitation for a large crowd to gather and did not give any thought for the sensitivities of the grieving families. My family had to sit separately as no seats were available together. I wanted to be sitting with my other son at least, as I knew how rough this was on him. Seating became available as the Coroner went through his case list, as he deferred and postponed cases.

The only preparation we had for the inquest was from the Garda dealing with Matthew's case, which really was just a notice of the date and venue. He was unable to give us an approximate time when our case might be heard on the day. He did not know how public or private the inquest would be. We would like to have been aware and prepared for such experiences and be told important information such as; that the case could be deferred by the coroner, the involvement of the HSE, of the professionals who could be called on, the involvement of solicitors, the involvement of family members, the age limit of who could attend, that a jury would be involved, that we would have to sit and listen throughout the delivery of the brutal autopsy results of not only Matthew but that of all others also.

This can't be right. Those in the know seem to either assume that people would know how these things work or they haven't put themselves in the shoes of those who have been bereaved by suicide. I would hate to think that they don't care. If they showed concern on the day it went unnoticed as this belated effort in the midst of the organised chaos is wasteful. Instead, Matthew was reduced to a statistic in the most public of ways, his beautiful nature and short life coldheartedly erased. Change needs to reflect empathy for what the wait, the unknown, the public exposure to shame, official insensitivity and even inquest deferment can all mean for families.

Where was the neutral support, the comfort, the understanding? Where were the handouts or leaflets with basic information that could have helped even on the day? Why was there a need to announce unnecessary family information concerning my other son that could only have served to alert reporters present to a good story piece?

We all left the inquest that day in a bewildered state. We were unable to eat all day. No water was available to the families present. If we left the room who would call us? Why did we have to sit through the preceding cases to ours? Would the details of Matthew's case be in the paper? Could we have asked that our case be kept private? These and many other worries haunted us all as we travelled home in silence.

Coroner's Experiences of Presiding over Inquests into Suicide
Despite the stark coldness of the inquest process one of the most positive findings to emerge from our investigations for this book is the high level of empathy that is present among coroners. Coroner Terence Casey, related his experience of presiding over six inquests

in Killarney (RTE Radio 1, 5 May 2013) where five of these had been suicides:

> I saw the parents, the brothers, the sisters, uncles and aunts, friends of those young people sitting before me, and they all blaming themselves. People do blame themselves and they shouldn't. I'm afraid that is human nature. The pain and the suffering that is left behind in the families of those young people who take their own lives, is unbearable … It's terrible really to see the families coming into a coroner's court. They're afraid people will see them, walking in the door. It's a terrible situation when there should be no stigma attached to it. There's no blame on the families. On the 18 April when I had my last coroner's court I had as I say five cases of suicide. Now if you multiply that by four or five people per family and you put them all sitting, looking down at you, and one hearing the death in another family, and you have people starting to cry, and the whole area is starting to cry, there's tears flowing everywhere. I mean it has to move anybody, including a coroner. We see some horrific things in our job but I honestly believe that the suffering left behind by suicide is greater than the suffering left behind by any other type of death.

CHAPTER NINE

Mental Health and Psychiatry

Throughout history, society's unenlightened attitude towards mental illness and its often brutal system of incarceration has generated an enormous degree of stigma and fear (Salize et al, 2002, p. 2). People with perceived mental illness have always been regarded with dread or suspicion by society (Kemp, 2007, p. xiii) and have been isolated and discriminated against. This has placed mental illness in a central location within the Suicide Box. Deep mistrust and ignorance are tightly wrapped around the areas of mental illness and psychiatric services. Mental health clinicians are unlikely to adopt outside-the-box perspectives. They too are products of the powerful ubiquitous social and cultural influences dominant in society. Efforts to introduce change have brought a spate of criticism and rejection. Attempting to move in a new direction, no matter how beneficial, will likely involve a seismic shift.

Traditional Confinement of the Insane
According to the Irish Association of Suicidology (www.ias.ie), 'the stigma that surrounds mental health and suicide is ingrained in Irish society based on historical reasons'. Religion, the law and psychiatry have always had an influence on the definition of what constitutes normal, moral or sane behaviour. Religious beliefs as to the causes of mental illness throughout the ages have included possession by evil spirits, and a sinful and immoral nature. For centuries, the law has been the vehicle for involuntarily committing people who were

deemed to be insane to an asylum or psychiatric institution. A series of acts in Ireland from 1634 created cells for 'pauper lunatics' and 'idiots' in workhouses and houses of industry, before asylums were built to confine those who were declared insane. The psychiatric branch of medicine has incarcerated patients for centuries. Often people who exhibited challenging behaviours that were considered rebellious, non-compliant or overtly sexual, were handed over by their families for confinement in asylums, in appalling conditions, for various suspected mental or moral maladies.

Asylums were built to isolate the mentally ill from society (Prior, 2010, p. 6). Psychiatry was highly experimental and relied more on control, restraint and punishment than it did on any therapeutic discipline or science. This system persisted in Ireland until the late twentieth century when asylums began to close. A new system of treating mental illness has recently been introduced, by creating psychiatric units in hospitals, outpatient facilities and access to community care services. As humanitarian awareness and knowledge have developed, modern psychiatry has adopted more effective and humane treatments. These include psychotherapy and medication that can bring about improvements in many forms of mental illness, such as depressive disorders, psychoses, neurotic disorders and schizophrenia. The continued use of electroconvulsive therapy (ECT), formerly known as electroshock therapy, in which convulsions are electrically induced in patients, is an example of the resilience of antiquated practices. Anything that does not fit comfortably within the 'normal' box, as agreed by society, has, historically been aggressively suppressed. To break away from the dysfunctional mould that maintains stigma around mental illness, society needs to challenge its rigid view of 'normality' and its intolerance of what lies outside of this narrow construct.

Theories of the Mind

While religions traditionally concentrated on the nature of the human soul, scientists and philosophers grappled to understand the complex structure of the human mind. Early attempts at diagnosing and treating people with mental illness were highly experimental and often resulted in greater trauma. In the twentieth century psychoanalysts, such as Freud and Jung, developed theories, while psychologists conducted research, to explain the functioning of the mind and manifesting behaviour.

Developments in the twenty-first century reflect greater aware- ness as to the complexity of the human being. Theorists now advocate a more holistic model, and identify seven dimensions that the individual needs to integrate in order to experience wellness: physical, emotional, social, intellectual, spiritual, environmental, and occupational (Anspaugh et al, 2004; Hales, 2005). External social factors may also impinge on wellness, such as income, social status, social support networks, education, security of employment and actual working conditions, social environments, physical en- vironments, healthy child development, health service, gender and culture (Foster and Keller, 2007). Theories of psychosocial development and the importance of individuals having their basic needs met within their environment were devised by theorists, such as Maslow (1943), Glasser (1985) and Erikson (1994).

What begins to emerge as we review theories of the composition of the human being is the great complexity within each individual and the delicate balance required to maintain wellness. Within the Suicide Box, however, human complexity is denied. The social structures, including education and mental health, tend to simplify the sophistication and intricacy that is at the heart of every human being. Thus, schools standardise their curricula to suit students with particular learning styles and emphasise intellectual development over all other human dimensions. The mental health sector tends to advocate pills in an attempt to alleviate the symptoms of problems presented, including depression and various forms of emotional pain. Each individual's make-up involves physical, social, cognitive, cultural, intellectual, sexual and spiritual aspects, including past experiences lodged in the subconscious; unexplored potential awaiting discovery in the future, and present-moment awareness. All this complexity is reduced to mediocrity for the sake of conformity, compliance and our fevered efforts to reinforce the walls of society's box, so that the status quo is maintained, regardless of whatever awful costs result, even suicide.

Stigmas around Mental Illness
In the new millennium the emphasis of Western governments is on the promotion of mental health and the treatment of mental illness within the community. However, old stigmas and fears of being involuntarily incarcerated in an asylum, being held captive and powerless, forced to undergo invasive and painful treatments including electroconvulsive therapy (ECT) remain all too closely associated with the methods of psychiatry. There is also a strong public perception of the mentally ill as being dangerous and uncontrollable, thus contributing greatly to their stigmatisation (Angermeyer and Matschinger, 1995; Phelan and Link, 1998). A survey conducted by Robert Wood Johnson in 1989 showed that proposals to locate a mental health facility in a residential neighbourhood were met with more opposition from civil groups than proposals for shopping malls, homes for AIDS patients, factories, garbage landfills and prisons (Clarke, 1994, cited by Kemp, 2007, p. 58).

There are also archaic labels that are still used in general speech to define a person of unsound mind, such as 'mad', 'feeble minded', and 'lunatic'. It was not until 5 December 2012, that the United States

House of Representatives passed legislation to remove the word 'lunatic' from all federal laws (O'Keefe, E., 2012). Many people do not understand how mental illness develops and hence there is often a fear of the unknown. Research into people's attitudes to mental illness in Ireland revealed that six out of ten adults reported that they would not want people knowing if they were experiencing mental health problems (HSE, 2007, p. 12).

The fear of being labelled as mentally ill, with all the connotations and stigma that such a categorisation entails, certainly hinders open dialogue about the causes and effects of mental health problems in Ireland. A history of mental illness, even if the episode occurred decades previously, can follow a person for the rest of his or her life (Doctor X, 2007, p. 168). A case in point is the standard question that is often asked on employment forms: 'Have you ever suffered from a mental illness?' It is, therefore, a natural impulse to desire secrecy when a person has suffered a bout of mental illness or has made a suicide attempt. The need to hide feelings of depression or anxiety is contributing to individuals not seeking appropriate treatment when they experience suicidal thoughts or black moods (Pompili et al, 2003). Thus, people with mental illness who remain untreated are at greater risk of suicide due to stigmatisation. Dan's story below is an example of the stigma still experienced by individuals who are in need of treatment and support relating to their mental health.

Dan's Experience of the Mental Health Service
  I've been having a few problems for a while now. I went to my doctor and told him what I'd been feeling. He wrote out a letter and said it wouldn't take that long before I'd be called to see someone. I felt hopeful that I'd get some help that would sort things out. I wasn't too happy when I got a letter today inviting me to attend for appointment at the Mental Health Clinic. I've seen people drugged up to the eyeballs and out of it, hanging around outside there. If

you've to go into a place with all those around you, you wouldn't feel very good. I do see a crowd of zombies around that place and that doesn't make me feel good. You'd expect to be stuck in a queue with all the zombies around you. Someone might come out and shout out 'Is Dan ___ here?' They might even call out your address! I was waiting for the letter. I feel I need some outside help in moving me forward but this should be all completely anonymous. I just live up the road from the centre. Anyone could see me going in or coming out. I wouldn't like to be roped in with a whole crowd of doped-up, half-gone mental cases. I may end up in a very traumatic state if I go in there, being fired around from Billy to Jack. I have a few things I'd like to sort out but I'd like to do it with a private professional, someone in the know, but that would be costly. Then you're cutting out that part of it, of having to go to a place like that. Sadly, I think these places won't be good. You might end up with a straight jacket on you and you'd be put out before 'the team'. You're trying to slip along under the radar. I don't want anyone to see me in a place like that. What if my family saw me going in there? They look to me for support. The letter makes the place sound like an A&E, a very busy place where they haven't time to be worrying about you. I don't know what to expect or who I'd have to see. I don't want to go in to that environment.

Poor Quality of Mental Health Services

In Ireland, a longitudinal report into suicide (Malone, 2013) revealed that hospital emergency departments had turned people away who went on to die by suicide. A doctor working in the Irish health service, who chose to remain anonymous, highlighted in a recent publication the poor quality of mental health services in Ireland (Doctor X, 2007). Doctor X described the tragic case of a woman who called into a subsidiary hospital in Wexford along with her two children, seeking help in April 2005. She requested a phone number for social services but was told that the service was only available from Monday to Friday. She then asked for a phone number for emergency services but this was not available. She was directed to call Wexford General Hospital but she declined the offer and left. The following day, the bodies of the woman and her two young children were discovered. The mental health services had failed to prevent this tragedy even though they had been the last contact the woman ever made before taking the lives of her two children and then ending her own. When the inquest into the tragedy was conducted eighteen months later, it was found that the hospital where she had made her request for help still could not provide a list of emergency numbers for social services.

According to Doctor X (2007, p. 187–8), the main problems within mental health care in Ireland are: stigma stemming from lack of education and awareness; an under-resourced system with poor support from associated services; inadequate numbers of social workers and therapists to meet the needs of the population; widespread use of outmoded prescribing practices; lack of appropriate accommodation for long-term patients; and undue pressure on junior doctors to prescribe sedatives or other inappropriate medications. Although these are significant observations of the inadequacies of mental health care, there is an implicit acceptance of the large numbers of people who present with mental health issues. By exploring the Suicide Box from within, we clearly see this implicit acceptance of social problems, such as mental illness and suicide, which are treated as stand-alone matters and only dealt with as individual crises are presented. For suicide, this approach is assured of failure. For mental health care, a more important issue to address is why so many people suffer from depression, anxiety, stress and other emotionally related conditions in our society.

Prescription of Addictive Medication

The amount of medication prescribed for patients is of growing concern (Doctor X, 2007, p. 160). Counselling is not readily available, despite research findings that it is a highly effective treatment. Medication is, therefore, often the only treatment available. There is also the concern that people are labelled 'depressed' and treated accordingly when in fact the real cause is due to their life circumstances, such as bereavement, relationship difficulties, etc. Doctor X (2007, p. 161) estimated that about half the patients visiting a mental health clinician in Ireland are prescribed some form of benzodiazepine, with the prescription being repeated in the long term. This type of treatment may lead to the patient becoming addicted to the medication, with little long-term relief of symptoms.

Michael's Reliance on Prescribed Medication

After my mother died in April 2006 I got very depressed. I went to my doctor and she prescribed Paroxetine for me. My dosage was increased up to 30 mg early on as I could not cope with life. On a few occasions over the years I ran out of tablets or was unable to get them for some reason and I began to get terrible withdrawals such as a severe headache, a terrible sadness and even thoughts of suicide. I know, after eight years, I am addicted to them now and that someday I will probably have to face getting off them. I fear my doctor bringing up the subject of reducing or coming off the tablets but, thankfully, to date, she hasn't said anything.

Diagnosis and Treatment of Mental Illness

Research indicates that mental illness is increasing globally (WHO, 2003). It is reported that mental health problems account for up to 30 per cent of consultations with general practitioners in Europe and that depression continues to increase, particularly among adolescents (WHO, 2003). Recent research in Ireland found that 11 per cent of people said they had personally experienced a mental health problem (HSE, 2007). However, there is a danger in automatically accepting such research. As a diagnosis of mental illness is usually based on presenting indications, a misdiagnosis may occur when the symptoms are treated and not the cause. As we have seen above, the prescription of medication for emotional and psychological problems is common practice and, therefore, many people may be wrongly categorised as mentally ill.

Despite all reports produced on mental health and suicide, there are serious levels of misunderstandings and oversights about the causes of emotional and psychological dysfunction. For example, a recent Oireachtais Library and Research Services Report (2012) states that: 'In reality people have different levels of resilience to common problems in life, such as stress and bereavement. People also employ different coping mechanisms. It is more accurate to think of mental health, as something which fluctuates throughout a person's lifetime.' The implicit assumptions in this statement are that people are positioned equally in society, that their level of resilience and coping mechanisms are biologically based, with no acknowledgement of economic and social influences. Furthermore, this implies that people have equal access to similar types of treatment. Many governments adopt this strategy, perhaps due to social blindness or mere convenience. The real truth, however, would make public the private reality of the disadvantaged, and the inequalities that exist in accessing quality and timely treatments.

The Medical Mental Health Care Model
The current model for psychiatric treatment and care is based on the traditional medical model. This model treats mental disorders in the

same way as a physical condition, i.e. the theory assumes that there is a physical cause. A general practitioner or psychiatrist usually makes a judgement of the patient based on an interview. If it is judged that the person is exhibiting abnormal behaviour, the usual treatment is a prescription of medication, as outlined by Doctor X in the previous section. The medical model treats the person firstly by labelling him or her with a specific mental disorder, and then by prescribing medication in an attempt to alter the brain's chemicals, to affect a change in the 'patient's' emotions. This trial and error methodology is reminiscent of the scientific approach from a now-defunct past. The reliance of the general public on prescribed medication is proof of the effectiveness of the medical model in negatively educating, informing and disempowering individuals to maintain their own life situation, no matter how detrimental to their well-being. The doctor is cast in the role of social protector, so that no matter what is going on in a person's life that is causing enormous pain, whether that be due to an unhappy marriage, a career that is stifling, or a life that is devoid of meaning, a prescription of medication is used to alter emotions and maintain the person within their social circumstances.

Julie's Story

I married Tom when we were both nineteen. Coming from strict Catholic backgrounds we restricted our intimacy before we got married. When we did become intimate we were completely incompatible and this transferred to all other areas of our relationship. Tom didn't seem to need the emotional and physical contact I craved. From being a confident, happy girl before my marriage, I began to feel ugly and untouchable. Years went by and I became very sad and introverted. I began to think of ways of ending my life. I told my doctor and he put me on tablets to help me cope. An old friend arrived one day when I was at a very low ebb, and I broke down and told her about my sorry situation. She had attended counselling for her own unhappy marriage and was beginning to feel good about herself after many years of pain. I decided I would try counselling although I was pessimistic of a positive outcome. I had begun to realise, though, that no matter how many tablets I took my situation was never going to change. I hated waking every morning wishing I was dead. Today I have got back much of my former happy view of life although this did mean separating from Tom, who refused to make any effort to work on our marriage.

The Recovery Model

In 2006 the Irish government launched a new mental health policy, *A Vision for Change* (2006). At the heart of the document is a commitment to replace the antiquated medical model with a new, holistic recovery model. This policy document is designed to build positive mental health services throughout the community and to provide community-based specialist services for people with psychological and emotional dysfunction. It is planned to develop holistic programmes in consultation with service users. This model is currently being utilised in the social care area, particularly with people who have intellectual or physical disabilities. In contrast to the medical model, the recovery model supports an individual's journey to recovery. This person-centred approach invites active participation by the person concerned and his or her wider social network, with an outlook for recovery that offers hope.

Although the recovery model is not a part of the construction of the Suicide Box, we feel it is beneficial to contrast both the medical model and the recovery model in this section. In line with, and recommended by, international best practice the shift towards healing needs to be located within the person, instead of being driven by judgemental directives and chemicals. Thus, the recovery model offers an holistic alternative to the one-dimensional medical model. The table below summarises some of the main differences between the medical and the recovery model.

Table 2: Comparison of Medical and Recovery Models

Medical Model	Recovery Model
Doctor/Patient centred, with focus on symptoms	Person-centred, with focus on the person's needs
Focus on confinement, rest and medication	Focus on wellness and recovery
Patient Passive (Outcome determined)	Person an Active Participant
Individual Disempowerment. Medical team driven	Individual Empowerment. Holistic wellness team support
Inequality of power and status imbalance	Equality (Person is valued, respected, and listened to)
Discharge focus, with some follow-up reviews with Psychiatrist	Journey towards recovery focus. Support network established to scaffold progress
Only medical history and symptom-driven details are important	All aspects of a person's life are important and relevant, their constructed unique life
Black & White view around illness	Multi-coloured view of persons holistic problems
One-dimensional view of person	Holistic view of person
Guiding principles or conceptual framework: little hope is given for returning to 'normal' life	Guiding principles or conceptual framework: hope of a meaningful life (despite serious mental illness); recovery is a process, an outlook, a vision
Permanent feel to condition that is stigma ridden	Belief that recovery from severe mental illness is possible
Emphasis of returning to former life, even though it may have been the catalyst for the person's pain	Recovery does not necessarily mean getting back to where the person was before

Needs to show linear progress. Mood fluctuations may determine release, more medication or even ECT (formerly Electric Shock Therapy)	Progress occurs in 'fits and starts' and, like life, has many ups and downs
Focus on medical model fosters pessimism and isolation	Optimism and commitment enlisted from all concerned
Involvement of social network not encouraged or invited	Recovery is believed to be profoundly influenced by people's expectations and attitudes
Developing non-medical support would upset the hierarchical framework model	Requires a well-organised system of support from family, friends or professionals
Maintains the archaic ways of doing things	Requires services to embrace new and innovative ways of working
Emphasis is on survival and existence	Looks beyond mere survival and existence
Beyond rest, medication, monitoring and professional advice, the life of the disempowered patient following release is left to chance	Encourages individuals to move forward, set new goals, and develop relationships that give their lives meaning

Source for content: Mental Health Foundation

Although the government's decision to introduce the recovery model is considered progressive and innovative by many, implementation of the plan has met with serious obstacles. According to Mental Health Reform, there is a lack of senior management within the HSE (Health Service Executive) who are engaged in the policy development of the new model (www.mental healthreform.ie). Leadership and accountability within the HSE has largely been absent and there is also the failure of management to grasp the complexity of the implementation process. In this period of transition between two diagrammatically opposed models, a chaotic and ineffective system has resulted that has caused severe problems for those who present with any form of psychological or emotional difficulties.

Dichotomy of Models

The Irish government's policy, *A Vision for Change* (2006), purports to be service-user driven, with its central vision being the creation of 'a mental health system that addresses the needs of the population through a focus on the requirements of the individual'. The plan is certainly pioneering and the government is to be applauded for this fact alone. Yet, it is the individuals who use the mental health services who must attest either to the success or failure of the psychiatric system currently available.

Much of this section has focused on the inequalities between patient and doctor over centuries of experimental treatment in mental health and psychiatry. Status and power are highly valued within the Suicide Box even to the detriment of mental and physical well-being. There is a disconnect between the government's plan of transformation, the view at the functional level that attempts to cope with its impoverished resources, and the real experience of the service user, currently caught in the crossfire. Since the tendency of human beings is to opt for continuity rather than change, it would be indeed tragic if the person-centred recovery model was scuttled during this time of transition, due to the predominance of the medical model and those who maintain it.

CHAPTER TEN

Education

Education derives from the Latin word *educo*, meaning 'to draw out'. Thus, the original concept of education was to bring out children's innate talents, to nurture and develop these skills for the enjoyment and benefit of both the individual and society. However, the notion of education as being child-centred became corrupted and tainted. During the nineteenth and twentieth centuries, the educational experience of many children was laced with the pain and humiliation of being subjected to corporal punishment (The National Archives of Ireland). Today, education at primary and post-primary level is compulsory in many Western countries to ensure that citizens achieve a basic knowledge of subjects that are considered to be socially and individually beneficial. In the majority of schools, the emphasis is on the development of intellectual intelligence and the honing of memory through repetition. There is considerably less interest in the development of multiple intelligences and little accommodation for different learning styles.

There is also a failure to encourage students to express their opinions and feelings about subject matter; this would develop critical thinking and emotional intelligence that are both vital ingredients in the nurturance of bright, creative and involved citizens. This may be partly due to the system of standardised tests that requires a great deal of memory recall to obtain high scores, but also to further the objective of governments and industry: to create obedient, conservative and technically skilful workers to fill required roles in line with economic markets.

Ireland's high rate of suicide needs to be addressed by all sectors of society but most especially education. Schools have the unique opportunity to foster health and well-being in all children, as it is compulsory to attend school from the age of six to sixteen. Schools need to teach subjects that are relevant to securing lucrative employment. The problem, however, is that schools fail to prepare students to understand their inner world that is a complex blend of many separate but interlocking facets. Good mental health and well-being requires a delicate balance to be achieved and maintained between many composite elements of the self. Recent government policies on education promise sweeping reforms that will place a strong emphasis on personal development through the introduction of Social, Personal and Health Education (SPHE) in primary schools, and the issuing of guidelines to introduce the programme entitled, *Well-Being in Post-Primary Schools* (Department of Education and Skills, 2013). The challenge, however, is to ensure that schools consistently implement these programmes with well-trained teachers, viewing them as central to the emotional well-being of children and teenagers, and not as an adjunct to academic subjects.

Throughout life, people need to adequately fulfil their basic psychological needs, and to create purpose and meaning even when they encounter great setbacks and disappointments. Schools are in a unique position to teach and foster positive ways of thinking and being. Since education is compulsory, even if other aspects of a child's upbringing are problematic, school life should be so rewarding and personally satisfying that children become happy, emotionally resilient and compassionate adults who are equipped with powerful tools to cope with the vicissitudes of life. All too often teenagers fail to find constructive ways of meeting their needs. The education system occupies a central location within the Suicide Box due to the present level of bullying, stress and feelings of inferiority that it generates in children and adolescents: its emphasis on intellectual intelligence and a convergent learning style, and its system of grading increases pain and low self-esteem in some students.

Emphasis on Intellectual Intelligence

In most schools the emphasis is on the development of intellectual intelligence and the honing of memory through repetition. The importance of developing a student's emotional intelligence that may greatly increase self-awareness, empathy and relationship skills is largely ignored. Due to the constraints of a narrow curriculum that focuses on industrial needs rather than human diversity, teachers usually do not have the time or the resources to focus on children who have a specialised intelligence. Despite the emphasis on intellectual intelligence, the main focus is on memory recall and not on the development of critical thinking. A recent study by the Economic and Social Research Institute (McCoy et al, 2014), surveyed 753 young people, three to four years after completing the Leaving Certificate. Over 90 per cent of those in higher education that were interviewed for the study felt their school work didn't prepare them for project work and the independent thinking that was required in college. According to the authors of the study, 'many felt ill-prepared for the world of work, for adult life and for going on to college. Just over half felt that their second-level schooling prepared them for their course.'

Emotional Intelligence

Our emotions are powerful forces that act as an internal gauge, signalling whether or not we wish to draw close or distance ourselves from a person or situation. The initial onset of an emotion is mostly outside of our conscious control. Our subsequent behaviour, however, may come from a place of greater awareness when we learn to observe the constant changes in our emotional state. There is much that can be learned about our emotional system that can be of great benefit in our day-to-day lives, especially in managing stress, hurt and anger.

The theories of emotional intelligence were first developed during the 1970s and 1980s by a number of psychologists, primarily Howard Gardner. The concept views the usual measure of intellectual intelligence as too narrow, stressing that success in life requires that a person becomes socially and interpersonally adept. A person who has a high level of emotional intelligence will also have high levels of self-esteem, self-awareness, compassion, empathy, and adaptability. These traits help people to understand themselves at a deep level, to understand the feelings and motivations of others, to communicate clearly, and to create mutually satisfying and positive relationships. A key component of the development of emotional intelligence is to improve mental health by reducing stress for individuals and organisations, by decreasing conflict, improving relationships and understanding, and increasing stability, continuity and harmony.

Several studies conducted in Europe, the United States and Asia found that when a person has a high level of emotional intelligence he or she is less likely to suffer depression (Downey et al, 2008; Baron R., 1997; Berrocal et al, 2005; Extremera et al, 2006; Tsaousis et al, 2005). Research emphasises the importance of schools adopting programmes that develop emotional intelligence, thereby bolstering the mental health of students.

Multiple Intelligences

Howard Gardner brought intelligence out of the academic realm and placed it in the context of real life. He defined intelligence as (2011):

'A property of all human beings; A dimension on which human beings differ (No two people – not even identical twins possess exactly the same profile of intelligence); the way in which one carries out a task in virtue of one's goals.' Gardner defined seven types of intelligence: linguistic, logical-mathematical, musical, spatial, bodily-kinaesthetic, and two forms of personal intelligence, one directed towards others and one directed towards the self. According to Gardner (2011), educators need to know as much as possible about the unique intelligence profile of each student. The teacher should then assess and teach in ways that will bring out the child's capabilities – the original aim of education. Subjects should also be taught in multiple ways to make use of each person's unique combination of multiple intelligences.

Different Learning Styles
When children sit in a classroom surrounded by fellow classmates, it is imperative that they are given the best possible opportunity to understand and interact with the subject matter that the teacher is discussing. The extent to which learning styles can affect a child's experience of education has been studied by a number of scientists. Skehan (1989, 1994) purports that our ability to learn is affected by many individual differences including age, aptitude, general intelligence, modality preferences (e.g. visual, auditory, kinaes-thetic), motivation and sociocultural factors. Mariana (1996) suggests that individual personality affects how a child will interact in the classroom. Kolb (1984) proposed that there are four different types of learner: diverging, assimilating, converging, and accommodating. According to Kolb (1984), every person learns in a very different way and, in a school setting, a teacher needs to accommodate teaching methods and the materials used to meet these needs.

Convergent learners are a teacher's dream within the Suicide Box. These children can work alone and are best at finding practical uses for information (Kolb, 1984). While convergent learners are the least skilled socially they are, paradoxically, the most likely to achieve high grades and become society's doctors and high-level carers, often with poor bedside manners. Divergent learners find school a difficult environment, as focusing on a set curriculum opposes their learning style (Kolb, 1984). They are often considered to be poor students but may flourish in later life. Albert Einstein, Marie Curie and John Lennon are examples of divergent learners. While children from this learning style have a greater social awareness and would make the best social carers, they do not usually achieve the required grades within the Suicide Box.

Accommodator learners have the most hands-on approach (Kolb, 1984). However, school does not have the time or the structure to optimise their abilities. They take creative risks and enjoy challenging experiences because they dislike routine. Similar to divergent learners they will be seen as poor fits for academic requirements. Again a lifetime of low self-esteem is often a legacy left by early school experiences for accommodators. Assimilator learners have a strong control-need and like the clean and simple predictability of internal models as opposed to external messiness (Kolb, 1984). Being focused on abstract ideas and concepts, they are strong in inductive reasoning and creating theoretical models. The assimilator learner is likely to do very well in academic subjects. However, their social skills and emotional intelligence may need much development.

Josephine's Story
    When my son Brian was eight years old, he was not doing well at
    school and it was recommended by his teacher that he transfer to a
    school for children with intellectual disabilities. Brian couldn't focus

in school and spent much of his time daydreaming. I knew he was very bright but only if he found something interesting. For Christmas and birthdays he'd request unusual presents, such as a telescope or a microscope. He loved to look at the stars and had a fascination for the natural world, such as falling snow, sunsets and weather changes. I chose not to send him to the special school because of the stigma associated with it but also because I knew that Brian had a different type of intelligence that didn't do well in a school setting. Brian's time at school was a waste. He was never made to feel good about himself and none of his natural talents were ever highlighted. After he left school it took him a number of years to get on his feet. Everything he learned was self-taught, through online courses that taught using videos. He recently achieved national recognition for his work on a film documentary. He has also travelled the world, has set up his own business and has developed a great confidence in his abilities. I don't know what would have happened if I had gone along with his teachers' recommendations when he was eight.

System versus Learner

Although these four learning styles have been identified by research, each individual falls into a position along the learning style spectrum, with a leaning towards a particular learning style. Convergent and assimilator learners excel in the present day educational system as they are the best match: to fulfil society's needs, to flourish under current teaching methods and within the timescales of curriculum demands. While these learners do well academically, the system often leads them into ill-matching careers, such as medicine, where the person has great technical knowledge but may lack the necessary social skills. In contrast, the divergent learner tends to have better people skills and is likely to become the doctor with the caring bedside manner, should the system permit this. This is just one example of how the current system of education defines success for itself but takes no responsibility for the large number of people it fails. Accommodator learners stand little chance of success as defined by society and often their experience of attending school is one of failure, as experienced by Brian above. It is when they exit the educational system that these learners often find their niche, develop their skills and eke a living from their own resources.

Career mismatching is one of the factors that causes much dissatisfaction and stress at work. In research conducted in the US, 25 per cent of employees viewed their jobs as the number one stressor in their lives (North-Western National Life Insurance Company, 1992). Also 75 per cent of employees believe that they have more on-the-job stress than a generation ago (Princeton Survey Research Associates, 1997). Therefore, it is of great importance that natural talents are recognised and valued and that people are allowed to pursue suitable careers in spite of any grades achieved.

Tom's Recollection
Tom, a dentist for over thirty years, told us:

> From my earliest memories my siblings and I were driven to high academic achievement by my parents. I feel that my path in life was channelled by the pressure to meet their expectations. Assimilating information was relatively easy for me and I achieved high grades in all exams. Becoming a doctor or a dentist became the only choice for me and I was carried on the crest of that wave of assumed success. It was only after this wave had come to shore that I began to realise that I had somehow been driven onto a life road that left me feeling that something was not right for me. I had all the trimmings that suggested that I was a success but I was desperately unhappy. My standard of living was little compensation for how I was feeling. Working in people's mouths every day had little interest for me. I would have much preferred to be working with the whole person in some capacity. I can't remember when I began to use

alcohol as a means of helping dull the pain. Suicide has often entered my thoughts as a solution. My siblings also show similar unhappiness in their careers and alcohol seems to play a role in their coping systems too.

Curriculum and Student Stress

The experience of attending school and of being pressurised to do well academically, especially in state examinations, can take its toll on children's mental health. Comparisons between classmates in terms of test scores can lead to some students feeling inferior. In Australia it was found that the NAPLAN literacy and numeracy tests caused students to feel stressed and some were concerned they were not intelligent enough to sit the tests (Dulfer, 2012). Teachers stated that some children felt sick and were visibly upset before the tests while others no longer wanted to go to school due to the testing.

In Baltimore, Maryland, USA, teenagers were interviewed as part of a study into teenage stress (Center for Adolescent Health, 2006). Results found that schoolwork was the greatest source of stress for 78 per cent of students. In Ireland, My World Survey (2012) revealed that: 'Adolescents who ranked themselves at the "bottom of the class" were more likely to experience more severe symptoms of depression and anxiety.'

According to the Department of Education and Skills in Ireland in *Well-being in Post Primary Schools* (2013): 'The onus is on schools to provide a broad and balanced curriculum. Approaches to teaching and learning should take account of the diverse needs and learning styles of all young people.' An educational system that emphasises students' unique learning styles and celebrates multiple intelligences could provide every child with a positive learning experience. It appears that educational theories as to what constitutes quality learning for students have finally filtered down into government reports, yet the practical implementation of new policies that could bring about real change remains elusive. The broad-sightedness of this government view is highly commendable but it is interesting that it transfers responsibility to schools to create a balanced curriculum when the rigidity of the system is set at government department level, leaving little time for any autonomy for schools to take into account diverse needs and learning styles.

In the meantime students continue to experience stress, feelings of low self-esteem and the erroneous belief that they are not intelligent enough because the current school system does not support different learning styles or multiple intelligences. A rather worrying aspect of a report by the National Suicide Research Foundation (2013) on the risk factors for 190 suicides completed in Cork during the period September 2008 to March 2011, found that 38.7 per cent of the people who died by suicide had experienced problems with school as a negative and traumatic life event in childhood or early adolescence (Arensman et al, 2012).

Bullying in Schools
Being bullied at school is one of the most serious problems that students face globally. Bullying behaviour has been defined under six distinct headings: verbal, physical, gesture, exclusion, extortion, and cyberbullying. Much has been written about bullying in schools and workplaces. These well-written and well-meaning approaches have focused on the destructiveness of such behaviour on the victim. In spite of this, we have seen little positive change in the frequency and devastation caused by bullying in schools. A survey carried out in the United States on behalf of the Department of Education (Neiman and Hill, 2011) found that 30 per cent of students were bullied in middle schools daily or at least once a week and that 20 per cent of students were bulled regularly in primary and high

schools. A report into bullying of young people across the European Union found that one in five (19%) of young people had been bullied (EU Kids Online, 2011).

In Ireland, the ISPCC (2011) conducted a national children's consultation survey of 18,000 young people. Results showed that 26 per cent of respondents from secondary schools said they or someone they knew had been bullied; 22 per cent of respondents from the primary group said that they or someone they knew had experienced bullying; over half of the students stated that they would not tell anyone about bullying because they would be afraid that it would make the bullying worse. A survey that interviewed nine year olds (Growing up in Ireland, 2011) found that 40 per cent of boys and girls had been victims of bullying within the past year.

Based on the conservative figure of 20 per cent of children being bullied in Irish schools, and taking the 2011/2012 figure of 884,813 students attending primary and secondary schools (CSO, Statistical Yearbook of Ireland, 2013b), we can estimate that approximately 177,000 children in Ireland suffer from the effects of bullying each year in our schools. However, these statistics only tell half of the story. Just like society's usual focus on the individual in cases of suicide, all attention is placed on the targets, thereby omitting the source of bullying, i.e. the perpetrators. Are there 177,000 perpetrators of bullying that are excluded from the phenomenon? Can we explain why our usual responses to bullying are aggressive and war-like when we choose words like 'combat' 'fight' using a 'shield', etc? Are we aware that the perpetrators are also children?

Bullying, like suicide, is another social phenomenon that is highly emotive because of the devastating effects that ensue. The current response to bullying in schools is to react when an accusation of bullying is made. This is usually after the behaviour has progressed to full-blown bullying. The vast majority of targets of bullying behaviour suffer in silence. A minority of targets who make a complaint have to state their case and defend their accusation. The perpetrator most often denies the allegations and the target experiences a period of isolation and scrutiny. In informal situations the target may have to leave the environment as the only real solution. In these circumstances perpetrators experience, by default, a huge boost of personal power and are more likely to repeat their behaviour on a fresh target.

A report into bullying in Irish schools conducted by anti-bullying groups entitled *Action Plan on Bullying* (2013) was recently submitted to the Minister for Education and Skills. The report recommended a whole-school/community approach to tackling bullying. Part of the Programme for Government commitment stated that 'we will encourage schools to develop anti-bullying policies and in particular, strategies to combat homophobic bullying to support students (*Action Plan on Bullying*, 2013, p. 5)'. As part of the report's recommendations, funding for training of parents and members of the Board of Management was to be made available. During 2013, a mere €60,000 was provided to schools to fund this important training (Department of Education and Skills, 2014). This amounts to approximately €15 per school in Ireland which is a good example of the top-down approach which wastes effort and money, however paltry. The report also emphasises that schools have a duty of care and a legal requirement under the Equal Status Acts and the Employment Equality Acts 1998–2008, to take reasonable and practical steps to prevent harassment of students and teachers occurring. While this recommendation appears apt, there is currently no government funding made available to schools to implement an all-school/community approach to bullying that would require training of staff, seminars, meetings with parents, and involvement from the wider community on an ongoing basis. A problem seems to arise between government sentiments and its subsequent actions, as if a perceptible disconnect exists between its head and its heart.

Political short-sightedness has resulted in vital social projects being left to chance with inadequate funding. This is one of the most serious obstacles to real social change.

Effects of Bullying

Bullying in school can have serious effects for both the target of bullying and the perpetrator. Being bullied at school has been the trigger for some young people experiencing suicidal thoughts (Kaltiala-Heino et al, 1999), depression (Hawker and Boulton, 2000; Rimpela and Rantanen, 1999) and bullying has also led to suicide (Anti-Bullying Centre). Students who have been victimised by peers are also more likely to suffer illnesses, school avoidance, poor academic performance, low self-esteem, increased fear and anxiety (Hawker and Boulton, 2000; McDougall et al, 2009; Boulton and Underwood, 1992; Olweus, 1978; Salmivalli et al, 1998; Slee, 1995; Kaltiala-Heino et al, 1999). When teachers are bullied in school by peers or students the effects can also be very damaging.

Bullying has also been linked to extreme anger, aggression and violence, and to delinquency and criminality in later life (Olweus, 1993a). Studies of bullying also show that students who use bullying behaviour in schools are more likely to use antisocial behaviour in other settings and in adulthood. Approximately 60 per cent of boys who were classified by researchers as bullies in grades six through nine were convicted of at least one crime by the age of twenty-four (Olweus et al, 1999).

Laura's Experience of Being Bullied

I suffered from bullying at home, so when a group of girls targeted me as their victim I suppose I was ripe for the picking. I felt in the beginning that they just didn't like me, that I was unlikeable. Then I began to wonder what was wrong with me. I felt ugly and weird. I can feel emotion coming up for me as I recall this. If you are told something often enough you begin to believe it. I used to get palpitations. I lived in dread of what was going to happen.

On some level I thought I deserved it. I began to see things as being my fault and internalising the hurt prevented me from saying anything. I didn't want to admit that I was a victim, or to apply the tabooed word 'bullying' to what was happening to me. I had no trust or confidence in telling teachers. At fifteen I considered suicide. I was very depressed and told my mother. I changed schools and felt safer even though the bullying continued by text. I remember feeling so drained as texts came in. Then in a moment of helplessness I decided to text them back and forgive them, as thinking about it was hurting me so much. I felt panic doing this but I also felt stronger to have done it. I had to do something to stop the pattern of power they wielded over me. To my surprise they stopped texting me from then on. I later learned that they targeted a friend after I left.

Why do I think they bullied me? I can now see that there was no reason. I asked one of the bullies on her own why she picked on me. She said maybe she was a bit jealous because my life was so perfect. If only she and the others knew how far from perfect my life was. They could not have been aware of my unhappiness at home. I think that they were only doing it because of their own insecurities. They needed power in their lives. They probably felt good to have power over me, to make me feel completely alone in the group and isolated. I used to be so much happier alone in the art room. After I moved to a new school it took three years to get some confidence back.

What I learned from being bullied is to avoid people who aren't good for me. I feel annoyed when people say suicide is a selfish act as they have no idea how the mind works when abuse is taking place. I've learned to value myself as a person and have learned to meditate which I find really helpful. I know the effects of having been bullied stayed with me though. Sometimes the bad feelings are activated when I hear a certain word or a certain tone of voice. This is when I realise the terrible effects of being bullied.

A Culture of Bullying

When a culture of bullying exists in a school, teachers and students may be subjected to an escalation of bullying behaviour. Students learn what is acceptable behaviour from adults and subconsciously begin to mirror their demeanour, manner and conduct and to imitate their goals, intentions and desires (Hurley and Chater, 2005; Meltzoff and Prinz, 2002). When bullying behaviour is used by teachers to coerce or intimidate teachers or students, this signals that bullying is a powerful and effective behaviour used by adults to subdue others. In such a school, it becomes irrelevant as to how many anti-bullying policies are pinned to walls or the number of programmes that have been put in place to engender respect or empathy. A culture of bullying destroys the entire life of a school. The school principal's style of leadership is the most important factor of all for creating positive staff relations, and for shaping the ethos, atmosphere and culture of the whole school (Mortimore and Mortimore, 1991). If the school principal uses bullying behaviour to maintain authority when interacting with teachers, students or parents, then there is little hope that a positive environment will be created in the school.

Sexuality and Relationships

During adolescence, young people undergo enormous physical, emotional and psychological changes that prompt them to have many questions about their bodies, sexuality and relationships. Awakening sexuality brings new, intense feelings but also anxiety about body image and fears for females around becoming pregnant. The feelings of elation when young people first fall in love are universally known. According to anthropologist, Dr Helen Fisher (2004), when we fall in love, our brains create dramatic surges of energy that fuel such feelings as passion, obsessiveness, joy and jealousy. Psychologist, Dr Shauna H. Springer (2012) concurs with this premise, stating that all relationships begin with feelings akin to a 'cocaine rush'. A feeling of addiction to the beloved is also common. This may explain why the feelings of loss after relationship break-up can be so intense.

Teenagers are reluctant to consult parents, siblings and friends about sexuality due to embarrassment. Also, they may not want to attend a doctor because of fear of lack of confidentiality. Much shame and embarrassment comes from adults' hang-ups about sexuality, as many are weighed down by religious, moral and political teachings over millennia around reproduction, sin, and 'pleasures of the flesh'. There may still be a fear that discussing sexuality outside of this pinhole view of reproduction may unleash a Sodom and Gomorrah of biblical proportions on society. Much confusion also originates in the media's portrayal of overt sexuality and social pressures to become sexually active. Schools are in a unique position to train teachers in these sensitive but vital areas that affect every person throughout life, or to contract experts who are skilled in working with adolescents to overcome embarrassment in talking about their developing sexuality, managing intense feelings, sexual orientation, romance and ensuing emotions around love, rejection, abusive relationships, disappointment and loss following a relationship break-up.

The Need for Information on Sexuality
Adolescents spend a lot of time thinking about sex and relationships. Since many teenagers are embarrassed asking questions about these topics, the Internet provides vast amounts of information that can be readily accessed while preserving anonymity. A study of the topics that most interested adolescents (Suzuki and Calzo, 2004) included teenagers' changing physical, emotional, and social selves.

Romantic relationships were the most frequently discussed topic on the teen issues bulletin board, while sexual health was the most frequent topic on the sexuality bulletin board.

Schools can play a vital role in initiating discussions around what constitutes healthy and dysfunctional relationships. Since relationship break-ups so often involve intense feelings, young people need to learn how to take care of their emotions in relationships. Skill-building programs and the promotion of healthy relationships need to be introduced into schools. These programs need to focus on how to remain safe, if sexually active; minimising the risk of sexually transmitted diseases and pregnancy; being involved in healthy relationships that support and nurture; discussing gender stereotypes that limit genuine communication; and respecting relationships of all sexual orientations. Relationship break-ups can also be a difficult time, especially since there may be many emotions to process and one's confidence may be seriously dented. Relationship problems and break-up have been identified as significant risk factors in suicide (O'Neill and Corry, 2013; Wiley et al, 2012; Arensman et al, 2012). It is, therefore, imperative that educators develop programs and initiate discussions about healthy ways to express emotions when dealing with the break-up of relationships.

Gay, Lesbian and Bisexual Youth
Sexuality and relationships become a mental health issue for some young people when they feel their sexual orientation is not acceptable to family, friends or society and they need to deny their sexual feelings or keep them secret. Feelings of low self-esteem or poor body image may be intensified if a young person feels unattractive. Roffman (2010) outlines challenges that may negatively affect the development of gay, lesbian and bisexual youth: 'Despite

progress, GLB youth must still cope with a culture that is often hostile. Stigma still surrounds homosexuality. GLB kids face many of the same obstacles as earlier generations: poor self-esteem, family rejection, stigma, social isolation, self-harm, and risky behaviour. In school, where kids should feel safe, GLB youth are often taunted and bullied.' When a teenager perceives that his or her sexual orientation is socially unacceptable it can cause deep insecurity, distress and low self-esteem. The coming-out process, where a homosexual tells family and friends about his or her sexual orientation, can feel overwhelming, particularly if there is rejection or negative reactions. Schools could play an important role in championing positive non-heterosexual role models and of discussing the right of every person to express their sexuality in a loving and positive way.

Education in Mental Health
The role of schools in educating teenagers about their psychological and emotional selves and how to maintain good mental health was a central recommendation of a longitudinal report into suicides in Ireland (Malone, 2013, p. 9). Young teenage deaths from suicide were of particular concern: 'As this age of risk corresponds in great measure with school teen-years, it is time for a national analysis of psycho-education (especially mental health literacy) and intervention strategies for young people.'

Studies into suicide (European Commission, 2011; Malone et al, 2012; Malone, 2013) and self-harm (Headstrong, 2012; NERF, 2013, p. 1) make it crystal clear that children and teenagers need to be educated in the following areas to reduce mental illness, depression and suicide: the importance of expressing thoughts and emotions; learning to relax and to live in the present; learning about life's stressors and how to cope with unexpected problems and setbacks; the benefits of talking to a trusted person to bring another per-spective to problems; recognising the early signs of depression and how and where to seek support; developing a positive philosophy and learning how to create meaning throughout life.

At present, schools give little attention or merely pay lip service to the most important subjects of all: how to remain sane, positive and reasonably content despite the challenges that every human being has to face. Within the Suicide Box there are countless external forces that tug at an individual's power, adversely influencing their decisions in a defective society. Frequent classes and discussions about mental health and all of the foregoing areas, facilitated by teachers who have received prior training, would go a long way towards increasing emotional awareness in our youth.

CHAPTER ELEVEN
Work

For the vast majority of people across different cultures and societies, the life experience necessitates attendance at an educational institution, followed by decades spent working in order to eke out a living for self or family. There may be periods of unemployment that bring their own difficulties, and times when people change jobs or career, yet work is the usual activity undertaken by the majority of people during their lifespan. Ever since the structure of work shifted from an agrarian, home-based system to industrialisation in the nineteenth century, workers have been at the mercy of their employers, of economic fluctuations and technological changes. The struggle for better working conditions was largely led by workers' collectives and unions. State legislation to protect workers' rights and to ensure welfare in times of unemployment gradually emerged, providing a modicum of security.

Research in the 1960s showed a management style on the laissez-faire-autocratic spectrum that maximised both profitability and happiness in businesses (Blake-Mouton, 1963). However, it became evident in the 1970s and 1980s that managers generally had opted for a management style that had more to do with a desire for personal power and control than profitability or raising happiness in the workplace. In a study of 46,000 workers in the USA, 40 per cent of workers described their jobs as very stressful, identifying work-related stress as an important and preventable health hazard (Goetzel, Anderson et al, 1998).

Within our social structure, the work that a person performs and the salary that is received largely determine his or her social status and lifestyle. Thus, there is an enormous pressure exerted on the individual to secure lucrative employment – usually through scoring well in state examinations – and then struggling to maintain that position, or to supersede it through promotion. Many of the problems inherent in the educational system are carried forward into the workplace. Both systems follow the hierarchical structure of authority; examination results are the measurement of success for schools and they are usually the basis for recruitment at work; bullying behaviours that are present at school and ineffectively dealt with, re-emerge in the workplace to cause further pain and trauma. Also, the unfortunate trait of human greed and the need for power and control over others, combined with the relentless drive to make profits and the disregard for workers' welfare, promotes a culture where bullying and harassment may flourish. The recent global recession also placed great economic pressure even on the most benevolent of employers. Thus, the degree of job satisfaction, the level of happiness and work-life balance as experienced by workers during times of economic prosperity, suddenly vanished. The stark reality of looming poverty and economic survival took its place.

Within the workplace there are many types of personalities to negotiate. The world of work is fraught with stress: the need to be a team player but also to compete for promotion; the requirement to meet deadlines, to achieve targets or to work in stressful situations where mistakes could have catastrophic results. The greatest stress of all, however, is when a worker is bullied, harassed or isolated. Masquerading among us are socially unskilled people with poor empathy abilities, who are mistakenly hired for skills that on the surface look positive such as drive, knowledge and efficiency. On the job, their self-serving flaws and inadequacies emerge to often destroy people's lives and the companies that hired them. Despite recent legislation in Ireland, stating that employers have a duty of care to their employees to create a safe working environment, workplace bullying and excessive levels of stress are still a frequent experience. In a study conducted into bullying in the workplace in the United States, 54 million Americans are bullied each year (Namie et al, 2014). Work is, therefore, placed firmly within the Suicide Box, as the effects of bullying and stress on large numbers of workers can cause serious physical and emotional trauma, leading to depression and suicide.

The Irish Situation

A recent study into workplace bullying conducted by Peninsula Ireland reported that six out of ten employees have been bullied at work, but that most are too frightened to report it (Ring, 2013). More than 40 per cent of workers claimed to have been bullied by their manager. The survey conducted among 524 employees during 2013 revealed that 62 per cent felt bullied or intimidated in the workplace; 43 per cent claimed to have been bullied by their manager; and 67 per cent were too frightened to report the bullying.

In Ireland, legislation introduced to protect employees from harassment at work puts the onus on employers to create an harassment-free workplace as part of their duty of care to employees (Safe, Health, and Welfare at Work Act, 2005 and 2010; Safety, Health, and Welfare at Work (General Application) Regulations, 2007; Employment Equality Acts 1998–2011). The Employment Equality Bill (1998) outlaws sexual harassment (section 23) and general harassment in the workplace (section 32). Discrimination is outlawed on the following distinct grounds in section 28(1): 'marital status, family status, sexual orientation, religious, age, disability, race, colour, nationality, or ethnic or national origins, and traveller community.' Therefore, in the workplace in Ireland, it is an offence to harass a person, or to treat anyone less favourably, on any of these grounds.

Since the onus is placed on employers to safeguard the health and safety under Irish law, firms need to put certain policies and training in place, to show their diligence if a case of harassment is taken against the firm. It is, therefore, important for firms to establish and display an anti-bullying and harassment policy, to ensure that its management style is conducive to the carrying out of that policy, to train a designated employee to deal with any complaints of bullying and harassment, and to provide training to all staff as to what constitutes bullying and harassment at work.

Despite the best efforts of legislation recently enacted to minimise bullying and harassment at work, bullying behaviour is still allowed to fester and wreak havoc in the workplace. The truth is that a properly run business can never tolerate bullying behaviour within genuine management leadership. Recent statistics highlight the worsening situation for workers (Ring, 2013). Certainly within the Suicide Box, where the emphasis of our educational system is on intellectual intelligence and in the provision of adequately skilled workers for industry, there is a stark lack of interest in developing emotional intelligence to equip students with vital people skills. The onus, therefore, is placed on families to teach these life skills to their children. When parents do not have the capacity or understanding to undertake such a task, it is largely left to chance whether or not the child becomes a well-balanced, empathic adult or an angry, controlling perpetrator of bullying.

Bullying Culture at Work
Bullying at work, as defined by the Health and Safety Authority in Ireland (HSA, 2007), is 'repeated inappropriate behaviour, direct or indirect, whether verbal, physical or otherwise, conducted by one or

more persons against another or others, at the place of work and/or in the course of employment, which could reasonably be regarded as undermining the individual's right to dignity at work. An isolated incident of the behaviour described in this definition may be an affront to dignity at work but as a once off incident is not considered to be bullying.' Examples of bullying or harassing behaviour include the spreading of malicious rumours; insulting or humiliating a worker; exclusion or victimisation; unfair treatment; or deliberately undermining a competent worker by constant criticism. Bullying may be carried out by a single perpetrator against a fellow worker or may be part of a general culture of bullying.

When a bullying culture exists in a workplace, there is no attempt made to satisfy worker's basic psychological needs, such as their self-esteem needs. Since the advent of industrialisation and the rise of capitalism, businesses have used boss management to coerce workers into doing specified tasks by the promise of reward, or by the threat of punishment (Costigan, 1998). The boss manager is typical of the Theory X manager as portrayed by McGregor (1960), who devised two management styles which were basically sets of assumptions about worker's behaviour. Theory X managers regard workers as being lazy and irresponsible, requiring control and coercion. Theory Y managers believe that workers enjoy their work, and are thus viewed as responsible, committed and creative members of the team, who contribute significantly to the organisation's goals. McGregor's concept has been helpful in identifying extreme types of management styles.

Employees in a boss-managed workplace are controlled through micromanaging, where rules and regulations are strictly enforced. Workers feel actively discouraged from airing their grievances or obtaining impartial representation, as disagreement with management or company policy is viewed as highly undesirable. Bullying, stress, sexism, racism, and favouritism are rife in such a workplace. Since worker's social needs are ignored, this leads to low staff morale and a general state of discontent. A high degree of conformity is expected in a boss-managed firm. Individuality, creativity and personal flair are viewed with suspicion. Workers are promoted on the extent of their obedience to management. Therefore, it is often the case that, psychologically, the weakest and most pliable workers are promoted to managerial positions. The following story is an example of what employees are still likely to experience within the Suicide Box, when their well-being at work is of low priority.

Joan's Experience

I worked in a government department for eighteen years. When I entered my civil service job in 1990 I was elated and I did so well with the work. Even though I wasn't a great socialiser I loved my job and the people I worked with. Then in 2003 my immediate boss retired. I could see that the new Principal Officer was a very different person. Change came like a tsunami. The office was redesigned, negatively changing the dynamics. Then the roster changed making our time off and social planning less certain. I still loved the work so I believed I could weather it, until her focus turned to me. After a private introductory talk, which she was having with all the office staff, I felt demeaned, as she was critical of me as a person. All the work I believed I did well became full of flaws. She moved me to a corner cubicle to 'avoid me being distracted'. I felt more and more powerless every day. I could hardly sleep at night and felt sick at the thought of going to work. After a year of this I felt broken. My colleagues behaved differently towards me. Some showed concern but none wanted to get involved.

I eventually went to my doctor who prescribed sleeping tablets and antidepressants. I was now beginning to become the person the office bully was painting me to be. My work was now of a lower quality, my timekeeping was getting worse and my attitude at work was less

121

interactive. I was advised by my employee assistance officer to talk to my union representative. They advised me to take account of the daily incidents and if the behaviour persisted that I was to warn her that I found her treatment of me to be unwelcome and if she did not stop I would have to make an official complaint of harassment and bullying.

It was as if she knew that I had looked for help as her bullying became more subtle. Three years had now passed and my life was totally fragmented. I now had a poor sick record and thoughts of suicide were constantly there. Finally the pressure was too much and I had to go on sick leave that became long-term. I considered taking a case against the bully but I couldn't face the years of stress that legal action would entail. The union support was poor as my abuser was a union member too and they felt conflict dealing with two members.

I now feel I am unemployable. Being bullied is a devastating experience. It creeps up till you are sapped of energy. Management avoided any involvement in the matter. My last communication from them was that they have agreed to grant me a half pension. They just want this to go away rather than deal with it. My abuser is still in her position.

Profile of a Perpetrator of Bullying

In a boss-managed organisation, bullying is an inevitable feature of the work environment. For many employers, employee welfare is an irritating distraction from the real point of being in business. While work will always carry inherent but manageable stressors, employers that allow unnecessary and unmanageable stress for their employees are as guilty as the socially unskilled tyrant they selected and empowered to destroy lives. A perpetrator of bullying misuses a position of authority or capitalises on a situation of favouritism to coerce, persecute, or oppress others by using force, threats or name-calling, or by undermining co-workers. Perpetrators of bullying are emotionally immature, unstable and power-hungry, with little or no respect for fellow workers. They may also have sociopathic or psychopathic tendencies. Bullying may be overtly aggressive or may be covert. It may be very difficult for the target to obtain tangible proof. An example of this is where a bullying manager adopts a strategy to discommode a worker by heaping on excessive volumes of work, or demanding that work be completed in unreasonable deadlines. Thus, it may appear to management that there is a work performance problem whereas, in truth, excessive stress is being generated by unfair treatment of the employee.

Lack of Management Training

One of the most effective ways of tackling bullying and harassment in the workplace is the promotion or recruitment of managers who possess a good level of emotional intelligence, the ability to motivate and delegate, to lead rather than to boss, and the character and maturity to take responsibility for the health and welfare of their department. This needs to be coupled with adequate training in the areas of people skills and conflict resolution. A manager who feels out of his or her depth from lack of training may suffer from high stress levels, generated by lack of knowledge and fear of failure. This kind of pressure may bring out behaviour in a newly appointed manager that is uncharacteristic, such as bullying, intimidation and abuse of power.

According to Tucker et al (2000), educational institutions have traditionally focused primarily on the importance of IQ (Intelligence Quotient) with less attention being given to other types of intelligence. However, it is vital that emotional intelligence, namely intrapersonal and interpersonal competencies are included in courses of study in business schools. In Ireland, the importance of training managers to international standards of excellence has been highlighted by The Management Development Council (2010). In a recent study by McKinsey and Company (2009) it was found that management practices in all manufacturing sectors in Ireland lag behind performances amongst similar firms in the highest-performing countries (the US, Germany, Sweden and Japan), where Irish firms are ranked number 10 out of 14 countries. Irish firms employing between 50 and 250 employees are ranked number 12 out of 14 countries.

Effects of Bullying at Work

It is a common experience for workers who are being systematically bullied to feel demeaned, inadequate, and deeply distressed. Many feel too embarrassed and ashamed to talk about what is going on in their workplace. This is especially true for men, who find it very difficult to admit that they are being bullied, particularly if they work in a 'macho' environment such as prisons, the military, the police force or the fire service. Constant, petty criticism and failure to meet impossible deadlines eats away at self-esteem, eroding years of positive reviews and appreciative managers, stripping away layers of experience and competence.

The effects of bullying on a worker are often crippling. Feelings may include powerlessness, hopelessness, anger, hatred, rage, and the desire to seek revenge. Workers may be so fearful of going to work that they may vomit and feel physically ill. In many cases, a person's self-respect among colleagues, and the means of one's livelihood come under siege by constant bullying and intimidation. When worker's basic survival needs are threatened and their self-respect is being systematically eroded, thoughts of suicide may occur. Actual suicides have occurred as a result of workplace bullying.

Occupational Stress

Occupational stress is defined as (NIOSH, 2008, p. 1) 'the harmful physical and emotional responses that occur when the requirements of the job do not match the capabilities, resources, or needs of the worker'. While some degree of stress is a factor in every employee's work life, when stress becomes excessive and continuous then serious problems may ensue. Occupational stress has been designated as a hazard for certain occupations, particularly health care workers (NIOSH, 2008, p. 2), flight attendants (NIOSH, 2012) and those working in banking (Bunn and Guthrie, 2010).

In the health care industry, stressors have been identified as (NIOSH, 2008, p. 2): inadequate staffing levels; long work hours; shift work; role ambiguity; and exposure to infectious and hazardous substances. In the financial sector worldwide, stress is perceived as an escalating problem that can lead to suicide. According to Bunn and Guthrie (2010), a number of systemic factors contribute to the high rate of workplace stress in the banking industry, including a continual process of restructuring and change, combined with implications arising from the current economic climate.

Work stress is also associated with change, particularly in work practices. An employee may have been doing the same job in the same way for years, when suddenly a new manager is appointed or policies are introduced that require new skills, thereby challenging the worker's confidence. Workers who endure excessively stressful conditions often experience anxiety and fatigue (HSA, 1997). They are more prone to making mistakes and having accidents. They are more likely to indulge in excessive smoking, drinking, eating or drug-taking. High levels of stress over a long period of time have been shown to contribute to heart disease, reduced resistance to infection, digestive problems and skin problems. Striving to meet impossible deadlines or to complete excessive amounts of work often leaves workers feeling anxious, inadequate, frustrated, depressed and out of control.

Sexual Harassment

Sexual harassment infringes the basic dignity of the individual, and can have a devastating effect on the health, competence, morale and self-esteem of those affected (Costigan, 1998). Workers who are being sexually harassed often feel powerless, frightened, demeaned, angry, humiliated, and isolated. Many feel they will be blamed for causing the unwanted behaviour if they report the abuse, so they remain silent. Others feel frightened that they will be demoted, suffer further victimisation or dismissal if they speak out. Feelings of anxiety and stress, loss of confidence, and bouts of illness are common experiences of those who are sexually harassed. Although the majority of targets of sexual harassment are women, men may also find themselves becoming the butt of sexual jokes and unwanted physical contact. It is particularly difficult for a male victim of harassment to come forward and seek support.

Violence

Violence is a serious form of bullying that may be inflicted on workers by co-workers, service users or members of the public. The physical effects of violence can range from cuts and bruises, to broken bones and life-threatening injuries that may leave the target scarred or disabled. Serious assault, even resulting in death, has become a real fear for some types of workers in the course of their duties. Occupations most vulnerable to attack are those that enforce the law (e.g. gardaí, army, prison officers and social workers), handle money (e.g. security workers, cashiers, bus drivers and shop assistants), and work in the caring professions (e.g. nurses). Working in areas where there is a likelihood of violence can lead to low staff morale and high levels of stress (Wynne, 1995).

Extent of Suicide in Particular Industries

According to the US Bureau of Labour Statistics (2009), the five occupations with the highest suicide rates were management occupations (34%), sales and related occupations (26%), protective services (25%), transportation (24%), production (19%) and construction (18%). In a recent study, suicide within the construction industry in Queensland, Australia was reportedly high (Heller et al, 2007). A total of 64 male suicides occurred over a seven-year period, representing a suicide rate of 40.3 per 100,000, significantly greater than the working age Australian male rate. A high suicide rate was also reported for workers in the construction sector in Ireland (Arensman, 2013). Findings revealed that over two-fifths (41.6%) of those studied who had died by suicide had been employed in the construction sector. This was followed by people who had worked in the agricultural sector (13.2%), in sales/business development (8.9%), those who were students (8.2%), those who had worked in the health care sector (6.6%) and the educational sector (3.9%). Up to a quarter of women who took their lives had been employed in the health care sector. One of the causes of suicides in the construction sector was reported to be due to the large number of men who had lost their jobs during the recession.

CHAPTER TWELVE

The Media

The media has undoubtedly contributed to the construction of the Suicide Box as it is a hugely influential force in our society, for good or ill. Its power to influence our thinking, feelings and behaviour has been well documented (Dearing and Rogers, 1996; Iyengar and Kinder, 1987; McCombs and Reynolds, 2002) and is briefly discussed in this section. Since the Suicide Box is a collective way of thinking that has become riddled with myths, half-truths and judgements, the media, being the vehicle for spreading communications globally, has too often failed to promote confidence and positive self-esteem in our youth. Instead, media journalism and broadcasting all too frequently indulge in stereotyping of minority groups, and the portrayal of a specific body type, most usually ultra-thin for females, muscular and well toned for males. Thus, the media habitually undermines all that is natural, beautiful and spontaneous, and instead, fosters feelings of low self-esteem in its most vulnerable readers and viewers. Feelings of low self-esteem are considered to be risk factors in suicides (Nelson and Galas, 1994). The importance of establishing responsible guidelines in the reporting of suicides and the need for sensitive reporting instead of sensational media coverage is also explored.

The Media's Influence on Society
The power of the media to influence, to sensationalise news and opinions, to stimulate, titillate and promise instant gratification has

never been greater. Technological advances in the early years of the twenty-first century have brought a new wave of revolution, where even school children can capture images on camera phones, type messages on laptops, phones, or digital tablets and distribute these around the world in seconds, using text messaging, email, blogs and social media sites. The media is above all else a billion-dollar industry that provides news, interviews, chat shows, comedy, sports coverage and drama for public interest and entertainment. The conglomerate that is funding the operation exerts enormous influence on the content and tone of what is being produced. Certain companies favour particular political parties, economic theories or social policies. All too often opinions can be touted as truths; highly stereotypical images and labels can be used to distort and foster prejudice; the blurring of truth with myths and fantasy is all too easily accomplished with the dazzling capabilities of modern technology.

It has never been easier for individuals to be duped and sucked into a world of fantasy and illusion that is ultimately all too artificial and hollow. The quality and integrity of the program, article or website created is determined by the collective aims of the writers, editors or producers, and the publishing or broadcasting company that is funding the project. The power of the media acts at different levels. As you read the following sections it may be a valuable exercise to examine whether you feel the influence is explicit, as in the case of blatant sensationalism, or implicit, as in the portrayal of particular body types as desirable.

Depiction of Minority Groups

Although the media often covers groundbreaking news stories and articles that raise society's consciousness and expose abuses and cover-ups, it is at least equally true that journalists, interviewers and film-makers regularly use stereotypes of minority groups, including those based on religious belief, skin colour, ethnicity, age and disability. Minority groups that are frequently stereotyped by the media are homosexuals, lesbians, and bisexuals.

Before the 1970s, almost no homosexual characters were depicted on television, and this absence continued until the 1990s (Wyatt, 2002). Although the portrayal of homosexuals is no longer taboo in television programs, depictions of real homosexual relationships are relatively rare (Brown, 2002). This creates a bias and a lack of positive role models in the media for non-heterosexual youth (Kielwasser and Wolf, 1992). The fact that there are no physical differences between heterosexuals and homosexuals means that programmes overemphasise the gestures, stance, clothing and tone of voice of their homosexual characters to enhance the effect.

The lack of positive or realistic portrayals of homosexuals in the media is particularly worrying when faced with researchers' findings that an estimated one third of young people who attempt suicide or take their own lives are gay or lesbian (Berkovitz, 1985). The concern has been expressed by Gross (1989, p. 135) that, since the mass media plays an important role in the process of social definition, this negative stereotyping of gay people creates further difficulties for their acceptance by the majority of society. This in turn makes it incredibly difficult for young homosexuals to develop self-acceptance and self-worth. Thus, the media carries enormous responsibility to use its vast talents and expertise to portray individuals who may be part of a minority group with realism and sensitivity, as human beings and not as gross caricatures.

Portraying an Ultra-Thin Female Body Image
The media receives billions in revenue from companies selling their wares online, in the print media, on TV and radio. According to

Dr Anthony Curtis (2012), from the University of North Carolina, 95 per cent of all the traditional media we receive every day is controlled by a handful of conglomerates, including the top Fortune 500 companies: Walt Disney Company, News Corporation, Time Warner, CBS Corporation, Viacom, NBC Universal and Sony Corporation of America. It is the task of the advertiser to create a scene that will affect the viewer's emotions. The greater the emotional impact, such as triggering feelings of desire, self-loathing, jealousy, or excitement, the more likely it is that the viewer will purchase the product.

We live in a world where appearance and body image have never been more important to our feelings of self-esteem. Images of thin, desirable females bombard us from every direction: on billboards, on our TV screens, in newspapers and glossy magazines, on posters selling everything from cosmetics to cars. The fact that these images are not representative of average women is creating self-loathing in many pre-teen and adolescent girls. In a recent study of a thousand women by Dove (*The Telegraph*, 2009), findings revealed that over 40 per cent said advertisements that feature women made them feel self-conscious about their appearance; 28 per cent said they were left feeling inadequate; 20 per cent said they were less confident in their daily lives as a result of such images. Dove also revealed that many of the images of models have been digitally altered or airbrushed to make their breasts appear larger or their waists appear smaller. Author and psychotherapist Dr Susie Orbach stated on behalf of the campaign (*The Telegraph*, 2009): 'On a daily basis women are bombarded with impossibly perfect images created by artifice, which they will always aspire towards, but can rarely achieve because these images depend on serious transformation by photographers.'

Puberty and teenage years have always been difficult to navigate, due to physical and emotional changes that lead to intense sexual feelings and the tentative formation of a sexual identity. Psychologically, there are two needs that persist throughout our lives but are most prevalent during this time of enormous upheaval: the need for love and the need to feel good about oneself (Nelson and Galas, 1994, p. 13). Self-esteem is generally regarded as the evaluation that the person makes about him or herself, that expresses a self-judgment of approval or disapproval about personal worth (Demo and Savin-Williams, 1992; Rosenberg, 1965; Suls, 1989). Low self-esteem has been associated with depression (Harter, 1986; Reinherz et al, 1989), alcohol misuse (Hull, 1981), binge eating (Heatherton and Baumeister, 1991), indulging in masochism (Baumeister, 1991), and suicide (Baumeiser, 1991). The unbearable pain of not feeling acceptable, beautiful or having the correct body shape as constructed by media images is a leading contributory factor in the onset of eating disorders (Orbach, 1993; Wolf, 1991) and may also be a factor in teenage girls self-harming and taking their own lives.

The portrayal of ultra-thin women in the media is, therefore, having a negative effect on the development of self-esteem and body satisfaction of females at every age, including children at school entry age (Dohnt and Tiggerman, 2005). The media prints and films these images of women, not for any aesthetic reason nor for any plan to cause harm, but as a requirement by lucrative advertisers to create dissatisfaction and hence desire in women, to convince them subconsciously that a specific product has the power to transform them into thin women who are worthy of society's approval. The truth, however, is that, unless our youth are educated to develop awareness, to keep questioning the motivation of powerful institutions, most especially the media, society will continue to cripple the most sensitive and vulnerable in every generation with its concocted images of beauty. The frightening side to this reality is that the media and advertisers are fully aware of the power that they hold. They know that the emotional upheavals they cause in people makes them vast profits. On the surface, the destructiveness of their behaviour is almost undetectable but their subliminal saturation of images is testament to their unsavoury intent.

Susan's Story as Told by her Best Friend Kate

I have known Susan since primary school. We each have a love of horses and used to spend a lot of our spare time at the nearby riding stables. I'm not sure when it started but all of a sudden I realised that Susan was getting very thin. I know her mother was very worried about her and brought her to a counsellor. I became worried when she had to go to hospital. I wasn't allowed to visit her for six weeks and when I did I cried when I saw her. She was only fourteen but she looked like a depressed thirty year old to me. She was shocked by my reaction and we held each other for a long time and cried together. At one point she blurted out that she hated herself. She said she was surrounded by images of perfect women but that her fat thighs and hips were abnormal in comparison. I couldn't believe what she was saying as I always thought she was gorgeous looking. Susan is due out in a few days and is going to have to be supervised closely for a while.

Media Portrayal of Males that Foster Self-Consciousness

Many studies have been conducted as to the effects that the depiction of idealised females in the media have on women, especially teenage girls. Recently, the effect that images of male models and desirable females have on young men has also been studied. A growing body of research indicates that, although men are less likely to talk about their feelings of insecurity, they do experience anxiety around body image and their level of desirability (Norman, 2011).

Traditionally, men were supposed to care little about their appearance, to be nonchalant about their weight, height or shape. The reality today, however, is that men are sensitive to their perceived level of attractiveness and to the portrayal of idealised males in the media. Since advertisers are now focusing more on young males as consumers of cosmetics, there has been an escalation in the number and intensity of advertisements that portray handsome males with perfect physiques. Studies show a significant relationship between the increase in idealised males in the media and the rise in eating disorders and body dissatisfaction in boys and young men (Smolak and Stein, 2006). Some studies indicate an incidence of eating disorders around 3 per cent for young women and 1 per cent for young men (Hoerr et al, 2002).

Recent research into the effects of lad magazines on male body self-consciousness and appearance anxiety reported some startling findings (Aubrey and Taylor, 2009). The first study conducted with undergraduate men, found that lad magazine exposure in Year 1 predicted body self-consciousness in Year 2. The second study revealed that men assigned to view objectified women in lad magazines reported significantly higher levels of appearance anxiety and appearance-related motivations for exercise than men assigned to view male fashion models. Thus it has been speculated that participants believed that in order to become romantically involved with attractive women, they would have to conform to an idealised appearance standard. The third study replicated the findings that exposure to sexually objectified women primed body self-consciousness in men, and also influenced men's lack of confidence in being romantically successful with women.

Stigma that labels eating disorders as mainly a female issue, makes it more difficult for men to admit that they have a problem around excessive weight control and body image. The fact that media portrayal of idealised males is having an adverse effect on the health as well as the confidence of an increasing number of young men is deeply worrying. As previously pointed out, men who suicide choose more lethal methods and we as a society are having to cope with the awful reality that young men are approximately four times more likely than women to die by suicide (Joiner, 2005, p. 29). Surely advertisements that have been proven to contribute to insecurity around body image should be required to carry a health warning? The promotion of mental health is a stated aim of most Western governments due to rising levels in mental illness, depression and suicide (Department of Health and Children, 1998). Researchers, therapists and psychologists concur that depression and poor mental health involve negative thinking, particularly in the areas of viewing of self, viewing of the world, and viewing the future (Beck et al, 1979). Therapists work with individuals to help raise their self-esteem, to increase positive thoughts and confidence. It is sadly ludicrous then that society is at cross purposes with itself, promoting a positive self-concept in the area of mental health, while simultaneously smashing the confidence and self-image, most particularly of teenagers, in the service of advertising and media expansion.

Robert's Insights, Aged Twenty-Eight

For men, body image is also an issue but it is part of male traits not to point this out, as to do so would draw personal negative attention. It wouldn't be a man thing to do. The media image portrayal of men includes: chiselled body, defined abs, and dictated maleness. There's no report given of the years of training, the cost of chiselling, personal trainers, and professional photography. Perfect male fashion models are not the male norm. Men are not as free to express this conflict as women are (as they did over the size zero uproar). Men are less free to express tension with the media portrayal of male-ness, hence the silence. That chiselled muscular look is impossible for most men. Brad Pitt spoke of his role in *Fight Club*, saying that such an image was impossible to maintain in reality.

Male social roles are too rigid, too ambiguous. There are too few roles acceptable. Even the male/female roles lack clarity. It has become too hard to maintain social expectations of these narrow roles, too hard to establish and express individuality. Society's quick identification of alternative or unacceptable traits for men include 'feminine', 'camp', 'geek', 'awkward', 'social outcast', 'a bit funny', 'loner', 'different'.

Media Reporting and Copycat Suicides

According to Pirkas et al (2006), there is strong evidence to suggest that suicidal behaviour is sometimes copied from descriptions of suicides reported in the media. If the suicide act is glamorised, it may lead to similar acts being attempted by vulnerable people. In the USA it has been estimated that one in five suicides is imitative of a previous suicide (Department of Health and Children, Dublin, 1998). This phenomenon is known as the Werther effect, so named after the main character in Goethe's eighteenth-century novel, *The Sorrows of Young Werther*, who took his own life. When the novel was published a spate of suicides followed, where victims used similar methods to procure death and dressed in similar clothes to those worn by Werther, with the novel being found at several suicide scenes.

The importance of journalists adhering to strict guidelines when reporting suicides is frequently cited by organisations working in the area of suicide. It is also vital that the media reports facts around suicide instead of feeding into myths that lead to irresponsible broadcasting and journalism. At all times a balance needs to be struck between representing the facts in the public interest, respecting the rights of bereaved families, and avoiding all references that could have a negative impact on vulnerable individuals (Irish Association of Suicidology, and The Samaritans,

2009). While there are responsible newspapers that strive for balance in their articles, there are many publications that seek to excite and feed the public desire for sensationalism.

Much research has been conducted into copycat suicides, suicide clusters, suicide contagion and the role of the media in fuelling these crises (Phillips, Lesyna and Paight, 1992). It has been estimated that 13 per cent of teenage suicides occur in clusters (Irish Association of Suicidology and The Samaritans, 2009). Overwhelming research findings indicate that the degree of increase in suicidal behaviour after newspaper coverage is related to the amount of publicity given to the story and its prominence in newspapers (Phillips, 1980; Philips, Lesyna and Paight, 1992). When suicide coverage appears on the front page, the likelihood of imitation becomes greater (Philips, Lesyna and Paight, 1992). Wasserman (1984) found that a significant increase in national suicide rates occurred when a celebrity suicide was reported on the front page of the *New York Times*.

Sensational Reporting
There are few events more distressing or incomprehensible as murder suicide, where one or more family members take their family's lives and then their own. The real causes of such tragedies are often complex and harrowing, involving social and economic factors, coupled with deep emotional and psychological issues. Just as suicide clusters can occur following the reporting of a suicide, so too there is evidence that reporting of murder-suicide cases can lead to imitation behaviours (Irish Association of Suicidology and The Samaritans, 2009, p. 14). These events usually have a deep and lasting effect on an entire community and attract national and international coverage. It is imperative that reporting in these cases is extremely sensitive, balanced and follows clear guidelines in

professional and responsible journalism. Some elements of the media, however, use such tragedies to indulge in sensational headlines, wild speculation, lurid fantasies and misinformation (Irish Association of Suicidology and The Samaritans, 2009, p. 14). This type of irresponsible and grossly insensitive reporting may greatly increase the distress of the bereaved at a time when they are in deep shock. While individual accountability cannot be discounted, a feature of the Suicide Box with regard to the media is that blame is usually heaped onto one individual. This is equivalent to a journalist taking a few pieces of a jigsaw, building a plausible story around them and presenting the story as a complete one. The full jigsaw, of course, would be less attractive or lucrative, would invariably dissipate responsibility to all aspects of society, and even onto the individual journalist for sensational reporting.

Reporting That Leads To Tragedy
Some sections of the media have done great work in sensitively portraying the reasons why people take their own lives, and in interviewing their loved ones in a decent and respectful way, giving them a platform to tell their harrowing stories, while also giving the public important information about the reality of suicide to reflect upon. Unfortunately, aspects of the media have also caused great pain through insensitive interviewing and the sensational reporting of events that humiliate and obliterate the character of the person being targeted. Since the development and maintenance of a person's character is of utmost importance in the society we live in, it is surely a serious matter when journalists or reporters disparage or humiliate people in the media. Certainly, there are laws that can be invoked against defamation of character, yet for individuals who are ridiculed or ruined in the national press or on TV, especially in a small nation such as Ireland, the mud usually sticks and there is little

choice but to suffer such slander or gross exaggerations without recourse to justice. Having one's character assassinated in the full glare of the media can have serious effects on an individual. In extreme cases, this can lead to feelings of overwhelming humiliation and ultimately to tragic consequences.

The following interview details the reporting of a recent story considered a public interest by a leading Irish newspaper. The subsequent tragedy is indeed food for thought for journalists when considering publishing material that can destroy lives.

Martha

I had lived in the same village as the man at the centre of this story for fifty years. I knew he was a hard worker and a dedicated family man. When his son took his life it took a huge toll on him. He lost his old astuteness and dedication to his work. It's fair to say he never really recovered. He was hospitalised and developed mental health problems. But it wasn't the tragic incident of losing his son alone that killed his spirit. It was an article that was printed about the man himself in a national newspaper that finished him off. A journalist contacted him about an article he was writing, accusing him of being a cowboy, a rogue and a fraud who was producing shoddy work, leaving his customers waiting for months before the work was carried out, and running up bills from creditors that he couldn't pay. The accused man pleaded his case, explaining how he'd been plagued by depression after his son's untimely death, how he was struggling to carry on his business, to keep his customers and to pay off his debts – like thousands of others in the country. He appealed to the humanity of the writer, stating that the proposed article would certainly destroy his business, would cause great pain and hardship to his family and would certainly cripple him in the small community where he lived and worked.

However, none of this mattered to the journalist. On the day that the article appeared, my neighbour bought the paper, read it, and immediately went home and ended his own life, hopeless, alone. If one journalist has this kind of power to destroy a man, with no sense of decency or basic feeling for a human being in a difficult situation, then something is very wrong with our laws, our media, our level of caring and consideration for each other. Nothing was ever done to expose this tragedy, this travesty. Neither the reporter nor the newspaper was ever challenged and the true story of what transpired was never publicised. But I know, and now you know, that the media has blood on its hands.

An Explanation for Sensational Media Reporting

The sensational manner in which suicide is reported is more understandable when viewed from within the Suicide Box. From this limited standpoint, apart from the fact that sensational stories increase media profits, there is also a tendency to opt for biological or individual explanations for events or for phenomena, such as depression, schizophrenia or suicide. This is no surprise since the media, and mental health and psychiatry, both occupy the Suicide Box. Reporting is, therefore, informed by the dominant psychiatric and medication model, as advocated within the mental health system. This simplistic model does not allow for any level of societal responsibility, in the shaping of attitudes, experiences and beliefs, and in the individual's accumulated emotional pain, due to the destructive effects of socialisation.

CHAPTER THIRTEEN

The Family

The family in its various forms has always been the bedrock of society, its role being central to the rearing of children in social values and norms. The structure of the family in Western nations remained static for centuries until an enormous social revolution dawned during the 1960s, proclaiming individual freedoms that challenged the traditional family unit. The changes in family life and social structures were very pronounced in Ireland where the teachings of the Catholic Church had for centuries been blindly followed with puritanical rigidity and a fanatical repression of sexuality (McGoldrick, 2005; 1996). The dawning of an age where individual freedoms, particularly sexual, were grasped by Irish youth, coupled with the advent of Vatican II, led to a wide split occurring between the guilt-ridden, older generation that looked to the Pope for guidance, and the newer generation that became immersed in popular culture, in progressive and experimental music, movies and fashions from Europe and the United States.

In the twenty-first century, families have never been more diverse and atypical. Stereotypes of male and female have also undergone radical transformation with the advent of feminism and equality legislation. Families have also had to absorb enormous advances in technologies that have brought many benefits but also problems, such as cyberbullying. Social problems, such as unemployment and lack of finances, confusion over male and female roles within the family, and the break-up of relationships that often cause deep pain.

The Irish Family

The position of the family in Ireland is enshrined in the Constitution (*Bunreacht na hÉireann*, 1937) and extolled as the natural, primary and fundamental unit of society and a moral institution that possesses inalienable and imprescriptible rights. The family (assumed to consist of a father, a mother and a child or children) once occupied a position of immunity and complicity from the state and the Church, where children could be beaten, neglected, mistreated and abused without intervention from any source. Recently, legislation in the European Union has acknowledged children's rights and has implemented a system for monitoring alleged abuse and neglect within families. Under Irish law it is now a serious criminal offence to abuse or neglect a child, to perpetrate domestic violence or to sexually or physically abuse any family member (Domestic Violence Act, 1996; Criminal Law (Sexual Offences) Act, 2006; The Child and Family Agency Act, 2013).

Families within the Suicide Box

Complex social and familial factors converge to contribute to trauma and heartache due to emotional abuse, domestic violence and child abuse, alcoholism and drug addiction. The degree of guidance, respect, positive affirmation and love that children receive from parents still largely contributes to their level of emotional and psychological development. While parents are not required to possess perfect child-rearing skills, the failure of some parents to provide for the needs of their children has serious consequences. A recent report found that mental maltreatment by a family member (16.4%), and physical maltreatment by guardians (15.8%) were experienced as negative and traumatic life events in childhood or early adolescence by those who died by suicide (Arensman et al, 2012). This places the family within the Suicide Box, as immense hurt and damage may occur during a child's formative years, when children fail to receive love, a sense of emotional security and ample nurturing.

Culture and Suicide

The family is one of the main vehicles where cultural norms are absorbed unconsciously and wholly accepted without question. Differences in culture also appear to influence the suicide rate across nations. For example, the Japanese suicide rate is twice that of America, three times that of Thailand, nine times higher than Greece and twelve times higher than the Philippines (Duignan, 2013). There is a legacy of suicide in Japan as practised by the samurai warriors and kamikaze pilots during wartime, so that suicide has always been considered an honourable death. The documentary created by Duignan (2013) singles out the media's failure in Japan to show the starkness of suicide and instead, to promote suicide black spots to attract tourism, hence creating an industry out of tragedy. Duignan's provocative documentary suggests that Japanese culture condones, encourages and is largely responsible for the fact that 300,000 Japanese people have taken their lives in the past ten years.

Repression in Irish Culture

In Ireland, the negative cultural influences on suicide are much more subtle. Repression, ridicule, belittling and shaming have played a major role in child-rearing in Ireland. Genuine praise is largely frowned upon. Children can, therefore, grow up to lack confidence and to have poor self-esteem. They learn to withhold praise, to hide their true feelings, and to use sarcasm and derision in their interactions with friends and loved ones. Feelings of deep shame, humiliation and inadequacy are then perpetuated, mingling with the Irish psyche of guilt, moroseness and sorrow. Although the Irish are renowned globally for being highly creative and articulate in literature, and for their deep expressiveness in art and music, they find a great difficulty in expressing inner feelings. McGoldrick (1996) sums up this immense paradox: 'Thus, although the Irish have a marvellous ability to tell stories, when it comes to their emotions, they may have no words.'

In an emotionally repressed culture, people learn to hide their perceived weaknesses, differences and failures for fear of ridicule. The repression of emotion has long been associated with the manifestation of health problems including asthma (Florin et al, 1985); cancer (Denollet, 1998; Greer and Watson, 1985); chronic pain disorders (Beutler et al, 1986); and cardiovascular diseases (Brosschot and Thayer, 1998; Jorgensen et al, 1996). Depression is most associated with a numbing of feelings, particularly grief, fear, anger and shame (Scheff, 2011). Scheff (2011) describes depression as: 'Anger turned inward against the self. If you fail to live up to some internal standard of who or what you are supposed to be, some internal watchdog notes your failure and begins to let you know that you haven't been all that you could be – depression.'

A culture that thrives on humiliation and shame, that fails to promote the open expression of emotion, creates many lonely, depressed, anxious and frustrated people who are living mediocre lives for fear of upsetting the status quo. When particular emotions become blocked people may be periodically taken over by the sheer force of the emotion, becoming pure anger, hatred or jealously. Eckhart Tolle (1999) calls this accumulation of unexpressed negative emotion 'the pain body'.

Gender and Emotional Repression
Studies suggest that gender differences in the way people express thoughts and feelings may be learned through socialisation. A male's

tendency to be inexpressive when disclosing feelings about the self may be part of the stereotyped 'masculine' gender role that avoids emotional intimacy (Shields, 1987). According to Polce-Lynch et al (1998): 'later in life, males' emotional restriction may render them more susceptible to health problems because their bodies unconsciously do the "emotional" work for them – in the form of medical problems such as ulcers, high blood pressure, heart problems.'

The fact that men tend to withdraw from close relationships at times of distress is viewed by the European Commission (2011) as a possible cause of the high number of young male suicides across Europe. According to the Samaritan's report (Wylie et al, 2012): 'Masculinity – the way men are brought up to behave and the roles, attributes and behaviours that society expects of them – contributes to suicide in men … Masculinity is associated with control, but when men are depressed or in crisis, they can feel out of control. This can propel some men towards suicidal behaviour as a way of regaining control.'

The socialisation of boys to lack emotional expression is in need of urgent reversal, according to Liam O'Neill, President of the Gaelic Athletic Association (GAA) (Fallon, 2014). O'Neill emphasised the importance of teaching children to talk about their problems and not to keep them bottled up. He also advocated 'a masculinity that doesn't centre around the fact that big boys don't cry and big boys don't show their feelings, because that's what locks the hearts and the mind of the child when they want later on as adults to express themselves, to say "I'm in bother here, I need someone to talk to".'

Keeping Deadly Secrets
Judy Pollatsek, a counsellor in Washington DC, states that one of the most common reasons for teens taking their own lives is living with a secret they can't share with anyone (Frankel and Kranz, 1994, p. 61). Studies have shown that feelings of deep shame that remain

secret may lead to violence and suicide (Gilligan, 1997). Secrets come in many forms. There are secrets that have their origins in past trauma and secrets that arise from something a person has done that triggers feelings of guilt and shame. Sometimes secrets develop due to a person's lifestyle or situation that is unacceptable within society. This is particularly true of sexual preferences and psychosexual identity, since there is still a taboo on sexual expression in society if it drifts outside the confines of the social definition of 'normal' sexuality.

Keeping silent about problems allows them to grow and become inflamed. The importance of expressing feelings, talking about problems, exploring past trauma and working through secrets is the cornerstone of psychotherapy. People who feel overwhelmed by difficult emotions or situations, and who see no way out of their pain except through suicide, may see things differently from another perspective if they talk to someone about their problem. Gail Griffith (2005, p. 3), mother of teenager, Will, was gradually admitted into her son's inner world when he attended a counsellor after attempting to kill himself on several occasions. It was only then that Griffith began to learn all about lethal secrets: 'It comes as a shock to learn that our children have secret lives – and that their secrets may be deadly.'

There are countless organisations set up to help the individual deal with personal issues. These organisations do excellent work, offering support to those in pain by facilitating the expression of their innermost thoughts. Yet they cannot offer any solutions that will make the person's experience within society, their family or community, any less restrictive or more accepting of their particular situation. If the individual finally chooses to disclose their secret to the world, the onus is on him or her to face the wrath of all of the social structures that make up the Suicide Box and deal with the ensuing chaos alone. The alternative is to remain in pain within the confines of the Suicide Box, under the guise of a social chameleon.

From our experiences, secrets have led to many known suicides: secrets that could not be revealed due to fear of rejection and ridicule, and secrets that were disclosed by another party that led to great humiliation that the person couldn't bear. We must consider as a society how we might embrace the complexity of human nature. Embracing humanity might mean broadening our collective social ego to include those features that a fear-and-illusion-driven society denies. How less stressful and unifying would society be if we could embrace our nature, warts and all, and work on features that progress us as a society rather than those that divide and destruct?

Josh's Insight, Aged Twenty-Three

It would be easier if I ended it all because then I wouldn't cause anyone any hurt. My family would be so ashamed if they knew about me. They might disown me. I keep imagining what my brothers would say. There's no way I could ever face them, and all my mates. Imagine what they'd say if they knew? I don't know how it started. I must have been around six when I began messing around with my sister's things. She was a lot older and she'd let me play with her stuff. I loved the way it made me feel. I always get such a rush when I dress up in women's clothes. It's like becoming someone else, someone much more free and adventurous. I'm not gay. I'd like to have a girlfriend but I'm so afraid of being found out. I feel such a freak. I often think about ending it all, that it might be better for everyone if I did.

Emotional Abuse

The positive emotional development of children is vital to their sense of self-worth and their level of confidence. When a caregiver is sensitive to children's needs and provides loving care, they develop the capacity to relate easily to others and to be self-confident. Such children display few if any signs of emotional dysfunction and rarely engage in anti-social behaviour (Grossman and Grossman, 1990). However, children may experience emotional abuse at the hands of a parent who is narcissistic or suffers from emotional hunger, due to their own dysfunctional childhood experiences.

When a caregiver is narcissistic and is unable to respond to a child's emotional needs, children suffer serious emotional damage (www.fortrefuge.com). A parent may use hostile and manipulative behaviours to control children, creating a fearful, sad and frustrated child. They may compare siblings, leading to feelings of inadequacy and worthlessness. They may threaten terrible punishments or dire consequences for even minor transgressions. Parents who reject their children through constant blaming, shaming and criticism run a high risk of rearing children who become depressed adolescents and adults with low self-esteem (Robertson et al, 1989, p. 134).

When parents are emotionally hungry and desperate to fill their feelings of emptiness and pain (Firestone, 2009), they may exhibit excessive touching, over-concern and violate their children's boundaries. Parents may foster an abnormal degree of dependency in their children, even to the extent of isolating them from peers. Emotionally immature parents may seek to fulfil themselves through their children, thus seriously hampering their development in self-esteem and social skills.

The importance of nurturing children's self-esteem as the basis for future mental health was reported by McGee et al (2001). Their findings from a longitudinal study linked low levels of self-esteem in mid-childhood years to hopelessness and thoughts of self-harm, and to suicidal ideation at ages eighteen and twenty-one. Dr Bernie Siegel, author and medical practitioner, proffered that the cause of much pain, and people's ensuing suicide attempts, is due to being unloved in childhood (2002, p. xii): 'I think that when you don't know what to do with your pain and are feeling unloved, suicide seems like a better choice than life.'

Domestic Violence

Domestic violence perpetrated in the home creates enormous pain and distress for every family member. Children are deeply traumatised by witnessing or experiencing violence at the hands of their parents or a live-in partner. The effect of domestic violence on children is detrimental to their safety but also to their emotional well-being. In a recent global study, it was found that more people die due to domestic violence than due to war, costing more than $8 trillion a year (Doyle, 2014). In the European Union, domestic violence continues to be a common occurrence, with one respondent in four reporting that a friend or family member is a victim (European Commission, 2010, p. 10).

Despite legislation, one in five women is reported to be abused by a current or former husband, partner or boyfriend, at some stage in their lifetime (Women's Aid Website). During 2012, 16,200 disclosures of domestic violence against women were reported to Women's Aid Services (Women's Aid, 2012). Our thinking, however, is limited to generalisations and stereotypes that are learned within the Suicide Box. It is a common misperception to solely equate domestic violence with the abuse of women by men. Both national and international research has begun to study the extent and the effects of domestic violence on men by their partners. Watson and Parsons (2005) researched domestic violence for the National Crime Council in Ireland and reported that approximately 88,000 men and 213,000 women in Ireland have been severely abused by a partner (Cosc, 2013).

Child Abuse

Within the Suicide Box, child abuse and domestic violence that occur within a family are surrounded by fears and stigma. There is now legislation in Ireland, mainly the Child and Family Agency Act

(2013) to protect children from abuse or neglect. Despite recent legislation, the fact remains that there are several factors that increase a child's vulnerability to abuse within the family and these include (World Health Organisation, 2002): being raised by a single parent or by very young parents without the help of an extended family or community supports; household overcrowding; a lack of income to meet the family's needs; the presence of other violent relationships in the home; and parents who have low self-esteem, poor control over their impulses, mental health problems, display antisocial behaviour or have unrealistic expectations for their children.

In some studies, between a quarter and a half of the children report severe and frequent physical abuse, including being beaten, kicked or tied up by parents (World Health Organisation, 2002). Research suggests that about 20 per cent of women, and between 5 and 10 per cent of men, suffered sexual abuse as children. Many children are subjected to psychological or emotional abuse, as well as neglect, though the extent of these abuses is unknown. All children are vulnerable to abuse, but the youngest children are the most vulnerable to maltreatment. In the United States, statistics show that 25 per cent of abused children are under the age of three while over 45 per cent are under the age of five (www.safehorizon.org).

The World Health Organisation (2002) has determined that child abuse can lead to many types of health problems and emotional difficulties, including suicidal behaviour. The association between childhood trauma, such as abuse or neglect, and suicidal behaviour is well documented. Neglectful parenting is an independent risk factor for adolescent suicidal attempts. This is true even when adjusting for other factors such as psychological disorders (King et al, 2001). Childhood physical abuse has been found to be a risk factor for suicidal behaviour in several studies (Roy, 2003; McHolm, MacMillan and Jamieson, 2003).

Tommy gives an account below of a child's private experience in an abusive environment. While Tommy's story may seem from another time, we can be assured that children today are still suffering unnecessary physical, emotional and mental pain within their private worlds, with suicide often presenting as a viable option.

Tommy's Reflections

I was born in the rural Irish Midlands in the 1950s into an angry world. Punching and fear filled my days. Suicide seemed a logical choice and was often part of my thinking. It was probably my mother's gentle spirit and wanting to protect her that kept me from killing myself on many occasions. However, there were times, like when I was about nine, when thoughts of my mother couldn't deter me from ending it. I took a rope to a little den I had discovered some fields away and just as I had prepared for the final event I heard and then saw our sheepdog that had followed my scent. For a moment I was happy to see her until I realised she was accompanied by one of my childhood tyrants who punched me and beat me home with the rope. The helplessness was spirit breaking.

I don't know how old I was when I first felt this feeling of helplessness. It was very early as I remember sitting on the floor playing with something when my father rushed in and grabbed my mother by the throat and hit her. I could do nothing. The fear I felt was so real. Everything seemed to revolve around that excuse for a human. His arrival to me was like the approach of the giant in *Jack and the Beanstalk*. I remember lying in bed petrified; worried while I listened to the wind and rain outside, after my father had thrown my mother out of the house earlier. Many years later she told me that on one of those occasions she went to a local church and was told by a priest that she had made her bed and now she must lie in it.

The local primary school was also run by a tyrant and a pervert. I was regularly beaten by him and I saw him put his hand up girls' skirts at his desk. No public investigation has touched this aspect of the rotten Irish society of the past. When I hid in a local wood the guards were called and brought me back to the esteemed pillar of society, alias Thug, to do with me as he wished. I felt that society colluded against me as a child. The deviant pillars of society were truly in charge. The surface has only been scratched as to the damage the powers that be have done.

Thankfully the truth about many of the Christian Brothers surfaced but in my experience it was the lay teachers they employed that were also capable of brutality and abuse against children and teenagers. There were three such thugs in the school I went to. They demeaned, humiliated and used fists and leather straps at will. We would regularly have to stand around the classroom, often for a double period, to recite an Irish poem or whatever we were told to memorise. Failure to recite the poem meant two lashes on the first occasion. Failure on each following round meant a doubling of lashes. Paradoxically, no one was allowed to learn the poem in the meantime, so the thug's fun was assured. I can still see the sweat on the face, the coat jumping into the air with the force of each lash, but the smirk on the face was the worst to bear. Then even more difficult to bear was the pain and the numb swollen hands, the sense of failure, the helplessness, the hating myself for living, the anger, the hating the world and the wanting to kill. Where are those tyrants now? Do they remember the evil they propagated and the negative world they contributed to? How do they justify it to themselves?

I am so happy to be alive now, to have survived the respected thugs who were allowed to run society, to see positive change occurring even if it means that society has to be dragged, kicking and screaming, into a civilised reality. They could have easily succeeded in turning me into a worse version of themselves, as I'm sure they achieved with many unfortunates, but I have learned to love life and my fellow man in spite of them.

Alcohol and Substance Abuse
Global, European and Irish reports and surveys are unanimous that the misuse of alcohol in Ireland is causing serious problems at all

levels of society, but most particularly in the spread of crime, disease, mental illness, family disruption (Corrigan, 2003) and suicide. Added to this appalling vista is the rising use of drugs by Ireland's youth. An EU survey in 2010 (TNS Opinion and Social) found that Ireland had the highest percentage of binge drinkers in the EU at 19 per cent. A European report into drug use found that 16 per cent of Ireland's young adult population (eighteen to thirty-four years) said they had tried 'legal highs' in their lifetime: this was the highest of any EU member state (EMCDDA). A report commissioned by the Irish Health Research Board in 2013 (Long and Mongan, 2013) found that 1.3 million people were harmful drinkers, while almost one in fourteen drinkers – 150,000 people – were dependent drinkers. Perhaps the most damning report of all was the recent global analysis on alcohol consumption (WHO, 2014). This report revealed that Ireland currently has the second highest rate of binge drinking in the world. The lack of government response to this epidemic of addiction was noted by a European report into drug abuse (EMCDDA, 2012): the level of Irish government funding for a national action plan on tackling drug abuse in Ireland is zero.

The consequences of drinking to excess have been well documented (Ramstedt and Hope, 2003). Irish men show high rates of consequences reported after excessive drinking compared to European countries, including, having regretted things said or done after drinking (31%); got into a fight (11.5%); been in an accident (6.3%), adverse consequences with work/study (12.4%), with friendships (9.6%), and with home life (7.8%). High levels of consequences for Irish women compared to other European countries studied were reported as follows: having regretted things said or done after drinking (21.7%); adverse consequences with work/study (2.9%), with friendships (4.3%).

The social effects of excessive alcohol are entwined with familial and individual consequences. A report on homelessness in Ireland has found that drug misuse is associated with becoming and remaining homeless (Keane, 2006). According to Alcohol Action Ireland (www.alcoholireland.ie/facts/case-studies-kids):

- ✦ Links between alcohol and crime are well established. Intoxication of both perpetrator and victims has been noted in a high percentage of instances of murder and sexual assault.

- ✦ Almost half of the perpetrators of murder were intoxicated when the crime was committed.

- ✦ 76 per cent of all rape defendants had been drinking at the time of the alleged offence.

- ✦ Alcohol has been identified as a contributory factor in 97 per cent of public order offences as recorded under the Garda PULSE system.

- ✦ One in eleven, or approximately 318,000 of the full adult population, said that they or a family member were assaulted by someone under the influence of alcohol in the past year.

Alcohol Abuse within the Family

Experts and clinicians in the area of alcoholism have reached consensus on the behaviour patterns of all participants within the family (Flanzer, 1993). An alcohol problem for one family member becomes a whole family problem with devastating consequences for each member. When a parent is an abuser of alcohol, the remaining family members will often erect enormous defences to minimise and rationalise the seriousness of their predicament. The abusing parent usually blames others for his or her problems, while the non-abusing parent accepts the blame, feels shame for the ensuing situation and struggles to hold the family together (Flanzer, 1993). The children most often develop feelings of inferiority. The alcoholic usually holds great power within the family as everything revolves around his or her misuse of alcohol. As the addiction takes hold, family members usually choose to cover up with enabling behaviour rather than expose the truth of the family's predicament. The non-abusing parent usually accepts the impossible role of carer for the entire family and may begin to believe that he or she deserves to be emotionally or physically mistreated and left without any intimacy. It is only when partners find the courage to face the truth of their spouses' addiction and to reach outside for healing and support that change for all concerned is possible, though in many cases the addicted parent is not prepared to contemplate change. This detachment from the alcohol-addicted parent and the enabling process are vital actions for all family members to take in order for true healing to occur. How the alcohol misuser responds to this detachment has to be a secondary concern at this stage as the healing has to be viewed in a holistic manner.

Alcohol and Suicide
Studies have established a close relationship between alcoholism and suicide (Kendall, 1983; Dooley and Fitzgerald, 2012), and alcohol consumption is considered to be a significant influence on the suicide rate of young men in particular (Walsh and Walsh, 2011). An Irish study of people from three counties who died by suicide found that more than half had alcohol in their blood; those aged less than thirty were more likely to have had alcohol in their blood at the time of death (Bedford et al, 2004). The World Health Organisation (2004) has estimated that the risk of suicide when a person is currently misusing alcohol is eight times greater than if they were not misusing alcohol.

Moll's Story

Moll's reflections epitomises the huge number of individuals who manage to live their lives as functioning alcoholics. It was only when a crisis happened in Moll's life that the extent of her problem emerged. Like Moll, all functioning alcoholics are like ticking time bombs. The sooner their crisis occurs the greater the chance of a return to a normal life and happiness. Sadly, many don't get that opportunity.

Ten years ago I contemplated taking my life. In August 2004 my partner broke up our relationship. This was totally contrary to what I had been led to believe would happen. Anyway for the couple of months after this I continued to work in my management position. It was really difficult as I was very consumed with grief. I continued to do the things that I normally did i.e. playing badminton, walking, and I even joined an acting class in an effort to be out of the house and not have to face the memories.

I met my ex a couple of times and talked about starting again but that didn't happen. Six weeks later he met a girl and got into a relationship very quickly. I found it next to impossible to accept this. I sat in a church in the dark every day in tears begging God for the answer. And answer he did. Less than three months into the break-up while sitting in the church a man sat in front of me and asked for some help to pay for his hostel bed that night. He had just been released from a treatment centre for alcoholism. I looked over my shoulder to see him after closing my purse but there wasn't any sign of him! I cursed at God very angrily and shouted into the empty church that I wasn't an alcoholic.

In those months, two glasses of wine went to one bottle, then to one and a half bottles a night. I managed to hide my condition by working mostly behind a closed door in my office. I hid it very well from my colleagues. I totally isolated myself from my family. From the minute I got home from work the door was closed and calls unanswered. I just spent my few hours each evening drinking and crying, totally devastated.

My friend, Niamh, called one night and found me drunk. She rang my sister who came over immediately. She couldn't get over the mess of the house as I'd always kept it so well. I woke up with a start the next morning, recalling a colleague who helped staff members with alcoholism to get into treatment centres. I phoned her and got an assessment very quickly and was asked to come three days later as they had a bed for me.

There were a couple of times in early sobriety that ending my life would have seemed the best option but thank God I did not go through with it. At times, early in recovery, I found it hard to trust myself. When crossing a bridge I passed every day I felt the pull of the water very strong for me. An underlying depression was diagnosed and treatment started. Art therapy, counselling and a solid commitment to recovery eventually helped. The wish to take my own life has now totally faded. Thank God.

Conclusion

The elements within the Suicide Box that have been created and are being maintained by our social structures are deeply engrained in our collective consciousness. What has clearly emerged is that suicide is largely a side-effect of society's dysfunction, where economic concerns are all too often placed before human needs. All the institutions researched have shown a serious lack of compassion and empathy. The general public's reaction to a suicide is usually one of shock and disbelief. This is understandable when suicide is seen as the act of an individual in isolation. However, now that the Suicide Box has been exposed, the shock factor of suicide must reside with the failure of society to serve, promote and develop the well-being of all its people. Likewise, those who practice discrimination, specialise in stereotypes, or inflict unnecessary pain on others must accept suicide as a possible outcome of such behaviour. In summary, the key problem areas that have been identified as contributing to the Suicide Box are:

⁜ The poor allocation of government funding for suicide and mental health.

⁜ The denial of the social factors that facilitate and enable suicide.

⁜ The economic disadvantage suffered by vulnerable groups.

⁜ Stigma and myth that partly stem from religious beliefs.

⁜ Interpretations of religious teachings that sullied human sexuality and aided the marginalisation of certain loving relationships.

⁜ The problematic and unfair punitive approach that underlies the justice system.

⁜ An inquest system for suicide that still functions like a criminal court.

⁜ Stigma and myths around mental illness that have their roots in a barbaric and ignorant era.

⁜ The poor quality of mental health services that are under-resourced.

⁜ The over-reliance on medication in the treatment of a whole range of emotional and psychological issues.

⁜ A one-size-fits-all educational system that favours intellectual intelligence, and convergent and assimilator learning styles.

⁜ The global occurrence of bullying in schools that causes long-term trauma, including depression and suicide.

⁜ Lack of education in important subjects for youth including self-care, sexuality, relationships and mental health.

⁜ Significant physical and psychological damage experienced by workers who have been subjected to sexual harassment, bullying, violence and stress in the workplace.

- ✦ The failure of workplaces to strike a balance between profitability and workers' well-being.

- ✦ Stereotyping of various minorities and the portrayal of a certain physique in the media that contributes to body loathing and low self-esteem in young people.

- ✦ The sensationalising and glamorising of suicide in the media, coupled with the lack of sensitivity when reporting suicides or other situations involving tragedy, human failing or misfortune.

- ✦ Lack of emotional expression within many families due to culture and socialisation.

- ✦ Learned practices of keeping deadly secrets in order to maintain a mask to gain social acceptance.

- ✦ Abuses that weaken and stunt the growing child including domestic violence, child abuse, emotional abuse, neglect, the effects of alcoholism and drug addiction.

- ✦ The social dependence on alcohol to extremely unhealthy levels and the denial of its impact on crime, domestic abuse, self-harm and suicide to often causal significance.

It has taken a radical shift in our awareness to begin to see the many lethal practices in our midst that have developed over millennia and that largely remain unchallenged. To begin to change these practices will demand an even greater leap forward in our thinking and actions. Our analysis of how the Suicide Box was constructed has provided us with the awareness of the most destructive elements that foster and facilitate suicide. This awareness helps to melt away the myths and stigmas that mystical thinking has created, allowing us to fearlessly move forward on our journey to dismantle the Suicide Box together.

PART THREE

Dismantling Its Structure

CHAPTER FOURTEEN

Working Together with Purpose

This book has many interviews and stories by real people about many aspects of society's dysfunction, in terms of suicide and pain. At this stage we hope that people just like Jennifer, who we introduced in Part One, have begun to realise that experiences of pain and confusion are not all of their own making, but often originate from diverse social failings. As we move forward towards a New Perspective, it requires certain qualities to be nurtured in all of us. These include:

✢ Outside-the-box thinking, in order to understand the concepts and themes discussed.

✢ Creativity and imagination.

✢ Openness to change.

✢ Challenging our embedded cultural perspectives.

✢ Willingness to challenge 'fixed' attitudes, values and beliefs.

✢ Suspending quick judgements of others and their ways of living.

✢ Being mindful in the present, and not being driven by a fearful past or an assumed negative future.

✢ Being driven by love and hope rather than by fear or hopelessness.

Tools for Dismantling the Box

In contrast to the fear-based understanding of suicide within the Suicide Box, we are embracing suicide as part of the human condition in this section. This in no way condones suicide as an acceptable way to die. However, with fearless and accepting hearts we may become more proactive and aware, by facilitating profound change at personal, community and societal levels. We ask you, the reader, to join us on this journey as we move through the old fears, stigmas and ignorance, to view suicide through new eyes of insight and awareness. We also wish to honour the many beautiful lives that have been cut short because they could not continue among us. Their legacy and gift to us is a wake-up call for vital change. By looking at the broader picture that this perspective allows, we may get a glimpse and a little understanding of what it was that triggered their final decision. By pushing suicide into a box, society has deprived us of viewing suicide, in all its complexity, as part of the spectrum of human pain. The past has been marked with terminations, hopelessness and darkness. We need to move forward with renewed hope and understanding, into the light of a New Perspective.

Key Features

It is imperative that suicide alone is not the focus of our campaigns, our debates and media discussions, but that we place the full gamut of unnecessary human pain before us. Whether we like it or not, suicide is just another way for human beings to die, albeit a preventable one. This approach may also lessen other unnecessary aspects of human pain, for example, bullying, drug abuse, self-harm, anorexia, and alcoholism, that so often are factors in suicide. By bringing suicide into the light, and onto the spectrum of human pain, we are creating a clearer picture of where we need to go.

Moving into the light, we need to admit that there are certain institutions that are getting it wrong, that add to the pain and ignorance around suicide, and this includes religion, the law, psychiatric institutions, schools, workplaces, the state, sometimes the family, and often the media. However, it would be inaccurate to imply that any individual or institution set out to create a society that would lead people to take their lives. It is more likely that systems, based on ignorant assumptions, evolved to protect societal structures rather than to nurture human needs. The fears, myths and stigmas that these institutions readily propagated were unfounded and deeply harmful to our understanding of the causes of suicide and of the nature of mental illness. In dismantling the Suicide Box and advocating a New Perspective we concentrate on Irish society. However, the New Perspective can also be applied to other societies. As we have seen from research and statistics, the same inherent dysfunction has also produced a Suicide Box appropriate to each social and cultural construction.

What Needs to be Dismantled?

There are crucial elements within the Suicide Box that need to be dismantled and transformed. Some of these require government backing and funding while many require an openness to view suicide, depression, mental illness and the expression of emotion in a new light, to begin to release the old myths and stigma that have kept us shackled and dwelling in darkness for far too long. The interviews in this section highlight the need for fundamental change in our social structures but also in our ways of thinking and behaving at work, at school and in our own homes. This book essentially takes a long-term view of the transformation that is required to understand the fundamental causes of unnecessary human pain that too often results in suicide. Adopting a compassionate and holistic outlook at all levels of society, we believe, is far more likely to reduce suicide and mental illness. However, to achieve this, immediate actions and ideas can be implemented across the spectrum of society to bring about short-term positive effects.

The format followed in the previous section, 'Understanding Its Construction', is also adopted here. We will, therefore, outline the areas where the dismantling of the box is most urgently required, in our collective attitudes and beliefs in the areas of politics and economics, religion, the law, mental health and psychiatry, education, work, the media, and the family. Our central theme in this section is that, social change is dependent on our willingness to change ourselves and on our ability to walk in the shoes of others.

CHAPTER FIFTEEN

Politics and Economics

The major areas that were identified as in immediate need of transformation when analysing politics and economics in the construction of the Suicide Box were: the poor allocation of government funding for suicide and mental health; the denial of the social factors that facilitate and enable suicide; and the economic disadvantage suffered by vulnerable groups. However, when we move our thinking outside the box, we realise that these areas are mere symptoms of core deficits in awareness by our government and state departments. Therefore, an investigation of these deficits needs to occur before we can move forward with any plan to dismantle key factors inside the Suicide Box.

We are about to enter a new period of relative prosperity. This is not a profound insight but a mere well-known historical progression or pattern of the system of capitalism. The noted years of 1850, 1890, 1930, 1970 and 2010 mark the centres of past historic economic depressions, that have occurred with clockwork-like regularity, every forty years or so. Similarly notable are the energies that have lifted economies from these recessions. These have included, respectively, the development of railway transport systems, electricity, mass production systems, and computerisation. These energies are utilised by those who are in the financial position to take advantage of them. They exploit these innovations to maximise profits until burnout occurs, leading to another economic depression. While this may be an oversimplification of events, it does show a clear pattern. However, what we can be certain of is that governments will continue to follow capitalist objectives, and without a great shift in awareness, investment in social change will continue to be miniscule, merely enough to stave off the possibility of social unrest.

Core Deficits in Awareness at Government Level

Since the political and economic system controls policymaking and the allocation of funding in the areas of the law, mental health and psychiatry, education, work, the media, and the family, any plan to fund vital social projects needs to be guided by innovative, out-of-the-box thinking. Thus, many of the flaws in the functioning of our social institutions that we discovered through our analysis of how the Suicide Box was constructed, need to be acknowledged and remedied by our political system before any real change can take place. Crucial changes that need to urgently occur at this level include:

- A decisive shift in thinking from the present cliff-top approach, where funding and policies are introduced when crisis point is reached, instead of planning for long-term change, where the community is fully involved and consulted. This requires a bottom-up approach to raise awareness and consciousness, as well as the implementation of practical changes that have the backing of the community. A relinquishing of the power of top-down approaches is a vital ingredient for positive progress. Instead, a sharing of responsibilities with the community needs to occur, energised and facilitated by government and county council bodies.

- The need for an open, fresh and holistic approach to the writing of policies and documents that is devoid of old narrow, conservative and stigmatised views that have kept us locked in the

Suicide Box for generations. This may require training of personnel at all levels of political life, particularly in consciousness-raising around important social issues, such as social inclusion, diversity, the need for empathy, etc.

✤ Policies and reports need to be based on empathy. This is particularly vital when policies are being introduced around suicide and mental health generally, where those who are drawing up the reports give adequate attention to the experiences, opinions and feelings of the true experts: the suicidal and the suicide bereaved.

✤ While governments love to publish reports and discuss these in the media on pressing social issues, such as bullying and suicide, there needs to be an emphasis on implementing changes identified in these reports. A poignant example of the lack of implementation of plans for long-term change is in the area of bullying in schools. The *Action Plan on Bullying* (2013) makes excellent recommendations for preventing bullying by establishing an all-school/community approach, yet the lack of government funding and practical direction to schools, leaves students as unsafe as ever, and schools open to prosecution for their failure to provide an adequate duty of care to staff and pupils.

Strategic Planning and Development of Policies and Funding
In this section we will look at the short-term haphazard approach adopted by the government to fund suicide prevention programmes. We also outline how a new long-term orchestrated plan might be approached at national level.

Present Short-Term Haphazard Approach

In the construction of the Suicide Box, it is clear that the Irish government's allocation of funding for suicide prevention is paltry. Although the government has increased its funding to the National Office for Suicide Prevention to €8.8 million for 2014 (HSE, 2014), it still lacks a coordinated strategy to prevent suicide or self-directed violence (European Child Safety Alliance: 2014, p. 76). The government's *Reach Out: 2005–2014* programme (Department of Health and Children, 2005) has been widely criticised for failing to implement the ninety-six key recommendations published. In the final year of its existence, tenders were only being sought to establish community-wide plans in suicide prevention in counties with the highest suicide rates.

Currently, government funding is mainly being allocated to train individuals in SafeTalk and ASSIST, two suicide prevention training programmes (HSE, 2014). Over €6 million is being used to fund statutory services and over thirty Non-government agencies (HSE, 2014). Many of these agencies, although doing admirable and necessary work at the level of the individual, are working within the old model constructed within the Suicide Box and essentially helping to maintain the social status quo. Within the new model this practice can be seen as merely placing plasters on gaping wounds, while ignoring the true poison underneath or how the injury happened initially. Using the present government strategy, even if all the funding possible were poured into the Suicide Box with its distorted perspectives, no fundamental, long-term social change could ever become manifest.

Long-Term Orchestrated Plan

To dismantle the political and economic strands of the Suicide Box there needs to be a long-term, orchestrated plan devised at national level. The overwhelming evidence that has been revealed during our analysis of the construction of the Suicide Box is that social institutions need to be infused with a new awareness of the spectrum of human pain that includes the full range of human emotions and responses, including suicide. In order to foster real change there needs to be a planned, orchestrated approach at government level, and not piecemeal efforts that waste important resources and keep us stuck in the quagmire. At the heart of the plan there needs to be an awareness, acceptance and acknowledgement of the many aspects of culture and socialisation and how these impinge on individual expression, development and self-awareness that contribute to individual emotional disorder.

Thus, funding must be earmarked for critical institutions, such as education and mental health, to implement important programmes in schools that impart practical life and self-care skills, in the funding of all-school/community positive, social skills programmes, and in the promotion of self-awareness and emotional intelligence to foster well-being. There are some changes that will make a huge impact in terms of lessening unnecessary pain, such as changing the archaic inquest system to a more compassionate and less traumatic experience for the suicide bereaved, and will require minimal funding. Significant advertising campaigns that counter old, negative cultural stereotypes will also reap many rewards, particularly those that starkly show the destruction to family and individual lives due to alcohol misuse, those that promote positive images of men who can openly express emotion, and those that foster diversity and an end to stigma for minority groups. Fundamentally and perhaps ironically, as governments have been shown to be incapable of bringing fairness, balance or equality to its citizens, supporting vital community programmes would be the sum of their involvement.

Providing Support and Opportunities for all Citizens
From the limited view of life from within the Suicide Box we can be forgiven for making value judgements regarding members of vulnerable groups, such as uneducated, social parasites or antisocial. This is a real example of the short-sightedness that arises from being immersed among the trees with no idea of what the whole forest looks like. In contrast, the outside-the-box view allows us to see the whole forest, its extent, the diversity of its make-up, its positive and negative aspects, how the whole affects the parts and vice versa. This view allows us to question common value judgements and beliefs. How members of society become marginalised and excluded due to the structure and demands of society becomes clear. The social engine driven with the singular focus of increasing profits and fuelled by self-serving greed can only benefit the drivers of this operation, while the vast majority of citizens eke out their living from the spoils of the system. Many can cope well within this arrangement and survive the manageable fluctuations in their lifestyles, as the profits manifest for the privileged. However, all too often, we see people pushed to the outer periphery, their opportunities for inclusion or benefitting directly from the system becoming less and less. While this, outside-the-box view may be reflective of critical analysis of a capitalist system, it is not in this case intended to be. For the purpose of dismantling the Suicide Box it is imperative that at least our politicians try to include human concerns when big economic decisions have to be considered. To date, the evidence has shown that our leaders have kept their eyes more on maintaining the status quo, within the Suicide Box, than on allowing all citizens to experience the full and natural potential of their lives while in this world.

CHAPTER SIXTEEN
Spirituality (Formerly Religion)

Some of the destructive aspects of religion have been the external manifestations of hatred and persecution of those with different beliefs, causing millions of people to die in the name of 'God'. Despite the fact that the message of all major religions is one of love, it has been a feature of religion that human failings, particularly the hunger for power and control, have led to the pollution of God's message and incredible abuses in the practice of these teachings. In dismantling the Suicide Box, it is imperative that we change our perspective from the limited and highly stigmatised term 'religion', to the all-embracing and universal term 'spirituality'. According to Dr Fergus Heffernan, 'spirituality means a sense of belonging; a connection, where we can hand over our pain in a dark moment. For the atheist that may mean belonging to a compassionate community. It's an integral part of being human that we belong and feel connected. It's so unfortunate that religion hijacked it.'

In 'Understanding Its Construction', a number of areas were highlighted as having enormous negative impact within the Suicide Box. These were stigma and myth that partly stem from religious beliefs; and interpretations of religious teachings that sullied human sexuality and aided the marginalisation of certain loving relationships. Past beliefs and practices adopted by religions that perpetuated myths, stigma and fears often led to the obliteration of the memory of those who had died by suicide. When we attempt to bury our loss, grief and pain, we increase the heartache and interfere with the onset of healing. No life should be defined solely by how that life ended. The unique tapestry of each life, with its many shades and textures, needs to be celebrated and remembered by family and friends.

In many countries there is a healthy division between state and religion, yet it is important to be aware of the continuing negative, conservative influences that derive from religious teachings, such as the repudiation of homosexuality that foster prejudices, biases, and intolerance, through judgemental and moralistic attitudes. It is surely the aim of all religions to offer moral guidance, to create meaning, and to offer hope and solace in this life and for the hereafter. Suicide is, therefore, a symptom of failure in these religious aims. The reason for failure is likely to be due to the thinking of disturbed individuals masquerading as God-loving within religions, rather than religions per se, as basic religious messages have remained steadfastly loving, compassionate and forgiving over millennia. The importance of all spiritual groups advocating inclusivity and empathy is highlighted in the following section. A wonderful example of a Jewish celebration held in honour of all its members who had died by suicide is also included.

Inclusivity and Empathy
There is an urgent need for religious officials to offer empathy, guidance, meaning, hope and solace today. There is a deep need for a true emphasis on love, compassion and forgiveness. Rigid thinking on sexuality has not served the Church well, as it has failed to encompass those features of the human condition that are freely included in all aspects of creation. The human interpretations of God's words have been highly problematic in spreading warped thinking and promoting sexual hatred. The subsequent sexual abuses perpetrated within the Catholic Church may have had their

origins in enforced celibacy. This practice began in the eleventh century, and had more to do with economics, by insuring that Church lands could not be inherited by the offspring of priests, than for any notion of morality (Sipe, 2004).

Religions are entitled to propagate their own teachings, but, such is the power and influence that religions may hold over members, it is vital that church officials filter out any negative, flawed, human interpretation that fails to offer empathy and deep compassion to those most in need. Surely, religions have a duty of care to all of their members and to all of humanity to promote civil rights and social inclusion.

In hindsight, one of the areas of key social change that can be facilitated by church leaders is the adoption of a more inclusive attitude, by sensitively becoming aware of the power of their words and actions to influence and affect members of their church. This is never more important than when one of their members has died by suicide. Without exception, the family and friends bereaved by suicide should be showered with deep understanding, compassion and love. This is also a powerful time to dissolve stigma and to be astutely discerning when it comes to adopting strategies that may hinder a grieving family's desire to celebrate the life of the deceased. Such a suggestion was made in a government document (O'Sullivan, Rainsford, and Sihera, 2011), where priests were requested to avoid mentioning 'suicide' or the person's life during a funeral service, for fear that this might glamorise the act. This view, however, may be unhelpful and may be yet another way of maintaining an inside-the-box mentality, based on fear, shame and secrecy.

At times of tragedy, when there is a sudden death due to suicide or some other cause, it is an opportunity to encourage the whole community to rally around the bereaved. A reminder by clergy or those officiating at funerals for the community to be aware of the importance of acknowledging the relatives of those who have died tragically when they meet them on the street, may go a long way to ending feelings of awkwardness or embarrassment when confronted by another's pain. It is at these times, by each person facing his or her fears and foibles, that destructive stigma and myths can be dissolved, by showing basic care and empathy for a fellow soul who is in need of a kind word.

Honouring Members of Religious Groups

Those who find comfort and support through the practice of a religion are never in more need of solace and hope than when they lose a loved one to suicide. This is the time when religious officials need to ensure that stigma of any kind is completely absent from funerals or religious services that mark the passing of a member of its congregation.

The aim of the Jewish Congregation Sha'ar Zahav of San Francisco is to remove all stigma associated with suicide (Lampert, 2012). On 7 August 2012, the synagogue held a public Yizkor to remember all those who had died in the seventy-five years since the first suicide took place at the Golden Gate Bridge. The names of all those who had died were read aloud during the service. It has been centuries since Judaism required those who died by suicide to be buried in a separate section of the cemetery. Even orthodox congregations allow mourners to recite Kaddish for their loved ones who had taken their own lives. However, according to Jenni Olson, co-organiser of the service, religion needs to remain focused on ending stigma and treating suicide with sensitivity and compassion.

Rabbi Angel was in favour of holding the service for a number of reasons, including her synagogue's most distinctive aspect: Congregation Sha'ar Zahav is an LGBT synagogue, built on progressive, inclusive ideals (Lampert, 2012). Rabbi Angel outlined her congregation's practice of honouring all their members, in life and death: 'Sha'ar Zahav is a community that strives to be radically inclusive. We know from our LGBT history that every life is a world, every life is a blessing, and every death is a loss. We're to honour their spirit and their soul the same way we would for any other death.'

Rabbi Angel felt that the service had an important lesson for all involved, and all those who would hear about it: 'I hope people who read about this think about how they might include tradition and symbols to remember those who have been forgotten.'

CHAPTER SEVENTEEN

The Law

Much of what our law provides serves us well, but when our human understanding of life is progressed, the regulations of law, based on old redundant views, can become a restrictive and destructive hindrance to human well-being and community growth. Similar to other institutions, established practices are deemed to be sacrosanct. For example, the punitive approach based on retribution is accepted as the only response to deal with the breaking of laws. This practice negatively affects social empathy as is all too evident in the inquest process following a suicide. These inquests still function like criminal courts although suicide has been decriminalised in Ireland since 1993. In the 'Understanding Its Construction' section the fundamental punitive approach that underlies the justice system was identified as being highly problematic and unfair. Also, the inquest system for suicide was found to function as a criminal court. In this section the adoption of a restorative approach is proposed. Also a new model for the inquest process in the case of suicide is advocated to reflect true social empathy.

The Need for a Restorative Approach
How can the archaic and restrictive punitive laws that we have been socialised to accept be dismantled to allow human beings evolve to a new paradigm? Zehr (2005) stated that the traditional punitive approach seeks to answer three questions: 'What laws have been

broken? Who did it? And what do the offender(s) deserve?' Zehr then contrasts what a restorative-justice approach entails with the questions: 'Who has been hurt? What are their needs? Whose obligations are these? What are the causes? Who has a stake in the situation? What is the appropriate process to involve stakeholders in an effort to address causes and put things right?'

The questions posed by the restorative approach are key to human advancement. This paradigm espouses healing for the whole situation that has been damaged. Unlike a punitive system, it does not dehumanise the event, store it for all time as a bad thing that happened and produce more long-term individual and socially destructive outcomes than the original offence ever could. According to Liebmann (2007), a good way of looking at restorative justice is to think of it as a balance among a number of different tensions: 'a balance between the therapeutic and the retributive models of justice; a balance between the rights of offenders and the needs of victims; a balance between the need to rehabilitate offenders and the duty to protect the public.'

As the legal system within the Suicide Box is hierarchical and status-driven, conferring great power and privilege on its operators, there is likely to be much resistance to change. However, the positive benefits to society as a whole would be immense. Adopting restorative approaches and solutions would be very different from the punitive system. Braithwaite (2002) wrote that 'Court-annexed processes and restorative justice could not be philosophically further apart', because the former seeks to address only legally relevant issues, whereas restorative justice seeks to expand 'the issues beyond those that are legally relevant, especially into underlying rela-tionships'.

The practical application of the punitive approach does not end in the courts. Its pervasive influence is felt throughout society. The tangible aspects of its application are felt to be appropriate as it satisfies the immediate natural emotional reactions, such as anger, and a desire for retribution. However, short-term solutions blind us to the long-term damage of the process that ignores the intangible, potentially healing aspects. These require insightfulness and far-sightedness to see the human benefits involved for society. Breaking the senseless and aggressive mindset of 'lock 'em up and throw away the key' may go some way towards producing more involved citizens than are turned out under the present system. As the vast majority of offenders are given a release date, the focus ought to be on how to make their return to society a better fit than prior to their imprisonment.

Many former prisoners interviewed spoke to us of their return to society, as though they had been pushed out, with less capacity to live than they had prior to their imprisonment. Many described their time in prison as being held in suspended animation until their day of release. Others stated that they still had the same problems, with other difficulties acquired while in prison. Restorative techniques could be adopted by identifying individual deficits. A unique sentence plan could then be developed to meet each person's specific needs. In this way, society would experience a reduction in recidivism and stem the production of marginalised individuals who are forced to act from a position of societal rejection on their release.

Many reading this may reject this position and respond that offenders get what they deserve or that they don't receive enough punishment. These feelings are understandable, especially if you have been personally offended against. However, a restorative approach would not be an easy alternative. Unlike the punitive system, a restorative approach would ensure that an offender would have to think of others, recognise the extent of the harm they caused, be accountable and accept responsibility for their actions. They would also be fully included in the process. Many of the former prisoners interviewed told us that being hidden away by the system in prison was easier than having to confront their wrongful actions openly.

The Punitive Inquest System

The current inquest system in operation in Ireland causes unnecessary stress and pain for families bereaved by suicide, in spite of the caring approaches and efforts being made by the coroner service and individual coroners. In some Irish counties, inquests into suicides have been relocated to hotels in an attempt to diminish the distress caused to families when giving evidence. However, the local hotel as an inquest venue is also problematic, as previously described by Miriam in Chapter Eight. Many families have reported feeling distressed when reminded of past family reunions at such venues, feeling ill when surrounded by the aroma of food, feeling that the whole episode was surreal, often with inappropriate background music, and the presence of groups of people chatting, laughing and clinking glasses. In this section, Anthony E. Walsh gives an account of an alternative inquest venue that he helped secure in Co. Meath during his time with Living Links that has the support and approval of bereaved families.

Transforming the Inquest System: Interview with Anthony E. Walsh

My work in the County Meath branch of Living Links, an outreach support organisation for families and individuals bereaved by suicide, opened my eyes to social empathy. It also showed me how embedded I was within the box, where I was kept from truly seeing the deep trauma that the suicide bereaved were being socially forced to endure, with practices that unnecessarily worsened their already drastic circumstances.

People of Insight and Empathy

Meath Living Links had already made attempts to bring together legal and human aspects in the most caring and least traumatic way, in conjunction with the coroner, Gardaí and media within an inquest model. The insightfulness and empathy shown by all those involved was commendable. However, the incredible efforts of the caring people in Living Links who were there before I joined, who tried to humanise the process, were often hampered by the priority given to the systemic legal aspects. For example, if a shortage arose on the jury, the coroner's officials would sequester members of Living Links to fill the jury places. This caused a dilemma for Living Links volunteers, due to the ethical boundaries that jury service raised for them in their work, and the sensitivity of the follow-up work they did with those bereaved by suicide. Sitting on a jury and making a determination on the context of a death by suicide effectively rendered a volunteer ethically impotent to work with the connected family. This, I discovered, was not apathy on anyone's part, but an example of how difficult it is to break through the thick social and cultural walls we usually accept without challenge. When negative actions such as these were presented, the speed of change and acceptance was immediate in Meath. The Coroner, John Lacy, was particularly notable for his compassion and eagerness to reduce the impact of trauma for families bereaved by suicide.

The Meath Inquest Model

The neutral venue chosen for inquests in Navan, County Meath is the Annex of Our Lady's Hospital. This was a far more suitable venue for inquests than county courtrooms or hotels. It did not have the coldness and criminal feel of a courtroom. It had none of the social associations of hotels, nor was it a venue that was likely to be visited again. The use of hotels is an example of choices that are made when we make assumptions from a position of ignorance and fail to listen to the people who know best, those who are bereaved by suicide.

In this setting, all the bereaved, whose loved ones died tragically by suicide or from other causes, are met in a non-threatening, neutral environment and brought to the dining hall where refreshments are available. An atmosphere of inclusiveness reduces feelings of isolation often felt by families bereaved by suicide attending inquests. In addition to refreshments, volunteers elicit and discuss ongoing concerns and worries, explain the inquest process as it applies uniquely to Navan, and present support options available to the bereaved following the inquest. The families then await the inquest of their loved one in a comfortable room. When the time comes to attend the inquest, the family is discretely called and the inquest is heard without an unnecessary public presence. Where a death is clearly self-caused or involves no other person, the jury is dismissed. This is a most positive development for families that reduces the criminal feel of the proceedings. The room where the inquest is conducted is also conducive to privacy. While it is the state's cold position that inquests are to be held in public, Coroner John Lacy's model limited unnecessary public inquisitiveness. As their loved one's inquest ends, the family connect with the trained bereavement workers outside. Details essentially presented at inquest, e.g. decomposition, lung and stomach contents, consequences of hanging, slowness or speed of death, extent of pain experienced, etc. adds immensely to a family's trauma. Volunteers often sit with families during the inquest. After the inquest, they help relatives to process what they have heard and to put it into some meaningful context.

A Path to Change

It was while attending inquests in Navan that I gained a number of important insights. If society is ever going to effect change in our suicide statistics, we must first change ourselves, our attitudes, and our unwillingness to take collective responsibility for the unnecessary pain that drives some people to suicide, and that ultimately affects us all. Our current attitude of treating suicide as the domain of individual families helps to maintain stigma and myths associated with suicide. I outlined the effort made in Navan to my dear friend Peg Hanafin, and, being a powerful advocate for social change, she joined me on a campaign to bring about necessary change, and to raise social consciousness for the plight of bereaved families. Peg has since written widely in the media on her new understanding and has received very positive reactions. Together, we contacted all coroners in Ireland and have received many responses from them.

The overriding tone of these responses shows the level of empathy and compassion that coroners have for families who attend inquests and the efforts they, and their inquest officials, make on the day. However, another dominant feature that emerged was that their hands are largely tied regarding necessary change, as both the funding and the inquest procedures are government driven. Several coroners emphasised the comprehensive report for change entitled *Review of the Coroner Service* (Department of Justice, Equality and Law Reform, 2000), the recommendations of which have never been implemented.

So much more can be done to change how suicide is viewed, and the inquest system is just one example of how we need to affect change.

CHAPTER EIGHTEEN

Holistic Well-being
(formerly Mental Health and Psychiatry)

When investigating the current system of mental health care and psychiatry in Ireland, the overriding factors to emerge were stigma and myths around mental illness that have their roots in a barbaric and ignorant era; the poor quality of mental health services that are under-resourced, and the over-reliance on medication in the treatment of a whole range of emotional and psychological issues. Now that we are dismantling the Suicide Box we need to look at the terms 'mental health', 'psychiatry' and any other labels that maintain the old destructive view within the Suicide Box. These terms are loaded with stigma and myths, their usage being synonymous with black and white thinking, and are, therefore, most unhelpful when moving towards a New Perspective. Thus, a multi-tiered approach to ending stigma is outlined below. The poor quality of mental health care and the over-reliance on medication derive from the old medical model, based on power-differentials between patient and doctor. In the 'Quality Holistic Services' section below, the merits of adopting a recovery model are discussed.

Stigma
Since the act of suicide is swamped in stigma, it is most unhelpful that the area that has been designated to treat it – mental health and psychiatry – is also caked in hundreds of years of fears and stigma.

We examined much of this in 'Understanding Its Construction'. In all instances of stigma, it is our thinking that needs to undergo a radical shift. This may be aided by education that exposes myths and fears, and offers alternatives, but also by changing negative associations, such as renaming an organisation or relocating to another building or environment, as recommended to reform the inquest system for the suicide bereaved.

The stigma pertaining to suicide can be reduced by viewing it as part of the spectrum of unnecessary human pain, as previously outlined. Thus, suicide is no longer a stand-alone phenomenon, a mysterious occurrence, but rather the most extreme act on a continuum of behaviours that people choose to deal with their pain. This also unites all people, as everyone experiences pain and develops ways of coping. It is the choosing of destructive behaviours rather than constructive ones that is the main difference between individuals. This perspective leads to a greater understanding and empathy for all people who experience unnecessary human pain, including those who have suicidal feelings and those who act on them.

The stigma that is inherent in the entire field of mental health and psychiatry can certainly be helped by the renaming of this sector. In Ireland, the government has undertaken to transform the medical model of treatment and care to the modern recovery model that is holistic and person-centred. The government is keenly aware that sometimes it is necessary to rebrand and rename one of its sectors. The government agency responsible for training, formerly known as FÁS, has recently been changed to Intreo, following adverse publicity around the schemes it funded during the Celtic Tiger years. It, therefore, seems a worthwhile plan to rename the field of Mental Health and Psychiatry to a title that reflects its new recovery model. The suggested title 'Holistic Well-being' would emphasise all that is positive, progressive and integral in the new paradigm that promotes a person-centred journey to overall health, and that takes account of individual needs, experiences and aspirations.

Quality Holistic Services

Once we begin to dismantle the Suicide Box we have a clearer view that mental illness is merely a symptom of the dysfunction in the person's overall well-being, and in their connectedness with their environment. The recovery model is holistic, respecting all aspects of the person, including physical, emotional, psychological, spiritual, sexual, creative, social and cultural. The Irish government has bravely spearheaded the adoption of a recovery model but has been attempting to use a piecemeal, incremental approach since its launch in 2006. Based on the importance of this change, attempting to appease all interest groups was bound to be fraught with difficulties.

In a review of the implementation of *A Vision for Change*, in January 2013, the Mental Health Commission (2013) advised that, while certain positive changes had occurred within the Mental Health system, there were still a number of issues that were hampering the progress of the policy's full implementation. These included the public service moratorium; the ongoing cutbacks in the public service; the decision to delay spending the additional ring-fenced €35 million during 2012, which impacted the staff numbers of Community Mental Health teams across the country; the need to progress the development of specialist services for the elderly, those with an intellectual disability and areas of rehabilitation; the need to move from a largely medicalised response to individual needs towards a more holistic approach, by filling the number of vacant psychology, social work and occupational therapist posts in the HSE teams. The Commission also highlighted the need for ongoing independent monitoring of the implementation of *A Vision for Change*.

Although the main points above are valid, the essence of the difficulties in implementing the recovery model is lost. While the Commission highlights practical considerations, such as staffing and funding, these would be necessary for the implementation of any model. There is a feeling here that what is special and beneficial about the recovery model is omitted, such as the whole community and social network aspects. What is missing, therefore, is the identification of key features that are vital to successfully implementing a recovery model, which requires a completely new, holistic approach to mental health care. After reviewing Irish and international reports on problems encountered during the implementation of the recovery model, we propose that the following features are incorporated into all levels of service provision, in order for a quality holistic service, based on care and well-being, to be available to the Irish public. This also includes a detailed case study of Paul who recently accessed the current Mental Health Care service in Ireland, whose level of care was still in line with the medical model. An outline of a fully implemented recovery model within the community is also given by way of comparison.

Importance of Community Involvement
A central tenet of the recovery model is that healing and recovery takes place within a network of relationships, including the service-user's family, friends, workplace and community, and is influenced by the greater society (Australian Health Ministers Advisory Council, 2013). It is, therefore, imperative that practitioners are aware of the significance of community participation for a person's recovery, including social determinants of health and well-being, such as being financially solvent or impoverished; having a loving home life as opposed to living in a stressful or abusive situation, or living alone; having a happy work life, versus hating ones career or being unemployed (Wilkinson and Marmot, 2003).

The Australian Health Ministers Advisory Council (2013) defines recovery as 'being able to create and live a meaningful and contributing life in a community of choice with or without the presence of mental health issues'. A person's social network is, therefore, vital to fulfilling one's need to belong, to contribute and to interact on a daily basis, where there is mutual respect and appreciation. It is the task of the practitioner working in partnership with the service-user, his or her family and friends, and the recovery team, to find the right combination of services, treatments and supports available, and to eliminate discrimination by removing barriers to full participation in work, education and community life. Glover (2012) views people in recovery as 'living, loving, working and playing in their community, or in other words, doing the things that people need or wish to do or enjoy doing every day'.

The government had promised the implementation of *A Vision for Change* by the end of 2014, but this did not happen. There are, however, many important elements, particularly those relating to services available within the community and involving the community, that have never been implemented. Paul's recent experience of mental health services in Ireland shows that we have a long way to go before the recovery model will replace the medical model.

Paul's Story

When my wife, Kathleen, died my whole world imploded. We were never blessed with children mainly because we married late. We were both retired and enjoying life together. I was an only child and Kathleen had one estranged sister living in England. We only had ourselves. There was no real warning given. Kathleen suddenly became ill and she died in hospital just two days later. I was devastated. People were good to me but after a few days the house was so empty. I thought I could hear Kathleen in the kitchen in the morning or hear her singing her happy little songs. I was ridden with guilt that I didn't look after her better and get the doctor quicker. I asked the doctor about this but he told me it would not have made a difference as she was too ill. That still didn't take my guilt away.

I couldn't understand why the world was carrying on as normal when my world was destroyed. Our neighbours and friends were good to me but they were having great difficulty dealing with me being so negative and depressed. I couldn't bear to be alone and I began imposing on their time. My doctor put me on tablets for depression, anxiety and for sleep. I hated taking serious medication but I had to because the pain was too much to bear.

A couple of months after Kathleen had died my neighbours became annoyed with me. I was told that the way I was carrying on wasn't normal, that it wasn't grief, and that I should get help. I was compared to other men who had lost their wives and got on with their lives. But these men had family of some sort at least living near them. I had nobody. I began to believe them as I felt I was going mad. My garden that I loved was now overgrown, but I didn't care anymore. Eventually, my doctor sent me to a psychiatrist and I was sent to hospital for an eight-week stay. I was terrified as I felt that I might never get out, end up as a zombie from medication or have to get electric shock treatment. The staff were great but I felt no better there. I was told to rest and my medication was increased. I attended different relaxation and activity classes but I couldn't relax. I met a patient there who had returned from electric shock treatment and it terrorised me. I asked to be let home after six weeks.

Back home the loneliness gripped me again. While the hospital was of little use to me, being abandoned on discharge was frightening for me. There were only a few people now who would come near me. I believe that word had gone around that I was in a mental hospital so I had to be mad. The psychiatrist told me that I was suffering from complicated grief but no one would believe that now. Three years on and the pain is easing for me. A friend recommended a counsellor and I found her to be really understanding. She listened to me and never judged me in any way. This was costly for me on my pension. I realised that as a society we are so poorly skilled in understanding grief. We have certain beliefs about how people should feel and behave that any variation on this is seen as abnormal. People also feel the need to advise when they should just listen and be there, and not feel that they have to fix anything. That's what I intend to do if ever I get the chance. I am not confident enough to get off the medication yet and I have probably become dependent on it. I still miss Kathleen so much but I have learned to have a different relationship with her now. I now know that I was not mad. I was just suffering from extreme loneliness. But people never mention Kathleen to me and still avoid interacting with me as if I am some kind of a social pariah.

A Fully Implemented Community-based Recovery Model

Unlike Paul's experience, a fully implemented community-based system of care within the recovery model would offer a range of services and programs that provide prevention and early inter-vention, medical and psychiatric treatments, support for physical health and fitness, and psychological therapies (Australian Health Ministers Advisory Council, 2013). Within this system, Paul would have been invited by his doctor to attend his nearest Community Care Centre. This care centre would be a welcoming and comfortable environment, far removed from the dour buildings associated with the medical model. In these pleasant surroundings Paul would have met a professional to discuss his particular needs. A team of care workers with various areas of expertise would also be available to him if required. A keyworker would be assigned to work with Paul on devising an Individual Care Plan to identify his particular needs, goals and any supports required. The aim would be to support and empower Paul on his journey, not to just cope with his loss and manage his pain, but to learn new meaning and self-discovery as he reintegrated into his community.

191

Much of the promotion of the Model would involve de-stigmatising mental illness and educating everyone in the community to realise that emotional or psychological difficulties can occur through the onset of stressful life situations, such as bereavement, job loss, relationship difficulties, etc. This facet of the plan would have been of particular help to Paul, as he could have invited his friends and neighbours to attend a meeting with his care team, to discuss the part that each might play in aiding his recovery.

The Individual Care Planning process empowers service-users through planning their own care programme to fit in with their unique goals, lifestyle, skills, etc (Mental Health Reform, 2013). In Paul's particular situation, he could have informed his keyworker that he would like to volunteer with a local animal shelter, as he had a particular affinity with animals. His interest in gardening could also have been explored and his keyworker could have empowered him to enrol for the year-long course in horticulture in his local college that he had planned on doing before Kathleen had died.

The service-user could then be informed by the psychiatrist as to all the possible benefits and risks of taking medication. The values and choices expressed by the service-user will then be fully respected by the psychiatrist. Paul could have chosen to take limited medication as an extra support during the initial phases of his Care Plan. Therapies that may be readily accessed within the community include psychotherapy and counselling, rehabilitation, psychosocial and recovery support, peer-support, and community development (Australian Health Ministers Advisory Council, 2013). Mental health services might also be provided by organisations that offer a broader range of health and human services, such as holistic complementary therapies. If these services were available to Paul, he could have availed of counselling, peer-support and a complimentary therapy such as reflexology, that could have helped him relax and sleep better.

Education in Practice of the Recovery Model

One of the main requisites for such a dramatic transformation requires a shift in thinking and understanding, and a change in work practices at every level. The philosophy and practice of the medical model has a tremendous hold on the medical profession, as well as the general public, as this has been the method of care traditionally practised for generations to treat mental illness. According to Mental Health Reform (2013), the implementation of the programme entails 'both structural and cultural change. It is about visibly demonstrating the values and having adequate laws, funding, staffing and facilities, but it also requires working from a recovery 'mindset' and adopting attitudes of hope, respect and empathy towards people with a mental health condition and their families and friends.'

The recovery model is now used in many Western countries. Internationally, the implementation process has encountered challenges, most specifically in the failure of health professionals to understand the essence of the new paradigm. In a study conducted in South-Eastern Australia, mental health consumers were asked about their experiences of the recovery-oriented services (Hungerford and Fox, 2013). Research participants stated that health professionals and service users were unsure of their roles or how to practice within the recovery model. It was reported that many health professionals took a 'hands off' approach in the name of recovery, rather than working in partnership with service users and community organisations. Solutions included more targeted, practice-focused education for consumers and health care professionals. Jacobsen and Curtis (2000), cited by the Mental Health Commission (2005), reported that in some states in the US, the implementation of the recovery model was severely hampered when existing practices based on the medical model were being renamed as recovery model programmes.

In Ireland, Mental Health Reform (www.mentalhealthreform.ie) states that 'successful implementation [of *A Vision for Change*] will require a paradigm change in how mental health is understood and how services are provided'. This 'cultural change' as outlined by the Mental Health Reform (2013) requires, 'national and local leadership, with those who hold senior positions both modelling the desired attitudes and behaviours and also demanding those attitudes and behaviours from all staff in the organisation. It also requires a dedicated process of reflection among staff.'

The effective implementation of the recovery model will, therefore, involve education and training in a number of key areas including a thorough understanding of its philosophy and practice, such as clarity of roles and programme structure; training to instil motivation and commitment to its person-centred approach; and the development of a 'team' mentality for achieving goals within a community setting.

Equality and Empowerment

For centuries, the medical model bestowed great status and reverence on practitioners, much akin to the adulation reserved for members of the clergy. According to Mental Health Reform (www.mentalhealthreform.ie), the recovery model, 'will challenge the traditional psychiatry power base'. One of the main principals of the recovery model is a person-centred approach, where the service user is, essentially, an equal participant in the programme. This approach could not progress or be successful unless there is a sense of equality and respect among all participants. The recovery model simply has no place for a practitioner who commands special status by virtue of position, title or academic attainment, as the resulting disempowerment is detrimental to the healing that the model promotes.

Equality may also be fostered through equal status being advocated for the service-user. Those who are making progress on their journey towards recovery are encouraged in some programmes to become peer specialists. Certification programs for peer specialists have become an adjunct to the recovery model in some locations (Frost et al, 2011). Thus, individuals who are in recovery from mental health issues are trained to work with fellow service-users, by providing education, advocacy and support (President's New Freedom Commission on Mental Health, 2003; Chinman et al, 2006). This further empowers service-users of mental health services and is also a crucial component of a recovery orientation (Hebert et al, 2008), similar to the system of appointing sponsors to work with new members, as advocated by AA (Alcoholics Anonymous) programmes. When peers are part of hospital-based care, the 'results indicate shortened lengths of stays, decreased frequency of admissions, and a subsequent reduction in overall treatment costs (Bluebird, 2008).'

While efforts to make fundamental changes for holistic well-being have been acknowledged and acted upon, albeit fragmentary, by the Irish government and its department of health, efforts to achieve any holistic headway for our children in education have been largely non-existent. The energy and the will required to achieve this will take a seismic shift in social focus.

CHAPTER NINETEEN

Education

In 'Understanding Its Construction', education was found to have a central location within the Suicide Box, particularly due to its emphasis on intellectual intelligence, and convergent and assimilator learning styles; the global occurrence of bullying in schools that causes long-term trauma, including depression and suicide; and its current lack of emphasis on important subjects to equip youth with vital life skills, including self-care, sexuality, relationships and mental health. The following sections make proposals for further dismantling of the Suicide Box in the problem areas exposed. While these are vital areas for change, they are merely examples of the type of dismantling that needs to take place in education.

Dr Fergus Heffernan is a psychologist, psychotherapist, Director of Services for RD Consult, and an educator in the area of stress management and how it relates to our mental health. In an interview with Fergus, the importance of correctly assessing a person's innate intelligences is highlighted. Fergus relates an example from his work with a teenage boy who was left feeling a failure, when he opted for a course of study in college that was a complete misfit for his own spatial and bodily kinaesthetic intelligences.

In the second interview, a new model for an all-school/community approach to counteract unwelcome behaviours, such as bullying, is outlined by Anthony E. Walsh. In the third section, there is an interview with Rose Tully, former primary school and special education teacher, on the importance of developing emotional intelligence in schools. Among many roles that Rose has filled, she has worked as National Secretary, Public Relations' Officer, and President for the National Parents Council – Post Primary for twenty-five years. This is followed by a discussion on ways to foster relationship skills, a holistic view of sexuality, and self-care in education.

Awareness of Multiple Intelligences: Interview with Dr Fergus Heffernan
Education and governments have been hijacked by industry. The decision of what to teach is governed by multinationals. Recent statistics show that 48 per cent of students dropped out from first year in college last year. First and foremost there's the pressure to go to college, and at sixteen or seventeen the fabric of your whole identity has to do with college. This is the message that is coming from schools and families. Schools' academic performance is measured by league tables. Teachers are being measured by the performance of their students' exam results and students are measured by staff based on their points. So everyone is locked into a system which ultimately creates a model of anxiety. Universities are stretched to the pin of their collar, trying to deal with first-year students who are on the wrong courses. Many of these courses have no bearing on real life, except for getting employment.

Recently I got a phone call from a mother who had attended one of my talks. She had a son who was nineteen, who had been home in bed for the past seven months, not communicating with the world or anyone in it. He had gone to university the previous September and had dropped out by Christmas. He then retired to his bed and dropped out of life. Obviously his mother was hugely concerned and asked me to meet him. A fine handsome, big fella arrived in my office two days later. He had gone to college to study applied biology. When I asked if he liked it, he answered, 'I hated it!' So I questioned him further. He finally admitted that he'd never done any science subject in school. I asked him why he had ever studied biology.

'All I'm after hearing for two years is that you have to go to college,' he said. 'The only message I seem to be getting is that if you don't go to college you'll never amount to anything. So, I figured out that I'd probably get 350 points max., if I worked my butt off, which I didn't.'

So he got his CEO form. He looked at every course that was under 300 points and loaded them in. It was a lottery then. So what came back? He was only a week in the course when he knew it wasn't for him. But now he's feeding into his whole sense of failure and he has no facility to talk about it. Then he dropped out and he didn't attend lectures at all up to Christmas, but it was only when the letter came home from college after Christmas that they discovered the truth. Then he felt guilty for letting down his parents, and everything began to feed into his belief that he wasn't good enough intellectually.

So after that he said, 'Sure, I didn't really know what I wanted to do.' 'That's a good honest answer,' I said, 'because 90 per cent of nineteen year olds in the country would say that, if they were allowed to say it.' Then I asked, 'And if you were to look into the future, what would you love to do? Say that money was no object.'

'Jesus,' he said, 'I play rugby with a local club and I'd love to be a rugby coach.'

'So why can't you be a rugby coach?' I asked. He said no one had ever asked him that question. I said, 'Maybe there isn't a course in Ireland, but there are plenty of courses in Britain. You could get your qualifications outside Ireland to be a rugby coach.'

Anyway, we met three or four times after that. We weren't dealing with therapy here. It's just that his mind had been messed with by the system. It shows how easily it can happen but also how quickly it can be brought back again when you are aware of the real problem. It is only by looking at the skewed educational model, and how young people and their parents are made to value it, that we become aware of its destructive elements, such as, its reliance on intellectual intelligence, the point's system and the college admission procedure. Mark ended up studying abroad. He has completed his first year and he says he loves the course. You know that Mark could have so quickly disappeared off the planet as so many others have.

Whole-School/Community Approach to Bullying: Anthony E. Walsh
In the following interview with Anthony E. Walsh, a new, all-school/community approach to dealing with disruptive behaviours, including bullying, is proposed.

The focus of the all-school/community programme provides a solution to deal with the social phenomenon of bullying in schools that has resulted in great trauma, suffering and even death. Countless theoretical reports have been published analysing the problem and identifying approaches to curtail the phenomenon. However, little effect has been achieved, as bringing theory into practice has proved problematic. A new programme, which we propose, is in response to all that has failed to be helpful from efforts in the past. It is an active intervention model that adopts a whole-school/community approach and provides a unique solution adapted from global research, insightful experience and outside-the-box thinking. This programme provides tools of change for students, teachers, parents, ancillary staff and the community. It is a cost-effective approach and has the potential to radically reduce school bullying.

The Solution
The solution involves a whole-school/community approach where all parties are given individual responsibilities and skills to practice during the roll-out of the programme. At present, prevention amounts to adopting a 'don't bully' approach, which leaves outcomes to chance, with little hope of achieving a change in culture for anti-social behaviours. Adopting a war-like stance towards bullying behaviour may be a natural response. Popular campaigns have fallen into this mode with slogans such as 'Let's Beat/Combat bullying' or the use of a shield. These show the underlying defensive and fear-based position that unintentionally fosters strong, negative feelings towards the person or child behind the behaviour. A change of attitude and understanding could result in a powerful learning and healing experience for all when we embrace human behaviours,

and manage them with patience and love. This programme could be delivered in a fun and meaningful way in every school to bring about a positive culture and attitude-changing experience with powerful long-term effects.

Our approach must, therefore, be truly proactive, i.e. pre-bullying, accepting bullying behaviour as part of the human condition, albeit unwelcome and changeable, and adopting restorative rather than punitive solutions to anti-social behaviour, such as bullying. This inclusive approach is likely to have a more healing effect on all concerned than the typical punitive responses. The idea here is that we separate the bullying behaviour from the child. In so doing, we embrace the needs of, not only the child who is targeted, but also the perpetrator. Both children have deficits, the former in confidence and the latter in empathy.

From this New Perspective, we are also likely to discover the reasons why bullying behaviour has occurred in the child and find creative ways to counteract this. In the long-term, children are likely to flourish and make happier choices in later life. Ultimately, society will derive the immense benefits by reducing self-harm and depression, and eliminating the loss of children to suicide due to bullying. The rarely considered side effects include a reduction of children with unresolved habitual bullying who go on to develop criminal and aggressive behaviours, domestic abuse and workplace bullying, leaving a plethora of victims in their wake. Overall, the freeing up of schools to do the job they need to do, while children are being emotionally empowered and helped to care for themselves, is a goal that we, as a society, surely aspire to.

Holistic Development

Holistic development encompasses the personal and social development of every child. Particular emphasis is placed on the emotional, spiritual and interrelational dimensions. In this section Rose Tully discusses the importance of developing emotional intelligence in schools. This is followed by a discussion on ways to foster relationship skills, a holistic view of sexuality, self-care and spirituality in education.

Interview with Rose Tully on the Importance of Emotional Intelligence
It has been a source of worry for me and indeed many involved in the education of our children that we are concentrating on academic progress and ignoring children's multiple intelligences and learning styles. Essentially, it's the whole area of emotional intelligence that's being neglected. The family are every bit as responsible for this too. We need to be sensitive to the differences between boys and girls. The past few decades have been particularly difficult for men. Their roles have diminished and changed. Men should not feel threatened because women are achieving equal status. They have also been forced to suppress their emotions to meet a socially acceptable male image. It is the lack of emotional development that causes much of the difficulty for children as they grow up. Suppressing and distorting emotional development in boys has been a definite contributor to the awful statistics we read about every day.

The present points system in the Leaving Certificate skews our values and distracts us from guiding our children towards meaningful and happy lives. If X gets 600 points, he or she is expected to go into high-points-requirement professions such as medicine or law. But if he or she wants to do arts or media studies and only needs 450 points, parents often feel that they are wasting 150 points. We have to get it embedded into the social psyche that it is never a waste for a young person to do what he or she is happy doing.

There's a blindness among many parents as they often try to live their assumed failed past through their children. All parents would claim that they only want their children to be happy, but then demand things of their children that often lead them on a lifetime of unhappiness. Surely, they would prefer to have a happy artist in the family than a suicidal doctor or dentist.

The Education Act of 1998 changed everything for parents in Ireland. It gave them a statutory right to be involved in the education of their children and the wider educational system. The time has come, I feel, for the next wave of change. It is only when the whole school and community work as a team, in a child-centred way, that we can facilitate real and meaningful change. Only people power will facilitate this change, and it can only come from the bottom up, not the other way round.

Relationships and Sexuality

Since we are social beings, the whole area of relationships is of utmost importance to our emotional and psychological well-being. It is, therefore, imperative that young people learn important skills that can foster and maintain positive relationships throughout life. Likewise with sexuality: this is such a central factor in our self-worth and our interactions with others. It is an important requirement within education that young people feel positive about their sexual orientation and that they develop an understanding of human sexuality. In the holistic view of the self, sexuality is yet another facet of our human expression, that it is interlinked and interconnected with all other parts. This is a very different view than the usual religious one that portrays sexuality as isolated from the rest of the self.

The presentation of sexual education must be given in a format that merges biological information with emotional, sensory and relationship components, similar to how we might discuss an appreciation of food or art. In early adolescence there is the need to receive information that is sensitively given and placed in the correct context, so that myths and misleading stories are not allowed to spread, causing confusion and anxiety. In older teenagers, emphasis needs to revolve around skill-building programs and the promotion of healthy relationships. Helpful discussions might include the responsibilities of being sexually active, remaining safe and minimising the risk of sexually transmitted diseases and pregnancy; focusing on the emotional component of sexuality; discussing gender stereotypes and the need for respecting all sexual orientations. In this way sexuality is no longer divorced from the whole person. Learning to respect and appreciate all aspects of relationships, including sexuality, may reduce the likelihood that any person is viewed exclusively in sexual terms.

The importance of adolescents being educated to recognise healthy and unhealthy relationships is imperative for their well-being. Without clear guidelines as to acceptable and unacceptable behaviour when dating, teenagers may misinterpret jealousy, constant text messaging or other forms of control as signs of love, rather than seeing these behaviours as a sign of potential abuse (Sorenson, 2007). Armed with such knowledge, teenagers would be more capable of distinguishing between constructive and destructive emotions, assertive enough to know which behaviours to accept and which to repel, with the confidence to verbalise these. Discussions around important characteristics to look for in a potential partner may inform adolescents that certain standards in values and behaviour are highly desirable, such as kindness, consideration, respect, empathy and tolerance. Challenging stereotypes of heterosexual males and females, gays, lesbians, etc. may also foster more realistic views of what it is to be a man, woman, heterosexual and homosexual, beyond stylised media representations.

Self-Care and Holistic Well-being

The ability to care for yourself, to know you are a person of value, a unique being of inherent worth – this is all too rare, yet it is the secret of happiness and well-being. Surely then, there can be no more worthwhile subject to teach than self-care. The human being is imbued with incredible strengths, physical, mental and spiritual, yet there is also a fragility; a weakening of the entire system if negativity is planted in childhood and allowed to grow and fester. There is also a deep need to connect with our inner world, to acknowledge the yearnings of our hearts and souls and to spend time reflecting, away from the demands of our busy lives. This section includes a discussion on how self-care, holistic well-being and the strengthening of self-worth can be nurtured, over a lifetime, despite problems and setbacks, on a daily basis, beginning in this moment.

The Practice of Mindfulness
In some schools, the practice of mindfulness is now included in their daily routine. The Department of Education plan to introduce mindfulness as part of the new Junior Cycle from September 2014 (*Irish Independent*, 25 August 2014). When practising mindfulness, students learn to observe what is going on internally, in their thoughts and in their emotions, and to develop techniques that bring calmness in stressful situations. It is also important that students learn how the mind and emotions work, as this may provide great insight in times of pain and confusion. Students can learn how to observe each thought and emotion without judgement, without labelling it as good or bad. Becoming aware that thoughts and emotions come and go in response to events, and that finding a constructive way of expressing emotions is vital to maintaining holistic well-being, offers students vital tools for self-care. The practice of mindfulness needs to be included in all schools as the benefits can be immense: the strengthening of awareness, increased health and well-being, decreased levels of stress, the cultivation of compassion and kindness, improved impulse control and the strengthening of relationships. It also deepens our understanding of emotions, thoughts, and habitual tenancies.

Healthy Expression of Pain

Emotional pain may become acute when the repression of emotion becomes a way of life, or when a sudden loss or tragedy occurs. Again, it is vital that educators include components in courses that deal with healthy ways of expressing all emotions, including pain, such as by talking about problems with a trusted friend, through physical activity, writing about feelings in a journal, or practising mindfulness. The key to emotional well-being is to find ways of expressing feelings on a daily basis so that they don't build up, leading to depression or deep pain. A combination of stressful events may also trigger great heartache. When troubling emotions are coupled with negative thoughts, the whole internal system strives to find a solution to restore the feeling of balance and peace. In the case of a physical ache that grows until it becomes agonising, so too a festering emotional wound may be left far too long before it is treated. Thoughts of suicide may arise in a troubled and overloaded mind as a possible solution to ending the pain that is beginning to become unbearable.

It is very important for educators to discuss the effects that an accumulation of emotional pain has on the whole person, and to explore healthy ways of expressing emotions, such as anger, frustration, fear or shame. Students also need to be instructed that, if suicidal thoughts ever begin to surface, it is vital to confide in a trusted person, such as a friend, a parent, a doctor, a therapist or by calling a dedicated suicide helpline, such as The Samaritans. Students should also be reminded that there are trained people who can offer support by exploring with them constructive ways of looking at their life situation.

Spirituality

Traditional religious education focused on a set of beliefs that were based on teachings that had been handed down over millennia. The intangible nature of the presented material required blind faith. In Ireland, we have recently witnessed what can happen when a church fails people who relied on it for spiritual support and guidance. There have always been branches of religions that nurtured more transcendental experiences and practices, such as the Gnostic Christians and the teachings of the Kabbalah of the Jewish faith. There needs to be a new emphasis on facilitating a personal experience of spirituality, where an individual feels empowered, imbued with a sense of meaning and connected to the whole cycle of life. This personal dimension of spirituality needs to be nurtured first and can then be enhanced by whatever religious tradition a person favours. Spiritual practices that instil inner balance and peace, and that enhance present moment awareness, such as meditation, may also be beneficial in dealing with life stresses. Students may be encouraged to discuss many facets of spirituality, including creating meaning, spending time in nature, developing a personal philosophy, and having a unique part to play in the unfolding of the universe.

CHAPTER TWENTY

Work

Significant physical and psychological damage is experienced by workers who have been subjected to bullying, excessive levels of stress, sexual harassment and violence in the workplace. It is often argued that employers struggle to keep afloat, particularly in times of economic recession, and that it is a necessary requirement for any firm to focus on maximising profitability. In this chapter we outline the importance for employers of maximising both profitability and workers' well-being. This is a vital strand in the Suicide Box that needs to be dismantled due to the human devastation that occurs in the workplace because of the singular emphasis placed by employers on profit-making. Instead, we argue that, if we apply a more compassionate approach to the business world, by ensuring that both the well-being of workers and profitability are equally prioritised, then the needs of all concerned will be maximised. This will minimise unnecessary human pain that sometimes results in suicide.

Maximising Profitability and Well-being

Many people's work lives are plagued with persistent levels of stress, particularly those outside of a person's control, i.e. constant high-pressured work, poor working relationships, unreasonable deadlines or unsupported restructuring. An essential transformation within the workplace will involve an adoption of a new ethos: to increase overall well-being and personal happiness for employees, while also decreasing absenteeism and increasing productivity for employers. With this approach, it is envisaged that workers will be more productive, enthusiastic, motivated and committed, possessing greater self-belief and a sense of belonging.

The Current System of Work

Companies need to keep pace with an ever-changing world in creating services that keep abreast of developments in the business world and our changing understanding of human nature. It is not only employees that suffer when profit is valued more than happiness and well-being. Businesses lose revenue and, hence, profitability, through high levels of absenteeism and low prod-uctivity. Current research across many studies shows that when these issues are addressed holistically and honestly, a workforce becomes happier, more enthusiastic, motivated and security-conscious. Distracted, unhappy and stressed workers are a hazard waiting to happen.

The following statistics are testament to the myriad of problems that face workplaces when important factors, such as employee happiness, dignity, respect, and self-worth, are omitted from businesses:

+ Stress is the second highest work-related health issue in EU member states (Health and Safety Authority, 2008). At any one time there are many thousands of workers in Ireland either out of work or under-performing at work with some form of mental health difficulty.

+ A recent survey by IBEC (2011) suggests that absenteeism is costing businesses around €1.5 billion, with workers missing almost six days a year on average.

⁑ Results from the largest workplace health and safety survey conducted in Europe (European Agency for Safety and Health at Work (EU-OSHA), 2010) revealed that four out of five European managers questioned expressed concern about work-related stress, and that stress at work is perceived by many companies (79%) to be as great a problem as workplace accidents.

⁑ In the United States, job stress costs employers more than $300 billion each year in absenteeism, tardiness, burnout, low productivity, high turnover, worker's compensation and medical insurance costs (The American Institute of Stress, 2002).

In contrast, happy workers have been shown to have, on average, a 31 per cent higher productivity rate and 37 per cent higher sales (Harvard Business Review, 2012).

Adopting Holistic Strategies

Before we move on to look at holistic strategies that can be adopted in the workplace, it is essential that employers acknowledge the devastating human consequences of business practices to date. Creating an environment where there are acceptable levels of stress, and where bullying or other forms of harassment are discouraged, requires strong and compassionate leaders who have been as well trained in people skills as in business and management practices. Part of this change involves acknowledging and accepting the often complex diversity of human nature, including the fact that some people misuse their power and exert control over others, by ensuring that human issues are given equal consideration in business models as profitability.

It is essential that we, in turn, acknowledge that bosses are often victims of the same stressful conditions as their staff. However, from all the research that has come into the public domain in recent studies, it is evident that employers need to become acutely aware of their workers' well-being. Holistic strategies need to be adopted by implementing better working and social conditions for both workers and bosses, to optimise happiness and profitability in parallel. Before another boom time takes place in the global economy, raising consciousness in business, with a thoughtful consideration of human factors, is likely to produce a happier and included workforce, and reduce the awful impact of future economic recessions.

Peter's Story

For me, my years as a prison officer involved a continuous erosion of any ambitions I had within the job. I wasn't interested in promotion but I loved the work. Over the years I presented a number of ideas to superiors but if they were implemented the credit was given to the superior involved. On confronting one superior I was told that I was only paid from the neck down. Similarly, personal issues were considered to come from a separate world and there were frequent reminders that what happened outside the walls of the prison was of no concern to prison management. Thankfully, the death of the dinosaurs and the arrival of fresh management heralded a new dawn in the prison I worked in. Unfortunately, my desire for involvement was well and truly killed off.

Blake-Mouton's Model

When reviewing the Blake-Mouton model of managerial styles, we were reminded of a story of a new clergyman who arrived in a village. On Sunday morning he gave a sermon that installed hope and meaning like they had never heard before. The following Sunday the church was full as the people awaited new words of wisdom. To their surprise the clergyman gave the exact same sermon. As the sermon was still powerful, the parishioners were forgiving and thought that he had some memory loss. However, on the third Sunday, to a packed church he gave the exact the same sermon. A few of the bravest parishioners decided that they would have to approach the poor clergyman and inform him of his lapse of function. They told him how wonderful his sermon was and how the whole parish was moved by his words, then gently added that he had given the same sermon for the past three Sundays. The clergyman responded that he was completely aware of his repeated sermon and said that he intended to continue with the same message until the people of the parish began to heed as well as to hear the words spoken.

The relevance of this story became clear when we came across studies from the 1960s by Blake and Mouton (1964, updated 1985). They developed a managerial grid that originally identified five different leadership styles based on the 'concern for people' and the 'concern for production'. In doing so, they clearly pointed out the leadership style that maximised happiness and profitability in business. Like the parishioners in the story above, the powerful message was heard but was not heeded, as perhaps the need for personal power and control was so intrinsically linked to the status of business ownership, free enterprise, and the focus on maximising profits. However, fifty years later, business leadership is often left to chance. The well-being of workers is generally given low priority. The resulting pain and unhappiness is experienced by vast numbers of employees, even contributes to the deaths of some by suicide.

Blake and Mouton's model of leadership has been updated over the years, as the understanding of human psychology and the damaging effects of unbalanced leadership styles became known. There are now seven different leadership styles referred to. These are:

+ The dictatorial style: These Managers try to control and dominate. Production is their main concern. They find employees' needs unimportant. Employees get paid for the work they do and high production is maintained with the pressure of rules and punishments. A dictatorial style is often applied by businesses in danger of failing or in cases of crisis management.

+ The indifferent style: In this style managers evade and elude. They have low concern for both people and production. Their main aim is to preserve their position of seniority, protecting themselves by avoiding trouble. Their main concern is to elude responsibility for any mistakes, which limits innovative decisions.

+ The accommodating style: Identifying characteristics of these managers is yielding and complying. They have a high concern for people and a low concern for production. They pay much attention to the security and comfort of the employees, in the hope that this will increase performance. The resulting atmosphere is usually friendly, but not necessarily very productive.

+ The paternalistic style: These managers prescribe and guide. They alternate between the accommodating and the dictatorial style. Managers using this style praise and support, but discourage challenges to their thinking.

+ The status quo style: This style is noted for its balance and compromise. These managers try to strike a balance between company goals and workers' needs. The difficulty with this style is that, in trying to satisfy the needs of both, they give away some of each concern, so that neither production nor workers' needs are met.

+ The opportunistic style: The basic aim of this style is to exploit and manipulate. Managers using this style adopt whichever behaviour maximises their personal benefits.

⚜ The sound style: This style is marked by participation and commitment. Managers here give high concern to both people and production. They encourage teamwork and commitment among employees. They count on making employees feel that they are vital elements within the business.

From the styles outlined above, identifying the leadership style most conducive to maximising profitability and well-being would not be too difficult. The inclusivity and human dignity offered in the sound style is most likely to produce high levels of workplace happiness and performance. Managers can use the grid system devised by Blake and Mouton (1985) to discover their own managerial style. Accurate measurement is important because of the tendency of managers for self-deception and exaggeration. It was found that 80 per cent of all managers who were shown the various styles, ranked themselves as sound or team style. However, when their style was analysed according to the grid, only 20 per cent were found to be using this style.

It is evident, therefore, that in order to dismantle the area of work within the Suicide Box that three distinct goals need to be achieved. The first is to ensure that workers' well-being is standardised, for all businesses, and not left to chance. This entails giving equal weight to human and production concerns. However, this may be difficult, as financial institutions place no importance on workers' well-being, as their only interest is in business models that show profitability, no matter how this is achieved. Secondly, the selection process of potential managers should include psychological profiling to ensure that individuals with poor social or empathy skills are excluded from management positions. This decision could be reconsidered, if proper training was given and psychological assessment indicated later suitability. This is a vital step for businesses to take in order to weed out those whose production skills are highly valued but who leave a trail of human destruction in their wake. Thirdly, management training needs to be centred on the sound or team management style, to reduce the likelihood of 'loose cannons' adopting their own destructive style at work.

The achievement of these goals will ensure that bullying behaviour or a culture of bullying will not be allowed to take hold. Under this new style of management, people skills will be considered a vital trait that companies seek in their employees, and on-going training in sound management style will safeguard against peer-to-peer bullying, and situations where workers suffer the harmful effects of exposure to excessive levels of stress. Ultimately, due to the damaging forces that are evident in workplaces within the Suicide Box, lawmakers must introduce policies that foster compliance, and that balance the drive for profits with workers' well-being and happiness.

CHAPTER TWENTY-ONE

The Media

From an examination of the construction of the Suicide Box, two key problem areas in the media emerged. The first is the stereotyping of various minorities and the portrayal of a certain physique in the media that contributes to body-loathing and low self-esteem in young people. The second is the sensationalising and glamorising of suicide in the media, coupled with the lack of sensitivity when reporting suicides or other situations involving tragedy, human failing or misfortune. The damage that exposure to constant unrealistic images of perfection and negative stereotypes does to young people and minorities is well documented. There is an overwhelming need for those who work in the media to be trained in two vital aspects that are all too often missing: empathy and sensitivity. However, the draw to satisfy the financial demands of employers, skewed views of what freedom of speech entails, the hampering of the freedom to express truths by some institutions, or the personal ego of the reporter make this a difficult task.

There are those who may feel that a soft version of censorship is being advocated. Freedom of expression is an important right of any citizen in a democracy, yet there are legal and moral limits to that freedom, such as the Prohibition of Incitement to Hatred Act (1989), that outlaws 'hatred against a group of persons in the state or elsewhere on account of their race, colour, nationality, religion, ethnic or national origins, membership of the travelling community or sexual orientation'. The Defamation Act (2009) protects citizens from attacks, such as libel or slander of their character. There is indeed an important balance to be struck between the freedom of expression, the general freedom of individuals to privacy when they are not convicted of any crime, society's wider moral and social responsibilities, and the freedom of all to human rights, respect and dignity. Too often reports are printed where there has been no illegality proven against the person, yet the media report has all the elements of accusation, judgement and conviction contained within.

Empathy as a Feature of Reporting

The sensationalising and glamorising of suicide, and the insensitive reporting of human interest stories involving any kind of tragedy, derives from many factors, including fears and prejudices that block empathy. Finance is required to print papers, to run networks and to pay salaries. Yet, the destruction of even one human being through character assassination, the stereotyping of some trait or body shape that promotes poor self-esteem in individuals or a minority group, or the ridicule or vilification of any group, is surely not a sound basis for economic prosperity in any society. It is not the reporting of facts that usually gives offence. It is the tone of the article, the tainting of facts by the inclusion of derogatory phrases that colour the story, making it more sensational and dramatic. Too many articles are written that portray individuals in an extreme light. Yet, the person's true life story may never be revealed. Even a judge in the most horrific of criminal cases considers mitigating circumstances. Some journalists seem to stifle any sense of empathy in case this may interfere with the sensational aspects of a story.

In this book we appeal to other facets of the reader, requesting that you join us on this journey as we move through old fears, stigmas and ignorance, to view suicide through new eyes of insight and awareness. We are also using words to express thoughts and opinions, yet there is no person being vilified or destroyed here. It is important to view society's failures in terms of a collective lack of awareness, rather than scapegoat any individual who must bear the brunt of our anger or hatred. It is time to face up to the role that each of us has played in blindly following those in authority, who have shown that they are driven more by short-term personal agendas and in-the-box thinking, rather than by long-term social needs.

In attempting to work outside of the Suicide Box, we have a much greater remit to insist that all reporting in the press and media follows a code of ethics, such as the *Code of Practice of the Press Council of Ireland* (www.nuj.ie), and the *National Union of Journalists' (NUJ) Code of Conduct* (www.nuj.co.uk), at least for now. The second code of conduct to be adhered to as per the NUJ's code states that a journalist: 'Strives to ensure that information disseminated is honestly conveyed, accurate and fair.' The fourth and sixth code items respectively declare that a journalist 'differentiates between fact and opinion; does nothing to intrude into anybody's private life, grief or distress unless justified by overriding consideration of the public interest'.

In terms of dismantling the effects of the Suicide Box and old, negative ways of thinking that need to be exhumed and liberated, it is imperative to spread the word, to newspapers and TV channel owners, to editors, reporters and journalists, that the reporting of all stories needs to be treated with empathy. In the *Code of Practice of the Press Council of Ireland* (www.nuj.ie), the following item, numbered 5.3, is worthy of note: 'Sympathy and discretion must be shown at all times in seeking information in situations of personal grief or shock. In publishing such information, the feelings of grieving families should be taken into account. This should not be interpreted as restricting the right to report judicial proceedings.'

The media surely has a duty of care to the public but also to the people it portrays in its pages and on its screens. In its various codes, the highest standards of journalism and reporting are openly stated.

Journalists and reporters are also taught the cardinal rule of story coverage: the need for impartiality. Adjectives that demean, and opinions that sentence and persecute, have no place in a mature, responsible media. The next tenet of journalism is surely the accurate and unvarnished reporting of facts. It is a tall order indeed to write or speak of any incident with complete accuracy, revealing utter truth, without bias. The immortal words of Marcus Aurelius, roman emperor (*Meditations*, c. 170), still ring true today: 'Everything we hear is an opinion, not a fact. Everything we see is a perspective, not the truth.' In dismantling the Suicide Box within the media, it is not perfection that is sought, but a new, fresh awareness that words have incredible power to inspire or to destroy. It is a reminder to all that, despite millions of codes of conduct and ethics being written and paid lip service, standards fall and individuals pursue their own unwholesome quests. Within each network or newspaper, empathy must be established as an important ingredient in the ethos of the organisation. This one change alone will hugely diminish un-necessary human suffering.

Sensitive Coverage of Suicide in the Media
There is certainly a need for sensitive reporting in cases involving suicide or self-harm. There is little doubt that articles would have a very different emphasis if journalists wrote from the spectrum of human pain, instead of from the old view of suicide as mysterious and unknowable. The need to adhere to media guidelines in the reporting of suicides was reiterated by Alan Gilsenan, film-maker and director, in *Media Guidelines for Reporting Suicides and Self-Harm*, (Irish Association of Suicidology and The Samaritans, 2009, p. 14): 'As a society, we must engage with the heart-breaking reality of suicide and self-harm, but we must only engage with it in a manner that is responsible, respectful and, above all, imbued with a genuine

humanity and a sympathetic understanding of the fragility of ourselves and those around us.'

The media has a vital role to play in dismantling the Suicide Box,
in preventing suicide but also in promoting the dignity of all human
beings by celebrating diversity in all its countless manifestations.
The first major transformation that must occur in the media before
it can play this role is the adopting of a new position of awareness
outside of the Suicide Box. All too frequently, reports such as those
referred to in the 'Understanding Its Construction' section are
written with obvious agendas of exclusion and division. This often
results in the marginalisation of those who do not fit in to a
perceived social norm and to the maintenance of the status quo. The
media can play a vital part in dismantling the Suicide Box by
discussing the true causes of unnecessary human pain that lead to
many human tragedies, including suicide. The media can be an
agent of great change by raising consciousness of important social
issues and campaigning on behalf of community efforts that
orchestrate practical projects from bottom-up models. A sense of
hope and inclusion can be fostered by emphasising the importance
of being respectful to each other, being non-judgemental,
understanding and empathic when any person we meet is in need
of support.

Within the Suicide Box we are all swamped with stigma and
myth-fuelled values and beliefs around suicide. Perhaps what needs
to be examined most is the choice made by journalists to report
suicide at all, as they may choose to do with other tragedies, the
details of which often go unreported. Responsibility also falls on the
individual to understand the part they each play in subscribing to
sensational articles. Again, coming from within the Suicide Box,
individuals are often fascinated by the mysterious phenomenon of
suicide that is perceived as being far removed from their lives.
However, if journalists were to inform readers of the spectrum of

human pain, and the fact that we each experience pain and for some that pain unfortunately results in tragic outcomes, then there would be nothing sensational about the reporting of suicide.

Mary's Story

Mary's husband died by suicide. Here she recalls her experience with the media.

> We live in a small rural village community in Ireland. My husband had a very high standing in the area and his death by suicide shook the whole community. Complicated personal issues dominated our family's life in the final months of his life. For me, these were difficult to deal with but were manageable. While I thought he was coping well, underneath he must have felt tortured. The community was aware of his difficulties and there was a lot of understanding. Soon after my husband died a reporter called and told me he planned to report on my husband's suicide in the local paper. I immediately felt panic. I didn't think anyone could do justice to my husband's name, connecting him with issues that may carry prejudice for people who didn't know the beautiful person he was. He had never hurt anyone but now this reporter spoke of his story as if it was a most newsworthy item. To our family he was still the same husband and father we loved. I pleaded with the reporter not to write his story but all he promised to do was write as sensitively as he could. I saw this as an unnecessary intrusion into our lives and a real danger of setting up my children for jeering and bullying if the story was printed. I drove in a panicked state to the town where the newspaper offices were and I sat for hours till the editor arrived. I promised myself I wouldn't cry but cry I did. He was very patient and understanding with me. I told him, off the record, the full details of my husband's story and why I felt that it should not run. He took me unawares when he reached for the phone and instructed someone to pull the story from tomorrow's paper, to replace it with some backup article and told me also that the article on my husband would not be run at all. I could hardly raise myself from the chair

with relief. I could not thank that man enough for his empathy for our situation. I returned home to my family that evening to grieve the loss of my husband and my children's dad without any further unnecessary painful complications.

CHAPTER TWENTY-TWO
The Family

From our earlier discussion of the family in 'Understanding Its Construction', a number of issues arose that need to be explored further in order to begin to dismantle the Suicide Box. These included: a lack of emotional expression within many families due to culture and socialisation; learned practices of keeping deadly secrets in order to maintain a mask that will gain social acceptance; abuses that weaken and stunt the growing child, including domestic violence, child abuse, emotional abuse, and neglect; and the social dependence on alcohol and drugs to extremely unhealthy levels, along with the denial of its impact on crime, domestic abuse, self-harm and suicide. In many Irish families, the adverse effects of socialisation become manifest, due to limited emotional expression that discourages the sharing of feelings and opinions. Thus, children learn to keep their innermost emotions and desires secret. This, in turn, creates a split within the self where children adopt strategies and pretence, too fearful of the consequences if they remain true to their own feelings, needs, talents or sexual preferences.

The importance for young people to feel respected, listened to and included in decisions was highlighted by a recent report by the Department of Children and Youth Affairs, conducted with teenagers in Sligo, Cork and Dublin (Keane, 2013). Young people who took part in the study stated that they felt included when they were: 'Being respected and not treated like a child in the family; being accepted and loved for who you are; having a safe place to be yourself; having a say and being included in decisions; having someone to talk to and rely on.' An interview with Dr Fergus Heffernan, psychologist, psychotherapist and educator, highlights the need for families to develop a new awareness that it is of paramount importance 'to encourage children to be true to their own unique nature'.

Abusive practices within the family that weaken and stunt children's development are perpetrated by individuals, but they also have cultural roots and hence require societal responses. This is also discussed in the following section.

Interview with Dr Fergus Heffernan

In an interview with Dr Fergus Heffernan, several of the important issues above are discussed, including the need for families to construct a plan for their daily lives, but most especially for dealing with crises when they arise. Fergus also stresses the importance of listening, allowing each family member to express their feelings and opinions, and for parents to resist the urge to project their own unfulfilled wishes and desires onto their children.

My Family's Experience

I grew up in a house bereft with mental illness and alcoholism. Looking back, it wasn't a desperately unhappy childhood but it was an incredibly anxious home, because we never knew what was coming next. My mother spent her whole life wanting to die and trying to die. The problem was compounded when I had my own children. So my son was reared in an anxious environment, where he was in anticipation and defence mode all the time, which doesn't give any growth to a child. He didn't want to go to school. He had pains in his tummy in primary school, he had eczema and asthma, but he was a smashing little hurler. He went off to college, and in first year was targeted for the hurling so he did well. He was in the top twenty-five lads so he really became special and his whole identity was created. He was also a handsome lad so the girls were never a problem. There was no anxiety, no eczema, no asthma but he never opened a book. In a house that was so anxious, academic achievement was never really pushed but he was told that he had to go to college. So anyway, he sailed through and he was on all the development squads.

Then about three months before the Leaving Cert, it all changed. The hurling was over now and he began to lose all the identity that had been created for six years. We totally underestimate for Leaving Cert students the amount of loss they experience, because probably the most important six years of life happen in secondary school. So my son must have been experiencing loss. So now there's the Leaving Cert that appeared on the horizon and he's really cast to the wolves. Since he was six or seven he's been an anxious child but you don't see that in a family. The golden rule is that you don't talk about what goes on in your house anyway, so there isn't that facility to process anything.

So one Monday morning in April before his Leaving Cert he stopped going to school. He retired to his bedroom and locked the door. He stopped communicating, washing, shaving, eating. He just couldn't cope. The Leaving Cert came eventually and he didn't do it. He went off one Saturday morning, the first Saturday in July. The Leaving Cert was over about a week, and he was bright-eyed and bushy-tailed, as though nothing had ever happened. His friends came around again and we thought we'd totally overestimated the Leaving Cert. Our world as a family didn't end so we said we'd chill out and make some effort to talk it through and create a place for dialogue.

So he went off on that Saturday night with his friends. Then about three o'clock in the morning there was a knock on the door and it was my twin, to tell me my son had hanged himself down by the canal. An old man walking his dogs came across him and he was able to get him down. He ended up in hospital and then in St Patrick's in Dublin for many weeks. He didn't want to be there, he fought with the system; he fought with everyone. He wouldn't take the medication. I was barred. He wouldn't let me near the place. He needed to be there but it's not the right place for an eighteen year old. That was the real horror story for us, with all our knowledge, we still felt such helplessness.

So we were fighting with each other and fighting with the system, blaming the school, blaming the world, blaming the hurling club and the county. But we did arrive at a place where we'd exhausted all avenues of blame and we asked can we change? This was the hardest moment of all and it took courage and conviction. We had looked inwards before, to blame ourselves, to say we were the worst parents in the world, but that's no good either. If we were really honest with ourselves we were doing the best we could – all of us do – but if you don't have the awareness, then your attitude is going to be wrong. When we began to look inwards, then acceptance came: It is as it is. We began to take ownership of our own anxiety and the managing of it. He had been in his room for so long and he had been suicidal. I'd been doing sentry outside his room so he couldn't get out but I stopped all that. I began writing notes to say, 'I trust you implicitly that you'll do the right thing, for you.' Now, we had to say that we'd accept whatever he did. We also said it would be extremely difficult to deal with if anything happened to him, but we did say, 'this is going to be your choice from now on.' It is as it is! That was the key to turning it all around.

Whenever a family arrives at a crisis, it's never one big thing that's to blame. It's the little things that we never did anything about. What happened is that they all came together at one point and became overwhelming and unmanageable. Anyway, one Sunday morning he disappeared at ten o'clock. He took off in his car and we were very worried about him. He arrived back at about five o'clock and came into the kitchen. He was screaming and roaring that he wanted to die, that he didn't know what he was going to do. I hadn't a clue what to do so I just held him.

Then suddenly there were just two people breathing. I hadn't realised what this mindfulness thing was all about but suddenly here it was. Then I realised that the moment is always safe. You mightn't feel good in the moment but if you can learn to stay with that feeling, the feeling can't do you any harm. It's the behaviour that we use to get away from the feeling that causes the difficulty. Stay in the moment. The moment is always safe. From that day on he just learned how to manage his own anxiety. He never took any more medication. He just learned what made sense. So he went off to Australia to work with horses. The only anxiety he got from me was 'you'll never make a living from horses'. But I knew the secret for him was in following his passion. You may not always have work, but it's all about the journey. Along the journey there will be potholes, but it's knowing how to get out of the pothole when you get into it. It's to accept that there will be potholes always: that's life. Now he's back, studying psychotherapy and psychology in Dublin. He attends college two days and then works with this firm, transporting thoroughbred horses around the world for the Arabs. They need a horseman who has to sit on the plane with the horse. Imagine after that high level of anxiety, now he can calm horses? The learning in that whole experience was phenomenal. We learned the Triple-A Rating: Acceptance, Attitude and Awareness for well-being in life.

What's wrong is that we're not allowed to be human anymore, because there are so many labels, measures and performance indicators, outcomes and deliverables. That's right across industry and in the workplace. There's no room for humanity and that causes anxiety. If you can learn to manage anxiety you'll never be suicidal again. It's not mental disability that we have in our genes, it's the journey of anxiety. Over time, things become more irrational and illogical. The more disconnect, then the energy changes, the mood changes: that's the cycle. Then at some stage irrationality becomes paranoia and you don't see it. You can't make decisions because there isn't clarity. Ultimately, suicide is the total disconnect from the conscious mind. All rationale is gone, there's only darkness.

Developing a Family Plan

As parents, the first thing you want to do is talk to each other. Have you the same opinions? Where do your opinions come from? That should be part of the plan. If you can have these discussions as parents, you're teaching the child from very early on to discuss things. With young children, ultimately you'll have to make the final call anyway, but you've created the platform for discussion. It's not about giving power over to a young child of six or seven. It's about giving children options and choices, and teaching them how to make informed choices. In a time of suicide, for example, the person is devoid of choices or options and has arrived at this one act as a way of solving their problems.

If parents have a discussion first about what might go into the plan, it could even include the attitude they'll adopt in times of crisis. Everyone in the family needs to be part of the plan. You're working on anxiety here too because everyone knows the plan, whereas anxiety is about the unknown. It doesn't have to be a very rigid structure. Simplicity is the key, yet sometimes the most simple things are the most difficult to manage. There are a lot of skills involved in living with evolving and maintaining a plan.

Teenagers often arrive in my office where parents want them to take honours in some subject or follow a certain career, and they have a completely different view of what they want to do. So I give them the space to look at the problem: what do you want, and what does mam and dad want? There are two separate plans. Now, hypothetically, let's say that your parents' model will never change. Now, is there any way that your model can change? Is there a little change you can make? This is so important because you'll end up in work or in marriage, where people are coming from different perspectives. I need to ask, what am I doing? Yet, I also need to be true to myself. It's the conflict between these two views that is creating the difficulty. So become empowered!

Responses to Abuses within Families

When we read material on families and parenting we are often left feeling that we can never achieve the perfection proposed. In reality, there is no perfection, no perfect parent and no perfect family. Winnicott (1964) suggested that we just need to strive to be 'good enough' parents. Probably a helpful guide is to accept that there will be negative times but to ensure that these will be interspersed with lots of loving and positive experiences. Rather than seeing our children possessively as ours alone, it may be more appropriate to see ourselves as representing the world, as their particular carers and protectors. It is our job to do the best we can to bring them to independence and maturity, maximising their natural flairs and abilities. In this way, they and their world will make the most comfortable fit possible.

Within the 'Understanding Its Construction' section, we identified family abuses that are far removed from perfection. Such abuses weaken and stunt the growing child and affect all family members. These include domestic violence, child abuse, elder abuse, emotional abuse, neglect, and the effects of alcoholism and drug addiction. Each occupies a large segment of the Suicide Box and, therefore, is in urgent need of being dismantled. It is a daunting task indeed to contemplate ways of preventing abuses occurring within the family. There is a public abhorrence to such elicit acts that occur behind the closed doors of some families. Yet within families there is a reluctance to admit the truth of what is happening and, instead, members tolerate all forms of abuse for fear of what may happen if family secrets become public. Within the Suicide Box, responses to family abuses are typically reactive. Abuses fester away until they burst like boils into public awareness. Behind these closed doors, family members are suffering severe pain and children are learning helplessness, sadness and hopelessness throughout their precious, formative years.

Despite legislation (The Domestic Violence Act (1996); Criminal Law (Sexual Offences) Act (2006); The Child and Family Agency Act, 2013), abuses still occur within families, often affecting the most vulnerable people within society. There is also support available from external agencies, yet fears still abound about contacting or using them. Parents may well ask: will my children be taken from the home? Could they end up in a worse situation in care? Who will support us? Where will we have to move to? Could we be in greater danger if we make a report? How will we cope with the public shame? These are just some of the questions that prevent a **recipient** of domestic violence or a non-abusing parent from availing of help. It is also imperative that the image portrayed by social services is softened, to be more empathetic and less threatening to those who are most in need of care.

A complete shift in our thinking, as individuals, as communities and as a society, is required in order to bring about real change to family interactions. Dismantling must involve breaking the old mould of waiting until abuses become evident and then dealing with them in a punitive manner. At this stage maximum damage has occurred with little possibility of healing taking place. Somehow we have to empower people, and most especially children, to make abuses against them known as early as their pain is felt. It is vital to present a healing community approach, to adopt restorative rather than punitive responses and to attempt to deal with core family issues before they develop to crisis point.

All children are vulnerable to abuse and neglect, but the youngest children are the most vulnerable of all, particularly those under five years of age (Safehorizon website). International studies into fatal cases of physical abuse have found that the most vulnerable children are young infants, aged less than two years (Adinkrah, 2000; Vock et al, 1999; Menick, 2000; Haapasalo and Peta, 1999). The effects of all forms of abuse on the developing child have, in some cases, been shown to cause brain damage, a shorter lifespan, high risk of suicide, psychiatric and behavioural problems, as well as the onset of learning disabilities in later life (Adverse Childhood Experiences (ACE) Study, 1995–7; Teicher, 2000; Teicher, 2002, Teicher et al, 2002; Teicher et al, 2006).

It is, therefore, vital that any signs of child abuse are detected immediately and that the child's welfare is safeguarded. In Ireland, a Public Health Nurse makes contact with every mother after the birth of her baby to arrange for home visits for health and developmental checks at three months, seven months, eighteen to twenty-four months and three to four years. Although these visits are mandatory, a refusal to allow a visit should immediately send a signal to the Community Health Centre designated to work with the mother and baby that something is amiss. Children begin school in Ireland at the age of five, so teachers must be aware of watching out for signs of abuse, depression or withdrawal in children under their care. At present then, the most vulnerable ages for a child are between four and five, when no outside agency can monitor the child's progress and level of well-being. It is imperative to the child's well-being that developmental checks and visits by the Public Health Nurse are extended until school-going age. If governments are reluctant to safeguard the welfare of infants due to economic restraints, then they may heed the findings of Professor James Heckman (2006), Nobel-prize-winning economist. According to Hecknam, the economic return to nations that invest in children's early years is higher than the return in investment in later childhood. Children whose brains are damaged due to abuse or neglect suffer the unnecessary pain of the abuse itself but, from current research, they may also be sentenced to a lifetime of disadvantage in terms of emotional, behavioural and cognitive functioning. It is, therefore, a priority that children's health and welfare is protected by having regular visits from a caring professional during those crucial years, from zero to five.

Parental Education

Since education is compulsory for all children within the state, parents are also directly involved with schools. Therefore, where an all-school/community programme is introduced that has the entire community's support parents may become further immersed in education that explores the causes of bullying behaviour and abuse. Parental seminars could include discussions on impulsivity, effective listening, damaging effects of power and control, misuse of drugs and alcohol and the negative effects when emotions become destructive. There are other important elements that could be included, such as the importance of developing empathy skills, becoming aware of social deficits that are disguised by violence and aggression, and the damage that is done to relationships when destructive behaviours occur at home or in school.

Exposing the Links Between Alcohol, Suicide and Pain

Alcohol is involved in many suicides and is at the root of countless family problems. The cultural use of alcohol varies, but for countries that tend to misuse alcohol they also tend to have higher levels of suicide. Ireland is one such nation that treats alcohol as a means of achieving a state of inebriation to enable social interaction, rather than a means of socialising as an end in itself. It is as though there is a need to self-medicate, to numb some inner pain that needs to be kept suppressed or released through a drunken state. In Irish society, alcohol has become linked with celebration, socialising and glamour. Non-drinkers are often made to feel like bores and spoilsports. Alcohol is central to socialising in Ireland to such a degree that no 'craic' can be had without it.

The state of Ireland's dependency has reached crisis point, as verified by the World Health Organisation's report (2014) that recently revealed that Ireland has the second highest rate of binge drinking in the world. The recent report published by the European Child Safety Alliance (2014, 18–20) found that the highest suicide rates, for those aged up to nineteen years, occurred in Ireland and Lithuania. It is indeed significant then, that Ireland has the second highest rate of binge drinking and that Lithuania has the third highest consumption of alcohol per person in the world. Many studies have found that alcohol and drug abuse are strongly related to suicide risk (Kendall, 1983; Harris and Barraclough, 1997; Kessler et al, 1999; Wilcox et al, 2004; Hope, 2008; Walsh and Walsh, 2011; Dooley and Fitzgerald, 2012; Arensman et al, 2012). It is certainly not surprising then that suicide, alcoholism, depression and drug dependence are perceived as being the most important mental health problems in Ireland (HSE, 2007).

Many tentative and piecemeal efforts are being made by politicians to deal with the social problems that alcohol and drug misuse causes. Alcohol is a poisonous chemical when taken in high doses over prolonged periods. Its effects on those who ingest it are unpredictable, and include criminality, addiction and suicide. All responsibility for resulting problems is typically levelled at the individual. Little responsibility is, therefore, taken by any other parties involved. Despite the seriousness of addiction and binge drinking, the Irish government has no national action plan on tackling alcohol or drug abuse (EMCDDA, 2012). While it has recently introduced some measures to limit the advertising of alcohol in the media from 2016, it has failed to impose a blanket ban. It also failed to impose any penalty on drinks companies that sponsor major sporting events (*Irish Independent*, 24 October 2013). This is a worrying omission since so much of Ireland's youth are involved in sports and are surely susceptible to the powerful influence of glamourous advertisements that link alcohol with sporting achievement, success and personal excellence.

The former Health Minister, Dr James Reilly, stated that (*Irish Independent*, 24 October 2013): 'Alcohol misuse in Ireland is a serious problem with two thousand of our hospital beds occupied each night by people with alcohol related illness or injury.' Despite full knowledge of the dangers that may ensue from continued use of alcohol, manufacturers still produce fancy drinks to attract young drinkers and create magnetic illusions. The sellers could be considered drug pushers except for the protection they enjoy under the law, and the government is happy to continue to rake in the vast revenue from taxes on alcohol. Yet our prisons are filled with alcohol-influenced crime and our homes continue to be destroyed by senseless abuse, dysfunction and heartache.

CHAPTER TWENTY-THREE
The Power of Community

From society's current perspective of suicide the sole focus is on preventing vulnerable individuals from taking their own lives. The assumptions inherent within this perspective are that suicide is a mysterious phenomenon that is perpetrated by dysfunctional individuals, without any reference to the myriad of social factors that contribute to deaths by suicide. Government funding to date, although minimal, has been ploughed into organisations that support this narrow individual perspective. Thus, the Suicide Box remains intact and no real change can occur, as we have seen by the continuing high rates of suicide and self-harm.

In contrast, the New Perspective, as proposed by this book, views the phenomenon of suicide as far more preventable if our social structures were transformed by collective responsibility. Within the present structure, most organisations funded for suicide prevention, are merely awaiting the arrival of those choosing to die by suicide from unbearable pain. That said, their absence would be devastating. While their main task on a surface level is to be ready to greet the arrival of those wanting to die, their principal work is less obvious: to counteract the damage caused by the social structures within the Suicide Box.

While researching community projects around suicide prevention we discovered several groups that functioned at an active human level. While these organisations are still essentially operating within the Suicide Box they are notably reaching back from the cliff edge, into the heart of the community, to deliver a message of care and hope. Ironically, such efforts are receiving little or no state funding. Instead, they exist through local community support. The three organisations we feature here are examples of community-based projects that are being run throughout Ireland. Our first interview is with Kay Quinn and Denise Hewitt, founders of Touched by Suicide, in Enniscorthy, Co. Wexford. This is followed by an interview with Mayor George Lawlor, founding member of Wexford Marine Watch. We also give an outline of the Loughmore Community Shop and Tea rooms in Co. Tipperary that was founded by Mary Fogarty and Maeve O'Hair, based on the Plunkett Foundation Co-op Model. We conclude with a brief summary of the core issues that have been identified in this section as being crucial to address, before developing a new paradigm to reduce unnecessary human pain and ultimately suicide.

Touched by Suicide: Insights from Kay Quinn and Denise Hewitt
When Kay Quinn's two sons, James and Harry, died from suicide, Kay and her friend Denise Hewitt set up a charity shop in Enniscorthy, Co. Wexford, called Touched by Suicide. Proceeds from the shop are used to fund local projects, such as helping Slaney Search and Rescue with expenses incurred after an accident, attempted suicide or suicide, paying for counselling for those who are suicidal, and helping out locals who have been hit by unemployment or loss of income during the recession. The shop is also a drop-in centre, where people come to remember loved ones who died through suicide, or to talk to Kay and Denise about problems that sometimes seem insurmountable. Kay talks freely about her own experiences around loss and suicide, and the way that she somehow managed to turn tragedy and heartbreak into a

beacon of light and inspiration for the entire community of Enniscorthy:

> When you lose two sons to suicide you look on life differently. You take nothing for granted. We started the shop for everyone, no matter what colour, creed or nationality. Locals call in to us, but we also have callers from all over the globe, people who spot our shop from the road and are drawn to call in. Some people make donations. The money helps to pay for our two counsellors, and for the twenty-four-hour helpline and text service we run. We also have local volunteers who help out. Sometimes we're asked to talk to local schools or colleges about suicide. It's important that people talk about suicide. Some people are carrying around a secret of suicide in the family for decades. There are too many secrets and too much stigma around suicide. When my sons died, none of my neighbours would come out the door the same time as me. They were afraid they'd say something that would hurt me. But now I've learned that we need to talk. I'd say to someone bereaved 'It's a nice day today' just to break the ice.
>
> When we started up the shop in 2007 we were just two ordinary women who joined together and put everything into our work. We trusted in a higher power to help us. I believe the body goes into the ground but the spirit lives on. When I lost my James and then my Harry, I could have turned to drink or I could have jumped in the river. I could have become full of anger. There's no use though in blaming anyone. You have to put your energy into something constructive and turn the negative into positive. We've gone from strength to strength. We treat people with respect and we're always there to listen to anyone who needs to talk. We just try to send out the message that somebody does care. One man calls in every so often. He's tried to take his life seven times. He goes away, gets the idea of suicide again in another few weeks, and then comes back to talk to us. We're always there when someone needs a shoulder to cry on.
>
> When we started the shop, some people who had trained in the mental health area told us we should be ashamed for setting up a

shop that draws people who are suicidal, or who want to talk about their losses through suicide, because we weren't trained. We've never received any support or funding from any politicians or from the HSE. The community here is very supportive and we love people getting involved. People do fundraising for us. Every penny is given back to the people who need it. People often call in for tea and toast and a chat. We want to see a smile on their faces on the way out.

Wexford Marine Watch: Interview with Mayor George Lawlor

In the context of Marine Watch what we're doing is not really the approach that is usually taken in the area of suicide prevention. We certainly refer people to counselling afterwards but firstly it creates an atmosphere of a community watching out, and I think this is the more important reason why it's been successful. That's much more important than any intervention we will ever do because the interventions are quite minimal. If you consider that in the three years prior to Marine Watch setting up, there were fifty-three jumps off Wexford Bridge, that's now just about down to zero. We're not walking along grabbing someone by the arm. We're sending out the message that there's an organisation manned by volunteers within the community, people all around us who care enough to do something and that means they actually care about you.

Initially, there were people who were sceptical about the project and there were those who wanted to see it fail. Obviously these were a small minority. When Wexford Marine Watch was set up there was a huge wave of support in the community for it, and there still is. People are greatly admired for being involved in the organisation. It's as if society is saying, 'By my supporting this organisation, either financially or with words of support, that's my contribution to tackling suicide.' I think society wants to help but in another sense it doesn't want to get involved, much because of the stigma attached to suicide and the old religious connotations. So, if society sees an organisation, be it Marine Watch or The Samaritans, and people can support and contribute, then they feel they're doing their bit to help.

However, even in their own homes they may be contributing to the reverse, contributing to people's strife or stress through a lack of awareness of the difficulties that people find themselves in.

One of the things that legitimised Wexford Marine Watch and gave us credibility from the start, was that we got all the relevant agencies on board: the Gardaí, the Ambulance Service, the RNLI, the Coast Guard, we got representatives from the local authorities and from businesses, and that immediately gave credibility to the organisation. There's a perception that if people of importance are involved it must be good! The local authorities have been extremely supportive. We wouldn't be able to function without their support. So that's what I would say to communities: get people who are respected and credible to be part of it. It's also important never to lose sight of what Wexford Marine Watch is all about, that our first and foremost duty of care must be to combat suicides in the Wexford Harbour area.

One of the things that has made us successful is that the people involved are ordinary run-of-the-mill guys and girls, people within the community who everyone can identify with, as being an ordinary factory worker, not a psychologist, just an ordinary person, with no qualifications in the area of counselling. So that makes Johnny down the road say to himself, 'I'm feeling this way but my friend down the road is with the Marine Watch, and he's sending out a message that he cares about me.' That for me is the very basic bottom-up approach. It's where communities are taking hold of the problem. The person who is contemplating suicide because of financial stress or whatever can see that the person doing the walking up and down the quay could be in the same boat, but this person is sending out the message that there is another way out.

Loughmore Community Shop and Tea Rooms
Loughmore Community Shop and Tea Rooms is a cooperative business that was set up in Loughmore, Co. Tipperary in 2012 by Mary Fogarty and Maeve O'Hair. So many services and businesses had closed down in the village that rural isolation was becoming a

sad reality. Villagers missed the social interaction that had once been a feature of village life, and those in rural areas were feeling completely cut off from their neighbours. Mary Fogarty and Maeve O'Hair became determined to set up some form of business to revive the spirit of the village. They discovered the work of the Horace Plunkett Foundation, based in England, whose model they decided to adopt. Maeve's sister offered them an eighteenth-century cottage located in the village. The villagers were invited to become shareholders in the new cooperative. The response from the entire community was very positive. The cottage was finally opened on 23 August 2012. The co-op employs three people, has twelve volunteers and is open seven days a week.

Mary Fogarty comments that:

It is a prime example of a community working together for its benefit. We now have the most beautiful and idyllic little shop and tea rooms and we are very proud of it … Everything we did to set up the business was done on a local level. We got local tradesmen to do all the work and purchased all our furniture from local suppliers. This meant a lot to them in these hard times. It is truly lovely to see the wheels of our cooperative in motion. We have nine food producers and ten craftspeople involved. All our food and crafts are supplied from within a five-mile radius of the cottage.

PART FOUR

Towards a New Perspective

CHAPTER TWENTY-FOUR

A Prerequisite for Social Change

Thank you for walking with us through the black and white world we have come to know. Hopefully, we have succeeded in making the Suicide Box visible to you, showed how it was constructed over time and how its dismantling is possible. What we present to you now will, we believe, allow the full spectrum of colour into our world and help bring an end to the social mediocrity, anxiety and pain in so many people's lives. This is the world that both Jennifer and Seán, who we presented to you earlier, deserve to inhabit in order to blossom, to delight in being alive and to experience all the variety and possibilities that life has to offer. If, after taking this journey with us, you are still content with your lot within the Suicide Box, then at least you will have made an informed decision. However, for those of us who dearly wish to create a better world by reducing unnecessary human pain, let us now experience what it could be like, if we adopt a New Perspective that attempts to achieve this.

While every society has a unique mix of social and cultural factors that facilitate unnecessary human pain and suicide, we use Ireland as our example. We do this, not just because of our familiarity with Ireland, but also because of its appalling history of allowing unnecessary human pain to be inflicted on its citizens, and its high ranking for suicides among all the countries in the world. During the dismantling of the key social structures from within the Suicide Box, several core issues were highlighted that are crucial to address in developing a new paradigm. These include: the need for a bottom-up, community model; the continual education of all sectors of society, particularly in the area of emotional intelligence; the requirement that a complete shift in thinking and awareness takes place in every sphere of public and private life. Special emphasis must be placed on emotional intelligence, as deficits in this area leave individuals vulnerable to bullying, self-harm, depression and suicide.

Individual Responsibility

Many individual responsibilities have also emerged throughout this book that are central to creating a new inclusive society if we are to reduce unnecessary human pain. These request that we:

✣ Allow the process of change to unfold.

✣ Embrace suicide as part of the human condition.

✣ Acknowledge and accept our collective responsibility for past wrongs.

✣ Be flexible instead of being rigid and judgemental in our thinking.

✣ Choose change rather than accepting continuity.

✣ Embrace the complexity of human nature, rather than simplify or 'box' life.

✣ Be prepared to examine and alter our attitudes.

✣ Balance reason with emotion.

✣ Acknowledge the link between suicide and unnecessary human pain.

✣ Maintaining an holistic view of the person.

A Model of Change for Ireland

As we have proposed, a bottom-up approach has to be activated to achieve success in a model for change. This may involve forming collaboration committees wherever possible in every county, town and village to develop an understanding of a new, inclusive approach to community life. A major part of this process is to invite active participation from those who are ostracised and marginalised by society. Obviously, due to generational damage, time will have to be allowed for this adjustment. An important principal will be to empower and break the cycle of learned helplessness that society fosters. Collaboration committees will be a fair representation of all possible service providers and delegates from all communities to express a reality of life today. Proven social entrepreneurs and campaigners, who express many of the ideas in this book already are ideally suited to empower communities to engage in the process. Care needs to be taken that the self-serving megalomaniacs among us are prevented from taking control. They, like flies, are attracted to the light. They may be entertaining, but once we hand over our power to them, destruction of the model would be assured. The focus on reducing unnecessary human pain must not be lost.

In many ways the 'Understanding Its Construction' section in this book represents society's appalling history, right up to today, in terms of the problems created by our social structures for individuals within the Suicide Box. The 'Dismantling Its Structure' section began to deconstruct these structures, to highlight areas of change that are most crucial to reduce unnecessary pain, including suicide. The New Perspective is an attempt to look differently at problem areas that were created within the Suicide Box. This includes examples of the work that can be done in key areas of society. There is no limit to the creativity that can be ignited to achieve inclusivity and to instil a sense of belonging within communities. We accept that our suggestions may pale in the light of the creative solutions that are to come, as at times of necessity human beings are capable of great inspiration. Based on the pandemic levels of unnecessary human pain that exist among us, change is necessary and high levels of inspiration are required.

CHAPTER TWENTY-FIVE
Evolving a New Perspective

The New Perspective involves a fresh approach to education, and to familial and social interactions. The objective is to help free up individuals to be more real with themselves and others; to recognise the importance of emotional expression; to consider all aspects of the human condition and to embrace human diversity in all its forms. Ultimately, achieving this vision would mean acquiring insights to explain our pain; showing empathy and compassion to all those who have suffered unnecessary human pain, and instilling empathy in those who have been empowered to abuse within the Suicide Box.

Achieving more meaningful results will invariably mean adopting new approaches, New Perspectives and new practices. These will not be focused on suicide per se, but on behaviours and practices that facilitate or enable suicide in society. Applying the principal of viewing suicide as part of a spectrum of human pain, and not as a stand-alone phenomenon, gives us greater scope to look more closely at ourselves, our society and our culture. From our investigation of the Suicide Box, our perception of suicide is clearly based on fear that is fuelled by stigma and myth. Little change can be accomplished within this view. Instead, we have to break through the wall of denial and learn to accept the painful fact that suicide is part of our complex human nature. This is not to condone or accept suicide, but no longer to deny it or react in shock when it occurs. Embracing suicide and acknowledging our personal responsibilities will enable us to take our social empathy to new heights and bring about change at crucial stages in people's lives. We can then examine the factors external to the individual that constrict his or her choices towards the development of efficacy and meaningfulness in life. In practical terms, we aim to offer pointers as to how these aspirations may be achieved. These are far from exhaustive and are merely intended as suggestions. Ultimately, a change in our ways of thinking about mental health and suicide is required at societal, community and individual levels.

A Social Blueprint

The following sections outline a social blueprint that focuses on the main changes required in the social structures as previously discussed. Within this New Perspective change occurs at all levels of society. This change is facilitated and driven by the community and gradually filters down to individual lives. For maximum effect, we have chosen to write this section as though transformation and social awareness has already occurred and we are now reaping the benefits.

Political and Economic Policies

Since Irish society has adopted the New Perspective to reduce the unnecessary human pain that had become inherent within the adopted system, politicians have acknowledged and admitted their powerlessness to deal with suicide. This is a human problem and, hence, governments, which focus almost exclusively on economic affairs, have little empathy or energy to facilitate human interventions. However, as truth became exposed, the Irish government discovered its political heart and released the power into the hands of organised, caring community members, and then supported them.

Spirituality

While much healing still needs to take place from the historical effects of religious cruelty, most especially on those who were unable to continue living due to intolerable pain, so much has been achieved by religious groups as the healing continues. The true basis of religious purpose has been rediscovered and this message of love has facilitated true spiritual development. Many religions have embraced this new wave of change. For example, in his document *The Joy of the Gospel*, Pope Francis challenges himself – and us – with three questions: First, 'why not look at things from a New Perspective?' Second, 'why not be open to doing things in a new way?' And third, 'why not have a new vision for the Church?' (Martin, 2013). Programmes of healing for people who still suffer from unnecessary human pain are well received by participants, regardless of their religious persuasion. Such programmes have proved to be powerful in heightening social empathy and awareness around suicide and other tragedies, and have been easily adapted throughout Ireland. The main aim of these groups is to help relieve people from the deep feelings of isolation and loneliness that can often be felt, following the sudden and unexpected death of a loved one. The support of enlightened spiritual practices provides great solace for all concerned. With full community and spiritual support, the suicide bereaved are allowed to fully grieve, until the overwhelming pain subsides and they feel ready to return to life without the physical presence of their loved one. In schools and in communities the recognition and nurture of the spiritual dimension of each person is fostered. Churches are slowly accepting and empowering this reality in all people. They have also separated the loving messages that are central to all religions, from the earthly, agenda-based ones. Levels of social empathy, love, compassion, tolerance and forgiveness have all risen notably as people now own their spirituality and have a direct relationship with their loving God.

The Law

Under the newly adopted societal approach great efforts have been made to humanise how people are treated under the country's laws. The whole legal system is under review to try to make the system fairer. Those who were most resistant to change, mainly due to personal advantage and power, were identified as obstacles to progress, and are slowly becoming redundant, as the social benefits of the restorative approach have become apparent. Wherever possible, restorative solutions are now being implemented. The emphasis is on inclusivity, restoration and the healing of lives. The application of a restorative approach within prisons has proven to be especially fruitful. Creating a sentence plan for every offender as they enter prison has resulted in each being actively involved in their personal development. Deficits from all aspects of their lives are explored, as well as unexplored gifts and talents. On release, individuals are describing greater positivity about their integration back into society.

Since it was found that some young people had taken their lives after getting into difficulty with the law for the first time, mainly under the influence of alcohol, police are now cognisant of such factors. They are trained to make every effort to ensure that their work does not adversely affect people's lives. Similarly, great strides have been made to soften the coldness of legal practices and to help raise social empathy. For example, the inquest system has been transformed. Neutral buildings have been acquired at little cost and are used to conduct inquests in an atmosphere of compassion and dignity. While incidents of suicide have become much rarer than the Suicide Box era, the inquest process now reflects society's acceptance that a loss through suicide is a failure for everyone, not just a particular family. As ignorance of stigma and myth is largely eradicated, families no longer feel the awful social consequences of suicide that prevailed within the Suicide Box.

Holistic Well-being

The Irish government has finally implemented the new recovery model. Its planned installation by 2015 failed due to resistance, mainly from some clinicians' difficulty in relinquishing their power bases and practices, enjoyed under the former medical model. However, knowledge of the destruction of the medical model became too public to ignore and the new model was finally implemented. Its new name 'Holistic Well-being' reflects the 'whole' view of a person that sets the service user at the centre of the process, with the primary objective of restoring him or her back to optimum health, within an environment that is conducive to happiness and development. There is continuing support and empowerment available until recovery and adjustment is complete. This is a reflection and an acknowledgement that the person is more than just a physical entity. Care is delivered from a multidimensional view, in full recognition of service users' constant transactional relationship with their environment. Mental health problems that people present are accepted as part of the human condition. The new recovery model has effectively broken down all stigma and fears relating to any dysfunction of the mind. Community involvement by the excellently trained and empathic Holistic Well-being teams has raised social understanding to new, remarkable levels. The old days that reflected a 'sick' society, with hospitals bursting at the seams and patients languishing on trolleys are long gone. The new model is focused on the individual's recovery. The former unhealthy overuse of medication and the unwise, constricted diagnosis of patients have been consigned to the annals of the country's negative history.

Education

While the government's former position advocated full responsibility to schools for dealing with issues such as bullying, they relented on this, due to new understandings and research. The addition of such a mammoth task to an already preoccupied teaching staff, whose focus was on developing the individual needs of students, meant that the new approach adopted had to involve a genuine community effort. This has been standardised throughout all Irish educational institutions, with schools feeling supported, and parents being fully involved. The bottom-up, government-supported approach has had resounding success, especially with the added boost of compassionate capitalism, where local businesses have rallied to support the new programmes. Many businesses have described their involvement as the best investment they ever made.

The newly implemented whole-school/community programmes have not focused narrowly on phenomena, such as bullying, as unsocial behaviours are now viewed as mere symptoms of an overall societal dysfunction. Instead, new programmes focus on the raising of awareness around destructive attitudes and beliefs. They outline the required responsibilities of all parties in the community in interesting and fun ways. This involves participatory practices for students, teachers, parents, school management, and ancillary staff. Features include the development of positive communication, emotional awareness, restorative solutions, and simple mindfulness practices that are formulated from global research and best practices worldwide. This has helped to develop a greater social conscious-ness, emphasising the importance of seeing ourselves holistically, as more than just physical beings. This also involves learning how the mind and the emotional systems work, to develop children's emotional expression and their awareness of the importance of self-care. Due to the many changes adopted, the long-term effects began to show sooner than expected. Resolving bullying behaviour in early stages and focusing empathically on the child perpetrator has had the dramatic effect of almost eliminating bullying behaviour in later school years. It is expected that this trend will continue, with reductions in crime, domestic abuse, incidents of societal aggression and workplace bullying, saving Ireland many millions annually.

Within the Suicide Box the almost total focus of education was on academic achievement, while the other dimensions were ignored for the majority of children. Likewise, the convergent and assimilator styles of learning were formerly favoured while other styles were ignored, leading to the development of teaching methods that only suited a minority of students. When these practices began to change, many children became empowered to explore their individual abilities, and a new, confident nation metamorphosed. The acceptance that the deficiency of emotional intelligence within the educational system fostered the existence of unnecessary human pain and suicide, was the main motivator for change. Trying to eradicate only the symptoms of deep underlying social problems, such as bullying, secret self-harming and suicide would always have been doomed to failure, unless the true causes of pain were acknowledged and transformed.

Our distorted confusion between what constitutes religion and spirituality has, after recent religious turmoil, left many in a spiritual void. Accepting that our spiritual dimension is vital for our well-being and has little to do with organised religion, was an important development for the Irish people. The negative elements of organised religions were hard to break. Schools finally made the distinction between a person's spiritual self and an external religious affiliation. Religious practices can now be appreciated in all their beauty and love, as God's word proposes at the core of every religious text. Rather than lose the means to strengthen spiritual development in children, ways were found to invigorate and develop their spiritual dimension, to help them to get in touch with divine aspects of themselves.

Work

The evidence presented in this book regarding the levels of unhappiness at work while within the Suicide Box is startling. Much of the unhappiness of employees was due to them opting for careers unsuited to their innate talents. Forces that directed their choices included the number of points they obtained in their final exam in school, the stress induced by having to seek higher-paid positions, and the problem of finding an appropriate match for their abilities and talents. Much of the unhappiness and unnecessary human pain was caused by workplace abuse, disrespect, lack of dignity, and lack of appreciation at work. This quickly led to burnout and apathy for vast numbers of employees. The government's acceptance of its responsibility for so much pain has brought laws and firm guidelines into workplace practices, to disable the behaviour of unscrupulous business customs and force compassion into the capitalist mindset. The management style that balances happiness in the workplace with profitability has been implemented nationwide. Happiness levels are notably higher and rising with each survey. The business world is delighted with the development as happier workers have led to an increase in production rates of between 20 and 35 per cent.

Psychologists have effectively found ways to ensure that socially unskilled people, who are drawn to management roles to satisfy their need for power and control over others, are now identified during the interview processes. Employing 'sound' managers who can focus on the creation of happiness and profitability has been a major development in reducing unnecessary human pain at work. The dovetailing of human and economic needs into all business models and plans has served to greatly reduce unnecessary human pain within workplaces. The realisation that happy workforces produce up to 35 per cent more profits is a major reason for this. It seems that those businesses that genuinely adopt a long-term aim to achieve a balance between workers contentment and company profitability become the most progressive and successful.

Within the workplace, employers have encouraged the use of workshops and staff meetings to give workers a sense of belonging and meaning in their work. Encouraging firms to support community projects was difficult initially but, as sponsorship resulted in a win-win situation for all players, more and more businesses got involved. Through advertising and by showing that compassionate capitalism is possible, powerful and cost-effective, whole-school/community programmes have been implemented with local business sponsorship. This has resulted in positive culture-changing behaviours that have greatly reduced bullying behaviour and unnecessary human pain throughout society.

The Media

As Ireland has acknowledged and dismantled its Suicide Box, the media now plays a powerful role. The promotion of the country's efforts to bring about this powerfully positive societal shift with a responsible approach to reporting, has propagated the required attitudes, and instilled confidence where it was waning. Instead of being accused of irresponsible journalism or held liable for contagion when copycat suicides occur, the media has become a powerful force for constructive transformation. The media has played a pivotal role in creating waves of positive change that have taken place in many connected ways throughout the country. The new ethos of reporters and journalists to report on stories that are of interest to the public, while taking into account sensitivity and empathy around human tragedies and misfortune has been applauded by all sectors of society.

The Family

The Irish family, after getting quite a battering through the ages from both Church and state, has emerged and blossomed under the New Perspective adopted. Families have learned to be wary of giving away their personal power into the hands of any earthly group and to trust in their personal ability to have a direct relationship with God. While an all-school/community programme connects with a great amount of families, it does not reach all of them. The plan includes, therefore, the training of skilled and passionate people to facilitate fun, educational workshops for communities to attend. The content of these workshops is not directly about suicide prevention, but is focused on those unhelpful attitudes and behaviours that facilitate unnecessary human pain, and contribute to suicide. Established programmes such as SafeTalk, Assist, and Question-Persuade-Respond (QPR), though delayed social responses to suicide prevention, continue to be powerful educational and crisis-prevention tools. However, the more proactive work is being achieved through the recruitment of trained volunteers throughout Ireland. Their selection and training is thorough to ensure that they have a clear understanding of the overall plan, its purpose and its application in society. Courses for couples who decide to form partnerships and raise children have become widely available. In the past, it was assumed that all parents possessed these important skills, but history has proven this to be otherwise. The skills now widely available include: the development of parenting skills, such as how to form a family plan; how to develop effective 'hearing' skills; resolving emotional issues utilising effective support; holistic human awareness; and learning to cope with children's challenging behaviours constructively and calmly.

Parenting (Family Plan)

Forming a family plan was first proposed by Dr Fergus Heffernan and its inclusion in the New Perspective made real sense. This prepares couples, who plan to raise children together, to develop meaningful responses to various issues and crises. A main contributor to much family trauma is the lack of preparedness to deal with crises as they arise. The uniqueness of each family is never lost when couples agree to devise a family plan together. They work on potentially difficult situations that may be encountered, discussing any number of hypothetical situations, so that they are prepared for many common problems and even crisis scenarios. Issues commonly discussed include how the family constructively expresses emotions, including anger, jealousy, sadness and anxiety. Developing important skills are part of the plan and these include: basic listening skills to learn to truly *hear* their child and each other; awareness of the effects of unresolved negative issues for the developing child in later life; the importance of allowing the expression of emotions; the importance of understanding how a child's brain develops, such as how it does not reach full emotional maturity until the age of thirty (Blakemore, 2005); and how overprotective behaviour can disempower children, leaving them with poor empathy abilities, lower levels of resilience, and greater vulnerability to stress.

The Child (Zero to Five Years Old)

The discovery of the vulnerability of the child, particularly from birth to five years old, was truly shocking. To deal with this problem a comprehensive, confidential and supportive programme of regular developmental visits has been set in place for every child until they begin school. Initially, there were some objections to this, with many claiming that Big Brother was watching them. However, when it became known that this was a case of real state empathy to protect children of this age, not just from neglect and death, but also from a lifetime of mental health issues due to abuse in the home, the programme became accepted and supported. Specially trained community nurses visit with children and their caregivers to ensure that their well-being is maintained. It has become an extremely useful programme as many medical problems have also been detected earlier than they would normally have been.

Community Change

The process of social change filtering from the bottom-up is a key concept of the New Perspective. In this way, individuals and communities hold great responsibility for being advocates of change, working together in a systematic way to reduce unnecessary pain and, therefore, suicide. Each community has heralded change for its own people, while also working in tandem with other communities throughout Ireland, sharing ideas, areas that need improvement, and their successes. The New Perspective that focuses on bringing balance to all members of the community through the acceptance that unnecessary pain can be fostered socially, and through the acceptance of collective responsibility for that fact, is now clearly understood. The diehard relics from the Suicide Box era who miss the power they wielded are easily identified now. They have become valuable reminders of why human beings need to progress to the next stage of evolution in a transactional relationship with our beautiful planet.

Methodologies to be Applied: General Population Approach

Meaningful results have been achieved in communities through the implementation of new approaches and practices. For example, the development of a plan for each county in Ireland was found to be the best way forward to meet each county's particular needs. This involved comprehensive and creative ways of developing social skills in families, schools and workplaces. These are not focused on bullying, self-harm or suicide but on behaviours and practices that facilitate or enable them to take hold in society. Destructive behaviours, such as bullying, boss behaviour, or ignorant attitudes, are all strongly advocated for change. Applying the principal of viewing suicide as part of a spectrum of human pain, and not as a stand-alone phenomenon, has given people greater latitude to look more closely at themselves, their society and their culture. This has led to the examination of factors that are external to the individual, and that constrict his or her choices towards the development of personal efficacy and meaning in life.

Adopting Positive Habits

Breaking the grip that alcohol has had on Irish society for aeons was a difficult task. The social acceptance and reliance on alcohol for social interactions had to be exposed. The process that Ireland had to undergo was similar to the work that an individual alcoholic has to go through in order to break his or her dependency. Research presented alcohol as a significant factor in many social ills, including suicide, crime, domestic violence, depression and self-harm, often at causal levels. Yet the denial was evident even at the highest level, as the Irish government chose, even in 2014, to allow ruthless alcohol advertisers to continue to present their attractive but highly destructive products at sporting events. Part of the difficult recovery period has involved helping society to adopt deferred gratification rather than the immediate-gratification attitude of old. This has powerfully transformed the Irish outlook towards alcohol, especially when included in the education of children. However, as in the

individual alcoholic analogy, a void appeared as alcohol consumption was reduced to normal, healthy levels. The introduction
of the new Holistic Well-being programmes in schools and within
communities has provided a complimentary alternative to fill this
void. The natural 'highs' achieved from exploring all aspects of
personal health development, such as nutritious food, individual
exercise programmes that are fun and flexible, creative activities that
foster the expression of people's natural abilities, and the availability
of mindfulness classes have become part of people's lives, helping
to free the Irish Nation from its alcohol dependence.

Volunteering
Great efforts have been made to tap into the vast pool of volunteers
available to help others in need. Volunteering has proven to be very
popular with elderly people who have so many skills and experience
to contribute to their communities. Under the New Perspective,
volunteer roles have been extended to areas where there was limited
services to the most vulnerable. This has been achieved in similar
ways to some of the features of the Garda Reserves. Problems, such
as demarcation, union issues, employee power and control, have
largely been set aside, in light of society's new levels of awareness
of social culpability for unnecessary human pain and even suicide.
This practice has become a powerful benefit, not just for service
users, but for volunteers and society as a whole. Under the New
Perspective, volunteers operate from the heart and not from the head
or the wallet. They regularly stand in until paid staff return to duty,
filling vital roles, especially helping to provide twenty-four-hour
caring 'human-presence' services to those who are most in need of
them.

There are safeguards for volunteers built in to the system to avoid
them being abused by unscrupulous managers and business owners.

Important lessons were learned from the Suicide Box era, such as, when many people on government schemes complained that employers gave them no training and were only using them to perform mundane tasks to benefit the company or department. Within the New Perspective, however, a high level of respect is given to volunteers. Their subsistence is paid where at all possible and they are given high levels of training in return for their care and diligence. The valuable experience that many volunteers have gained produces high quality and confident workers who quickly move into their chosen careers.

Social Inclusion

Past research demonstrated that our innate need to belong to a family, community and culture is a vital component for the development of personal resilience. The alienation of any individual or group is a major contributory factor to the onset of problems, such as alcohol and substance abuse, depression, self-harm, and suicide (Walker, 2008; The All Ireland Health Study, 2010). In the New Perspective, it has therefore been imperative to introduce cultural studies to schools that depict minority traditions in a positive light. When these programmes were implemented, the importance of social inclusion was gradually embraced by students and cultural diversity was celebrated in its many hues. This has been particularly vital to the development of young people, where discussions and dialogue now take place in an environment of learning and inquiry. A decline in narrow-minded thinking, stereotyping and half-baked beliefs has occurred around human differences. Since self-esteem is closely linked to how others perceive their family and culture, a celebration of each child's culture and heritage has added significantly to individual feelings of self-worth.

Changes among communities throughout Ireland have been absorbed into society as a whole. Currently, many communities are far advanced in their ways of thinking and in their practical approaches to organising voluntary groups in the prevention of societal causes of unnecessary human pain. These groups recognise the need for a caring and visible presence in certain suicide black spots, while also providing a means of social inclusion, and a focus on reducing social isolation, particularly in rural areas.

Media interviewers have embraced the new awareness of unnecessary human pain and have adopted a whole new way of communicating when confronted with caustic, destructive opinions. Such instances are calmly welcomed as opportunities to weed out those attitudes and opinions that have been directly responsible for maintaining the Suicide Box in its diseased state. The interviewees are no longer left thinking that they are 'entitled' to their corrosive opinion without being made fully aware of the consequences of what that entitlement means.

The success of these social endeavours has resulted in a great reduction of deaths by suicide and a downward trend continues. Communities have had great success in changing destruction opinions and attitudes. Thus, the problems caused by stereotyping, gossiping and discrimination are included in a series of fun and informative community-wide projects that the whole family can take part in. These include art exhibitions, theme weeks and drama presentations that show a direct connection between lethal attitudes and behaviours, and the increase in unnecessary human pain that often ends in suicide.

Diversity

The use of labels to describe minorities reflected more about society than it did about the people identified within these groups. Within the new paradigm, people have begun to actively seek ways to include others rather than to segregate them, as they embrace the complexity of human nature. In contrast to society within the Suicide Box, those now on the periphery of society are those who have been unable to lose their caustic attitudes or to adopt the inclusivity of society's new structure. In trying to undo the terrible damage where people were once stereotyped and marginalised due to race, sexual orientation, age, membership of certain groups, etc., active efforts are now being made to empower and involve them, to see the extent of their humanity, beyond the labels and boxes that they had been squeezed into. Ireland has already shown to the world its new all-embracing attitude in a public referendum to make marriage inclusive by recognising the love of same sex couples. Fears and biases continue to abate as people become socially and culturally educated. When community groups are being established, members of previously marginalised groups are invited and encouraged to be representatives, as the concept of real change is embraced.

Relationships
It was during the dismantling phase of the Suicide Box that Irish society became truly aware of the power of the skewed and twisted brainwashing it had received, mainly through the fearful patriarchal and ungodly teachings of a trusted church. The fears around sexuality made relationships and everything sexual seem perverted and deviant. Teachers were uncomfortable talking about relationships, and students, feeling the discomfort around sexuality, were set to continue society's dysfunctional and immature views that kept them ignorant of the true beauty and extent of human interactions.

As the New Perspective took hold in Ireland, social maturity began to blossom around an understanding of relationships. Quite quickly the realisation occurred that sexuality is just one part of a human relationship. Teaching about relationships became a joy, as teachers no longer presented them in one-dimensional terms, but always in the full light of human complexity. Students are now being prepared for life without having to sort through the subliminal fears that society had been giving for centuries with its skewed messages. Sexuality is now enjoyed as part of a deeper expression of love in relationships. Young people can explore the many factors that lead to healthy relationships, such as the powerful effects of unconditional love, mutual respect, and maintaining an holistic view of partnership as an ever-deepening friendship. This approach began to counteract the former damaging effects of society. Girls can now see through ruthless media and fashion industry efforts to objectify them and these once powerful institutions are quickly losing their destructive power. There is a female confidence building like never before, as women no longer have to compete with some external judgement of beauty, but can maximise their inner beauty. Boys have also been liberated by these insights. Being aware that females have many dimensions, not just physical and sexual, has enhanced boys' ability to interact with girls and to eliminate internal conflicts, confusion and rejection. This new approach greatly reduces self-loathing and raises self-esteem. Seeing ourselves and others in the light of all human dimensions has resulted in far fewer incidents of abuse and self-harm in Ireland.

The Elderly
In the New Perspective, due weight is given to the rights and needs of all citizens to direct their lives. In residential homes, programmes that inspire creativity and wellness are now offered to all residents. Each caring home also has a committee, comprised of elected residents, family representatives, community leaders and advocates.

These committees monitor the policies and practices of the home and deal with any complaints or suggestions that residents may have. Residents are empowered to organise their environment by arranging their own furniture, choosing their own wall pictures, tending their own plants, arranging outings, being members of active groups, such as those dedicated to gardening, singing, drama, etc. Thus, elderly residents in care homes feel useful, valued, respected and independent.

Self-Care

It has been a long struggle for individuals to begin to understand their true nature and to develop the awareness to live a positive life, instead of sabotaging their own happiness through poor relationships, work that doesn't satisfy, or behaviours that cause harm. Even within the New Perspective, there are times when people feel that their own thoughts conspire against them, making them feel inadequate, foolish, and not good enough. Shame, anger, sadness and desperation may lurk behind a happy-go-lucky façade that we turn to the world. Sometimes thoughts of suicide can loom, with false notions that those who love us will be better off without us. These thoughts can grow louder and stronger, until some kind of plan is hatched from a place deep inside where all our unexpressed pain has been stashed over a lifetime. No matter how much pain has gathered, no matter how many negative thoughts have accumulated, the mind can be restored to balance and our emotions can be healed. The simple truth is that it is never too late to teach oneself what society failed to teach and even kept from us: how to understand the workings of the mind and emotions; how to value and take care of the whole self; how to live, love and thrive, despite the failings of the world around us.

A central tenet of the New Perspective is to develop tools of self-care and resilience in every individual. The new emphasis on emotional intelligence, mindfulness, the workings of the mind and emotions, and programmes on self-care in education have transformed the ability of individuals to live a more balanced and holistic life, while also enjoying the expression of their unique set of talents. Certainly the individual now lives in a much more caring society, where values such as respect, self-expression and being true to oneself are espoused. Within education, every child learns the cornerstone of maintaining emotional health and well-being: learning to respect and value every unique facet that you possess. Children's education is also realistic, however, and far from hiding the fact that disappointments and setbacks are part of every life, emphasis is placed on ways that young people can learn to solve problems, to give and receive support, and to practise ways of balancing and healing troubled emotions. There are activities that young people now learn that can be built into their daily lives to enhance the good times and to help them through difficult experiences. Young people are also taught to be aware of their multifaceted nature and to ensure that all these parts are being tended to. Finally, there is the ability to create and to recreate meaning in life throughout the many changes and transitions that we encounter in our life cycle.

The Future with Hope

We thank you for making this journey with us as we explored the phenomenon of suicide from a very broad perspective. Feeling suicidal or losing a loved one to suicide are experiences no person should have to endure. Our aim has been to explode the topic of suicide beyond its tethered boundaries. We hope that you take away some of the important tenets of this book: that much of the pain felt by people is unnecessary and is often facilitated by external factors; that we often unconsciously enable unnecessary pain for others by ignoring or passively accepting social wrongs; that we can help raise social empathy through education and awareness; that modelling self-care by nurturing your personal power in all dimensions of your being gives power to others to follow that example. It is only then that you may recognise the role you can play, to create a world where people can maximise their multi-dimensional potential and become all that you are meant to be.

All That You Are

Don't allow this crazy world to destroy you.
There is still inherent beauty all around you,
In every shell, in every blade of grass.

Don't let society control you,
Your thoughts, feelings and inner soul.
Teach yourself to value all that you are.
Your task on earth is to awaken,
To know your true self
Then to share your truth.

See beyond the madness that dwells in darkness,
Always trapped in the mind.
Dare to set the past aside
To embrace this moment,
For only now you can be free.

Feel the laughter and the pain:
All is passing through you
Like wind rustling amid the leaves
Like water flowing in a stream.
Feel the breath move through your wondrous body
Bringing to life the deep mystery that you are.

Look upwards and glitter with the stars;
Look outwards and marvel at the ocean;
Look downwards and dance across the earth;
Look inwards and behold your dazzling light.

Beyond it all
There you are:
Resplendent.
Radiant,
Eternal.

Helpful Contacts

Alcoholics Anonymous
www.alcoholicsanonymous.ie   01 8420700

Aware, Helping to Defeat Depression
www.aware.ie   01 661 7211

Childline Online Support
www.childline.ie   1800 666666

Console, the Bereaved by Suicide Foundation
www.console.ie   1800 247247

Drug and Alcohol Information and Support
www.drugs.ie   1800 459459

Gay and Lesbian Equality Network
www.glen.ie   01 6728650

Grow (world community mental health movement in Ireland)
www.grow.ie   1890 474 474

Irish Association of Suicidology
www.ias.ie   01 667 4900

Living Links (outreach for the suicide bereaved)
www.livinglinks.ie   087 4122052

Mental Health Ireland
www.mentalhealthireland.ie   01 284 1166

National Suicide Research Foundation
www.nsrf.ie   021 4205551

Pieta House (centre for the prevention of self-harm or suicide)
www.pieta.ie   01 6235606

Samaritans, UK and Ireland
www.samaritans.org   116 123

See Change (Ireland's new national partnership to reduce stigma
and challenge discrimination associated with mental health
problems)
www.seechange.ie   01 8601620

Third Age (elderly helpline)
www.thirdageireland.ie   1850 440444

National Traveller Suicide Awareness Project
www.travellersuicide.ie   01 8721094

Turning the Tide of Suicide
www.3Ts.ie   01 2139905

References

3Ts: http://www.3ts.ie/about/who-are-3ts/

Adinkrah, M. (2000), 'Maternal infanticides in Fiji', *Child Abuse & Neglect*, 24:1543–55.

Centers for Disease Control and Prevention, USA, *Adverse Childhood Experiences (ACE) Study* (1995–7).

Alcohol Action Ireland, 'Almost half of the perpetrators of homicide were intoxicated when the crime was committed', Alcohol Action Ireland, http://alcoholireland.ie/facts/case-studies-kids/, accessed 2 September 2014.

Alvarez, A. (2013), *The Savage God: A Study of Suicide* (London: Bloomsbury).

American Foundation for Suicide Prevention, 'Suicide Warning Signs', American Foundation for Suicide Prevention, http://www.afsp.org/preventing-suicide/suicide-warning-signs.

Amnesty International (2012), *The State Decides Who I Am: Lack of Legal, Gender Recognition for Transgender People in Europe* (London: Amnesty International).

Angermeyer, M.C., Matschinger H. (1995), 'Violent attacks on public figures by persons suffering from psychiatric disorders: Their effect on the social distance towards the mentally ill', *European Archives of Psychiatry and Clinical Neuroscience*, 245:159–64.

Anspaugh, D., Hamrick, M., Rosato, F. (2004), *Wellness: Concepts and Applications* (6th edn) (Boston: McGraw Hill), cited in G. Miller and L. Foster (2010), 'A brief summary of holistic wellness literature', *Journal of Holistic Healthcare*, 7(1):4–8.

Anti-Bullying Centre, www.abc.ie.

Appleby, L., Mortensen, P.B., Faragher, E.B. (1998), 'Suicides and other causes of mortality after post-partumpsychiatric admission', *British Journal of Psychiatry*, 173:209–11.

Arensman, E., McAuliffe, C., Corcoran, P., Williamson, E., O'Shea, E., Perry, I. (2012), *First Report of the Suicide Support and Information System* (Cork: National Suicide Research Foundation).

Arensman, E., Wall, A., McAuliffe, C., Corcoran, P., Williamson, E., McCarthy, J., Duggan. A., Perry, I. (2013), *Second Report of the Suicide Support and Information System* (Cork: National Suicide Research Foundation).

Aubrey, J.S., Taylor, L.D. (2009), 'The role of lad magazines in priming men's chronic and temporary appearance-related schemata: An investigation of longitudinal and experimental findings', *Human Communication Research*, 35:28–58.

Aurelius, M. [c. 170] (2006), *Meditations*, trans. Martin Hammond, (New York: Penguin Classics).

Australian Health Ministers Advisory Council (2013), *A National Framework for Recovery-oriented Mental Health Services: Policy and Theory* (Australia: Australian Health Ministers Advisory Council).

Beck, A.T, Rush, A.J., Shaw, B.F., Emery, G. (1979), *Cognitive Therapy of Depression* (New York: The Guilford Press).

Bedford, D., O'Farrell, A., Howell, F. (2004), *Blood alcohol levels in persons who died as a result of accidents and suicide in Cavan, Monaghan and Louth in 2001 and 2002* (Ireland: North Eastern Health Board).

Berrocal, P.F., Salovey, P., Vera, A., Extremera, N., Ramos, N. (2005), 'Cultural influences on the relation between perceived emotional intelligence and depression', *International Review of Social Psychology*, 18:91–107.

Beutler, L.E., Engle, D., Oro-Beutler, M.E., Daldrup, R., Meridith, K. (1986), 'Inability to Express Intense Affect: A Common Link between Depression and Pain?', *Journal of Consulting and Clinical Psychology*, 54:752–9.

Biddle, L. (2003), 'Public hazards or private tragedies? An exploratory study of the effect of coroners' procedures on those bereaved by suicide', *Social Science & Medicine*, 56:1033–45.

Blake, R., Mouton, J. [1964] (1985), *The Managerial Grid III: The Key to Leadership Excellence* (Houston: Gulf Publishing Company).

275

Blakemore, S.J., Frith, U. (2005), *The Learning Brain: Lessons for Education* (London: Wiley-Blackwell).

Bleed, J. (2007), 'Howell's life insurance payout not a sure bet', *Arkansas Democrat-Gazette*, 19 February 2007.

Blom, A., Bracaille, L., and Martinez, L. (eds) (2007), *The Enigma of Islamist Violence* (London: Hurst and Co.)

Bluebird, G. (2008), *Paving New Ground: Peers Working in In-patient Settings* (Alexandria, VA: National Technical Assistance Center, National Association of State Mental Health Program Directors).

Boulton, M.J., Underwood, K. (1992), 'Bully/victim problems among middle school children', *British Journal of Educational Psychology*, 62:73–87.

Brent, D.A, Perper, J.A. (1995), 'Research in adolescent suicide: implication for training, service delivery and public policy', *Suicide Life Threat Behaviour*, 25:222–30.

Brosschot, J.F., Thayer, J.F. (1998), 'Anger Inhibition, Cardiovascular Recovery, and Vagal Function: A Model of the link between Hostility and Cardiovascular Disease', *Annals of Behavioural Medicine*, 20:326–32.

Carty, E. (2014), '2,400 Reports of Elderly Abuse last year', *The Irish Examiner*, 2 September 2014.

Braithwaite, J. (2002), *Restorative Justice and Responsive Regulation, Studies in Crime and Public Policy* (New York: Oxford University Press).

276

Bunn, A., Guthrie, R. (2010), 'Stress Testing the Banks: An Examination of Some of the Legal Issues Relating to Workplace Stress and Mental Harm within the Banking Industry', *Journal of Applied Law and Policy*, 3:105–21.

Center for Adolescent Health, John Hopkins Bloomberg School of Public Health (2006), *Confronting Teen Stress, Meeting the Challenge in Baltimore City: A Guide for Parents, Teachers, & Youth Service Providers* (Baltimore: The Prevention Research Centers Program, National Center for Chronic Disease Prevention and Health Promotion of the Centers for Disease Control and Prevention (CDC)).

Centers for Disease Control and Prevention (2012).

Chen, Y-Y, Chien-Chang Wu, K., Yousuf, S., Yip, Paul S.F. (2011), 'Suicide in Asia: Opportunities and Challenges', *Epidemiologic Reviews*, 34(1):129–44:10.1093/epirev/mxr025.

Child and Family Agency Act (2013), Dublin.

Childline (2011), Dublin.

Chinman, M.J., Young, A.S., Hassell, J., Davidson, L. (2006), 'Toward the implementation of mental health consumer provider services', *The Journal of Behavioral Health Services and Research*, 33(2):176–95.

Clarke, R.E. (1994), 'Family Costs Associated With Severe Mental Illness and Substance Use', *Hospital and Community Psychiatry*, 45:808–13.

Conwell, Y. (2001), 'Suicide in Later Life: A Review and Recommendations for Prevention', *Suicide and Life-Threatening Behaviour*, 31:32–47.

Corcoran, P., Arensman, E., O'Mahony, D. (2006), 'Research Trends: Suicide and Other External-Cause Mortality Statistics in Ireland: A Comparison of Registration and Occurrence Data', *Crisis*, 27:130–4.

Corcoran, P., Keeley, H.S., O'Sullivan, M., Perry, I.J. (2004), 'The incidence and repetition of attempted suicide in Ireland', *European Journal of Public Health*, 10:19–23.

Corrigan, D. (2003), *Facts About Drug Misuse in Ireland* (4th edn, Dublin: Health Promotion Unit).

COSC: The National Office for the Prevention of Domestic, Sexual and Gender-based Violence (2013), 'Male Victims of Domestic Violence', COSC, http://www.cosc.ie/en/COSC/Pages/WP09000005.

Costigan, L. (1998), *Bullying and Harassment in the Workplace* (Dublin: Columba Press).

Crosby, A.E., Han B., Ortega, L.A.G., Parks, S.E., Gfoerer, J. (2011), 'Suicidal thoughts and behaviours among adults aged ≥ 18 years – United States, 2008–2009', *Surveillance Summaries*, 60(13):1–22.

Crosby A.E., Sacks J.J. (2002), 'Exposure to suicide: Incidence and association with suicidal ideation and behaviour: United States, 1994', *Suicide and Life-Threatening Behaviour*, 32:321–8.

CSO (Central Statistics Office) (2012), Dublin.

CSO (Central Statistics Office) (2013a), *Births, Deaths and Marriages in 2012* (Dublin: Central Statistics Office).

CSO (Central Statistics Office) (2013b), *Statistical Yearbook of Ireland, Education for 2011/2012* (Dublin: Central Statistics Office).

CSO (Central Statistics Office) (2014), *Suicide Statistics 2011* (Dublin: Central Statistics Office).

Curtis, A. (2012), 'Mass Media Influence on Society', University of North Carolina at Pembroke, http://www.uncp.edu/home/acurtis/Courses/ResourcesForCourses/Media&Society/MassMediaInfluenceOnSociety.html, accessed 21 November 2014.

Cvinar, J. (2005), 'Do Suicide Survivors Suffer Social Stigma: A Review of the Literature', *Perspectives in Psychiatric Care*, 41:14–21.

Daly, M., Oswald, A., Wilson, D., Wu, S., (2011), 'Dark Contrasts: The Paradox of high Rates of Suicide in Happy Places', *Journal of Economic Behaviour and Organization*, 80(3):435–42:10.1016/j.jebo.2011.04.007.

Dearing, J.W., Rogers, E.M. (1996), *Agenda Setting* (CA: Thousand Oaks).

Demo, D.H., and Savin-Williams, R.C. (1992), 'Self-concept stability and change during adolescence', in R.P. Lipka, and T.M. Brinthaupt (eds), *Self-Perspectives Across the Lifespan* (New York: State University of New York Press), 116–48.

Denollet, J. (1998), 'Personality and risk of Cancer in men with Coronary Heart Disease', *Psychological Medicine*, 28:991–5.

Department of Education and Skills, the Health Service Executive and the Department of Health (2013), *Well-Being in Post Primary Schools: Guidelines for Mental Health Promotion and Suicide Prevention* (Dublin: Department of Education and Skills, the Health Service Executive and the Department of Health).

Department of Education and Skills (2014), '31 March 2014 – Minister Quinn announces €60,000 funding for anti-bullying training for parents: Funding will support the implementation of the Action Plan on Bullying', Department of Education and Skills, https://www.education.ie/en/Press-Events/Press-Releases/2014-Press-Releases/PR14-03-31.html, accessed on 2 September 2014.

Department of Health (1997), 'Major Risk Factors Contributing to Suicide', *Suicide Prevention Task Force Report 1997* (Victoria, Australia: Department of Health).

Department of Health (2013), *Healthy Ireland: A Framework for Improved Health and Wellbeing 2013–2025* (Dublin: Department of Health).

Department of Health and Children (1998), *Report of the National Task Force on Suicide* (Dublin: Department of Health).

Department of Health and Children (2005), *Reach Out: National Strategy for Action on Suicide Prevention 2005–2014* (Dublin: Department of Health).

Department of Justice, Equality and Law Reform (2000), *Review of the Coroner Service* (Dublin: Department of Justice, Equality and Law Reform).

Dervic, K., Oquendo, M.A., Grunebaum, M.F., Ellis, S., Burje, A.K. and Mann, J.J. (2004), 'Religious Affiliation and Suicide Attempt', *The American Journal of Psychiatry*, 161(12):2303–8.

Desjarlais, R., Eisenberg, L., Good, B., Kleinman, A. (eds) (1995), *World Mental Health: Problems and Priorities in Low-Income Countries* (Oxford: Oxford University Press).

Djernes, J.K. (2006), 'Prevalence and Predictors of Depression in Populations of Elderly: A Review', *Acta Psychiatr Scand*, 113(5):372–87.

Doctor X (2007), *The Bitter Pill: An Insider's Shocking Expose of the Irish Health System* (Dublin: Hodder Headline).

Dohnt, H., Tiggerman, M. (2005), 'The Contribution of Peer and Media Influences to the Development of Body Satisfaction and Self-Esteem in Young Girls: A Prospective Study', *Developmental Psychology*, 42(5):929–36.

Dooley, B., Fitzgerald, A. (2012), *My World Survey: National Study of Youth Mental Health in Ireland* (Dublin: Headstrong).

Downey, L.A., Johnston, P.J., Hansen, K., Schembri, R., Stough, C., Tuckwell, V. (2008), 'The relationship between emotional intelligence and depression in a clinical sample', *The European Journal of Psychiatry*, 22:93–8.

Doyle, A. (2014), *'Violence at home costs $8 trillion a year worse than war – Study'*, Reuters, http://in.reuters.com/article/2014/09/09/abuse-costs-domesticviolence-idINKBN0H419V20140909, accessed 10 September 2014.

Duignan, R. (2013), *Saving 10,000: Winning a War on Suicide in Japan* [film documentary], released 6 March 2013.

Dulfer, N. (2012), 'Testing the test: NAPLAN makes for stressed kids and a narrow curriculum', The Conversation (25 November 2012), https://theconversation.com/testing-the-test-naplan-makes-for-stressed-kids-and-a-narrow-curriculum-1096 5, accessed 2 September 2014.

Dunne-Maxim, K. (2007), *Survivor History Panel: Past, Present and What's Ahead*, paper presented at 19th Annual Healing After Suicide Conference, New Orleans, LA.

(EMCDDA) European Monitoring Centre for Drugs and Drug Addiction (2012), *Annual report on the state of the drugs problem in Europe* (Lisbon: EMCDDA).

Employment Equality Acts (1998–2011) (Dublin: Government Publications).

Employment Equality Bill (1998), (Dublin: Government Publications).

Erikson, E.H., Klein, G.S., Rapaport, D. (1994) [1967], *Identity and the Life Cycle* (New York: W.W. Norton and Co.).

European Agency for Safety and Health at Work (EU-OSHA) (2010), *The European Survey of Enterprises on New and Emerging Risks* (ESENER).

European Child Safety Alliance (2014), *What are European Countries Doing to Prevent Intentional Injury to Children: National Action to Address Child Intentional Injury* (Birmingham, UK: European Child Safety Alliance).

European Commission (2011), *The State of Men's Health in Europe: Extended Report* (European Union).

Evans, G., Farberow, N., Kennedy Associates (2003), *The Encyclopaedia of Suicide* (New York: Facts on File).

Extremera, N., Berrocal, P.F. (2006), 'Emotional intelligence as predictor of mental, social, and physical health in university students', *The Spanish Journal of Psychology*, 9:45–51.

Fallon, J. (2014), 'GAA has role to play in suicide crisis', *The Irish Examiner* (7 July 2014).

Firestone, R. (2009), 'Emotional Hunger vs. Love', *Psychology Today* (24 February 2009).

Fisher, H. (2004), *Why We Love: The Nature and Chemistry of Romantic Love* (New York: Holt).

Flanzer, J.P. (1993), 'Alcohol and other drugs are key causal agents of violence', in R.J. Gelles, D.R. Loseke (eds), *Current Controversies on Family Violence* (Newbury Park, CA: Sage), 171–81.

Foster, L.T., Keller, C.P. (2007), *The British Columbia Atlas of Wellness*, Canadian Western Geographical Series, vol. 42 (Victoria, Canada: Western Geographical Press).

Frankel, B., Kranz, R. (1994), *Straight Talk About Teenage Suicide* (New York: Facts on File).

Frost, L., Heinz, T., Bach, D.H. (2011), 'Promoting Recovery-Oriented Mental Health Services through a Peer Specialist Employer Learning Community', *Journal of Participatory Medicine*, 3:e22.

Fowler, K.A., Gladden, R.M., Vagi, K.J., Barnes, J., and Frazier, L., 'Increase in Suicides Associated With Home Eviction and Foreclosure During the US Housing Crisis: Findings From 16 National Violent Death Reporting System States, 2005–2010', *American Journal of Public Health*, 105(2):311–16: 10.2105/AJPH.2014.301945.

Gardner, H. (2011) [1983], *Frames of Mind: The Theory of Multiple Intelligences* (New York: Basic Books).

Gardner, S., Rosenberg, G. (1985), *Teenage Suicide* (New York: J. Messner).

Gilligan, J. (1997), *Violence: Reflections on a National Epidemic* (New York: Vintage Books).

Giroux, H.A. (2012), 'The "Suicidal State" and the War on Youth', *Truth Out* (10 April 2012).

Glasser, W. (1985), *Control Theory: A New Explanation of How We Control Our Lives* (New York: Harper & Row).

Glover, H. (2012), 'Recovery, Life Long Learning, Social Inclusion and Empowerment: Is a New Paradigm Emerging?', in P. Ryan, S. Ramon, T. Greacen, *Empowerment, Lifelong Learning and Recovery in Mental Health: Towards a New Paradigm* (Hants: Palgrave Publishers).

Goetzel, R., Anderson, D., Whitmer, W., Ozminkowsky, R., Dunn, R., Wasserman, J. (1998), 'The Relationship between modifiable health risks and health care expenditures: An Analysis of the Multi-Employer, HERO Health Risk and Cost Database', *Journal of Occupational and Environmental Medicine*, 40:843–54.

Goffman, E. (1968), *Stigma: Notes on the Management of Spoiled Identity* (Harmondsworth: Penguin).

Gonsiorek, J. (1993), 'Mental health Issues of Gay and Lesbian Adolescents', in L. Garnets, D. Kimmel (eds), *Psychological Perspectives on Lesbian and Gay male Experiences* (New York: Columbia University Press), 469–85.

Graycar, R. (1998), 'The Gender of Judgments: Some Reflections on Bias', *University of British Columbia Law Review*, 32:1–21.

Greer, S., Watson, M. (1985), 'Towards a Psychobiological Model of Cancer: Psychological Considerations', *Social Science and Medicine*, 20:773–7.

Griffith, G. (2005), *Will's Choice: A Suicidal Teen, a Desperate Mother, and a Chronicle of Recovery* (New York: Harper Collins).

Grollman, E.A., Malikow, M. (1999), *Living When a Young Friend Commits Suicide* (Boston: Beacon Press).

Gross, L. (1989), 'Out Of: Sexual Minorities and the Mass Media', in Ellen Seiter et al (eds), *Remote Control: Television, Audiences and Cultural Power* (London: Routledge).

Grossman, K.E., Grossman, E. (1990), 'The Wider Concept of Attachment in Cross-Cultural Research', *Human Development*, 33:31–47.

Growing Up in Ireland, *Growing Up in Ireland: The Lives of Nine Year Olds* (2011) http://www.growingup.ie/fileadmin/user_upload/document s/1st_Report/Barcode_Growing_Up_in_Ireland_- _The_Lives_of_9-Year-Olds_Main_Report.pdf, accessed 2 September 2014.

Guglielmi, M.C. (2008), *The Impact of Stigma on the Grief Process of Suicide Survivors* (Ann Arbor, MI: Pro Quest).

Hales, D. (2005), *An Invitation to Health for the Twenty-First Century* (Belmont, CA: Thomson & Wadsworth).

Halton Suicide Prevention Coalition, 'Addressing Stigma', Halton Suicide Prevention Coalition, http://www.suicidepreventionhalton.ca/suicidefacts/stigma1. php, accessed 2 September 2014.

Harris, E.C., Barraclough, B. (1997), 'Suicide as an outcome for mental disorders. A meta-analysis', *The British Journal of Psychiatry*, 170:205–28.

Harter, S. (1986), 'Cognitive-developmental processes in the integration of concepts about emotions and the self', *Social Cognition*, 4:119–51.

Harvard Business Review (2012).

Hawker, S.S.J, Boulton, M.J. (2000), 'Twenty years' research on peer victimisation and psychological maladjustment: A meta-analysis review of cross-sectional studies', *Journal of Child Psychology and Psychiatry*, 41(4):441–5.

Hawton, K., Haw, C. (2013), 'Economic Recession and Suicide', *British Medical Journal*, 347:f5612.

Hawton, K., Van Heeringen (2000), *The International Handbook of Suicide and Attempted Suicide* (New York: John Wiley).

Headstrong (2012), *My World Survey: National Study of Youth Mental Health in Ireland* (Dublin: UCD School of Psychology, and Headstrong: The National Centre for youth Mental health).

Health and Safety Authority (HSA) (1997), *Workplace Stress: Cause, Effects, Control* (Dublin: Health and Safety Authority).

Health and Safety Authority (HSA) (2007), *Code of Practice for Employers and Employees on the Prevention and Resolution of Bullying at Work*, Health and Safety Authority (HSE), http://www.hsa.ie/eng/Publications_and_Forms/Publications /Occupational_Health/Code_of_Practice_for_Employers_and_ Employees_on_the_Prevention_and_Resolution_of_Bullying_at _Work.html, accessed on 17 August 2014.

Health Service Executive (HSE) (2007), *Mental Health in Ireland: Awareness and Attitudes*, Health Services Executive (HSE) (2014), http://www.hse.ie/eng/services/news/newsarchive/2014arc hive/feb14/nospplans2014.html, accessed 2 September 2014.

Healy, A. (2012), 'People "with no religion" on the rise', *The Irish Times* (18 October 2012).

Healy, T. (2013), *Banks, Governments and Citizens* (NERI: Nevin Economic Research Institute: Research for New Economic Policies).

Heatherton, T.F., Baumeister, R.F. (1991), 'Binge Eating as Escape from Self-Awareness', *Psychological Bulletin*, 110:86–108.

Heckman, J. (2006), *The Economics of Investing in Children* (Dublin: UCD Geary Institute, Policy Briefing No.1).

Heller, T.S., Hawgood, J.L., Leo, D.D. (2007), 'Correlates of suicide in building industry workers', *Archives of Suicide Research*, 11(1):105–17.

Helliwell, J., Layard, R., Sachs, J. (2012), *World Happiness Report* (New York: The Earth Institute, Columbia University).

Hendin, H., Vijayuakumar and L, Bertolote J.M. (2008),'Epidemiology of suicide in Asia', *Suicide and Suicide Prevention in Asia* (Geneva, Switzerland: World Health Organization), 7–18.

Hebert, M., Rosenheck, R., Drebing, C., Young, A.S., Armstrong, M. (2008), 'Integrating peer support initiatives in a large healthcare organization', *Psychological Service*, 5(3):216–27.

Hoerr, S., Bokram, R., Lugo, B., et al (2002), 'Risk for Disordered Eating Relates to both Gender and Ethnicity for College Students', *Journal of the American College of Nutrition*, 21(4):307–14.

Hope, A. (2008), *Alcohol Related Harm in Ireland* (HSE, Alcohol Implementation Group).

Holt, G. (2011), 'When suicide was illegal', BBC News Magazine (3 August 2011), http://www.bbc.co.uk/news/magazine-14374296.

Horrocks, J., (2002), 'Self-poisoning and self-injury in adults', *Clinical Medicine*, 2(6):509–12, cited in Samaritans Information Sheet, *Self-harm and Suicide*, March 2005 (England).

Hull, J.G. (1981), 'A Self-Awareness Model of the causes and Effects of Alcohol Consumption', *Journal of Abnormal Psychology*, 90:586–600.

Humphreys, J. (2013), 'Suicide rate in prisons declines: Health professionals say reductions in overcrowding over the past 18 months has helped', *The Irish Times* (16 September 2013).

Hungerford, C., Fox, C. (2013), 'Consumer's perceptions of Recovery-oriented mental health services: An Australian case-study analysis', *Nursing & Health Sciences*, 16(2):209–15.

Hurley, S., Chater, N. (2005), *Perspective on Imitation: From Neuroscience to Social Science* (Cambridge, Massachusetts: MIT Press).

International Association of Suicide Prevention, http://www.iasp.info.

Irish Association of Suicidology, and The Samaritans (2009), *Media Guidelines for Reporting Suicides and Self-Harm* (Ireland: Irish Association of Suicidology, and The Samaritans).

Irish Business and Employers' Confederation (IBEC) (2011), *Employee Absenteeism: A Guide to Managing Absence* (Dublin: Irish Business and Employers' Confederation (IBEC)).

Irish Human Rights Commission (2010), *Assessment of the Human Rights Issues Arising in relation to the 'Magdalen Laundries'*, Irish Human Rights and Equality Commission (November 2010), http://www.ihrec.ie/download/pdf/ihrc_assessment_of_the_ human_rights_issues_arising_in_relation_to_the_magdalen_lau ndries_nov_2010.pdf, accessed 2 September 2014.

Irish Society for the Prevention of Cruelty to Children (ISPCC), (2011), *This will come back and bite us in the butt; Children and the Internet, National Children's Consultation Report*, http://www.ispcc.ie/uploads/files/dir4/12_0.php, accessed 2 September 2014.

Iyengar, S., Kinder, D. R. (1987), *News that Matters* (Chicago: University of Chicago Press).

Jacobsen, N., Curtis, L. (2000), 'Recovery as a Model in mental Health Services, Strategies emerging from the States', *Psychiatric Rehabilitation Journal*, 23(4):333–41.

Jehoel-Gijsbers, G., Vrooman, C. (2007), *Exploring Social Exclusion: A Theoretical Model Tested in the Netherlands* (The Hague: The Netherlands Institute for Social Research/SCP).

Johnsson-Fridell, E., Ojehagen, A., Traskman-Bendz, L. (1996), 'A 5-year follow-up study of suicide attempts', *Acta Psychiatr Scand*, 93:151–7.

Joiner, T. (2005), *Why People Die by Suicide* (Cambridge, MA: Harvard University Press).

Jorgensen, R.S., Johnson, B.T., Kolodziej, M.E., Schreer, G.E. (1996), 'Elevated Blood Pressure and Personality: A Meta-Analytic Review', *Psychological Bulletin*, 120:293–320.

Kaltiala-Heino, R., Rimpela, M., Marttunen, M., Rimpela, A., Rantanen, P. (1999), 'Bullying, depression, and suicidal ideation in Finnish adolescents: school survey', *British Medical Journal*, 319:348–51.

Keane, M. (2006), 'Homelessness and drug misuse: a continuing challenge for service providers', *Drugnet Ireland*, 18:8–9.

Keane, M. (2013), 'Young people appeal for a more inclusive society', *Drugnet Ireland*, 46:12–13.

Kemp, D.K., (2007), *Mental Health in America: A Reference Handbook* (Santa Barbara, CA: ABC Clio).

Kendall, R.E. (1983), 'Alcohol and suicide', *Substance & Alcohol Actions/Misuse*, 4:121–7.

Kennelly, B. (2007), 'The Economic Cost of Suicide in Ireland', *Crisis: The Journal of Crisis Intervention and Suicide Prevention*, 28(2):89–94.

Kessler, R.C., Borges, G., Walters, E.E. (1999), 'Prevalence of and risk factors for lifetime suicide attempts in the National Comorbidity Survey', *Archives of General Psychiatry*, 56:617–26.

Kielwasser, A.P., Wolf, M.A. (1992), 'Mainstream television, adolescent homosexuality, and significant silence', *Critical Studies in Mass Communication*, 9(4):350–73.

King, R.A., Schwab-Stone, M., Flisher, A.J., Greenwald, S., Kramer, R.A., Goodman, S.H., Lahey, B.B., Shaffer, D., Gould, M. (2001), 'Psychosocial and Risk Behaviour Correlates of Youth Suicide Attempts and Suicidal Ideation', *Journal of the American Academy of Child & Adolescent Psychiatry*, 40(7):837–46.

Kolb, D.A. (1984), *Experiential Learning* (Prentice-Hall, NJ: Englewood Cliffs).

Lampert, S. (2012), 'San Francisco Jews seek to remove religious stigma from suicide', *Haaretz* (12 August 2012).

Lickerman, A. (2010), 'The Six Reasons People Attempt Suicide: Suicide is far more understandable than people think', *Happiness in this World* (29 April 2010).

Liebling, A. (2001), 'Suicide in Prison: Ten Years on', *Prison Service Journal*, 138:35–41.

Liebling, A. (2007), 'Prison Suicide and its Prevention', Y. Jewkes (ed.), *Handbook on Prisons* (Cullompton: Willan), 423–46.

Liebmann, M. (2007), *Restorative Justice: How It Works* (London: Jessica Kingsley Publishers).

Long, J., Mongan, D. (2013), *Alcohol Consumption in Ireland, 2013: Analysis of a National Alcohol Diary Survey* (Dublin: Health Research Board).

Mahony, K.E. (1993), 'International Strategies to Implement Equality Rights for Women: Overcoming Gender Bias in the Courts', *Australian Feminist Law Journal* (Victoria, Australia: La Trobe University), 115.

Malone, K.M, Quinlivan, L., Grant, T. and Keller, C.C. (2012), 'Ageing towards 21 as a risk factor for Young Adult Suicide in the UK and Ireland', *Epidemiology and Psychiatric Sciences*, 22(3):263–7.

Malone, K.M. (2013), *Suicide in Ireland Report, 2003–2008* (Department of Psychiatry, Psychotherapy & Mental Health Research St. Vincent's University Hospital, and School of Medicine & Medical Science University College Dublin).

Martin, J. (2013), 'The Pope's Bold New Vision', CNN Belief Blog (26 November 2013) http://religion.blogs.cnn.com/2013/11/26/the-popes-bold-new-vision/, accessed 6 November 2014.

Maslow, A.H. (1943), 'A Theory of Human Motivation', *Psychological Review*, 50(4):370–96.

McCabe, S. (2014), 'Irish were bullied and treated outrageously during crisis – Legrain', *The Irish Independent*, 7 May 2014.

McCarthy, J. (2009), 'Abuse Report: A Catalogue of Horror', 20 May 2009, http://www.irishhealth.com/article.html?id=15548, accessed 31 August 2014.

McCombs, M., and Reynolds, A. (2002), 'News Influence on our Pictures of the World', J. Bryant and D. Zillman (eds), *Media*

Effects: Advances in Theory and Research (2nd edn, Mahwah, NJ: Lawrence Erlbaum), 1–18.

McCoy, S., Smyth, E., Watson. D., Darmody, M. (2014), *Leaving School in Ireland: A Longitudinal Study of Post-School Transitions*, ESRI Research Series, No. 36 (Dublin: The Economic and Social Research Institute (ESRI)).

McDougall, P., Vaillancourt, T., Hymel, S. (2009), 'What happens over time to those who bully and those who are victimized?' in S. Hymel and S. Swearer (eds), *Bullying at School and Online* [Special edition of Education.com].

McGee, R., Williams, S., Nada-Raja, S. (2001), 'Low Self-Esteem and Hopelessness in Childhood and Suicidal Ideation in Early Adulthood', *Journal of Abnormal Child Psychology*, 29(4):281–91.

McGoldrick, M. (1996), 'Irish Families in America', *The Aisling Magazine* (Issue 19), http://www.aislingmagazine.com/aislingmagazine/articles/TAM19/Irish%20families.html.

McGoldrick, M. (2005), 'Irish Families', in M. McGoldrick, J. Giordano, Garcia-Preto (eds), *Ethnicity and Family Therapy* (New York: The Guildford Press).

McGregor, D. (1960), *The Human Side of Enterprise* (New York: McGraw Hill).

McHolm, A.E., MacMillan, H.L., Jamieson, E. (2003), 'The Relationship between Childhood Physical Abuse and Suicidality among Depressed Women: Results from a

Community Sample', *American Journal of Psychiatry*, 160(5):933–8.

McIntosh, J.L. (1993), *U.S.A. Suicide: 1990 Official Final Data* (Denver, CO: American Association of Suicidology).

McKinsey and Company (2009), *Management Matters in Northern Ireland and the Republic of Ireland*, InterTradeIreland, http://www.intertradeireland.com/media/intertradeirelandco m/researchandstatistics/publications/tradeandbusinessdevelo pment/ManagementmattersinNorthernIrelandandRepublicofIr eland.pdf.

Meltzoff, A.N., Prinz, W. (2002), *The Imitative Mind: Development, Evolution and Brain Bases* (Cambridge, MA: Cambridge University Press).

Menick, D.M. (2000), 'Les contours psychosociaux de l'in-fanticide en Afrique noire: le cas du Sénegal' ['The psychosocial features of infanticide in black Africa: the case of Senegal'], *Child Abuse & Neglect*, 24:1557–65.

Mental Health Commission (2005), *A Vision for a Recovery Model in Irish Mental Health Services: Discussion Paper* (Dublin).

Mental Health Commission (2013), *Implementation of a Vision for Change is Slow and Inconsistent Across the Country* (23 January 2013) (Dublin).

Mental Health Foundation, http://www.mentalhealth.org.uk/help-information/mental-health-a-z/R/recovery/, accessed 4 August 2014.

Mental Health Reform, http://www.mentalhealthreform.ie/, accessed 4 August 2014.

Mental Health Reform (2013), *Recovery … What you should expect from a good quality mental health service* (Ireland).

Muldoon, M. (2011), 'Pressure on Irish government to increase suicide prevention budget: Mounting pressure over suicide issue', Irish Central (22 March), http://www.irishcentral.com/news/pressure-on-irish-government-to-increase-suicide-prevention-budget-118422179-237377601.html, accessed 2 September 2014.

Nagel, I.H., Hagan, J.L. (1982), 'The Sentencing of White-Collar Criminals in Federal Courts: A Socio-Legal Exploration of Disparity', *Michigan Law Review,* 80(7), Articles on Corporate and Organizational Crime (June 1982), 1427–65.

Namie, G., Christensen, D., Phillips, D. (2014), *U.S. Workplace Bullying Survey* (Bellingham, WA: Workplace Bullying Institute (WBI)).

National Debt Clocks, http://www.nationaldebtclocks.org/debtclock/ireland, accessed 14 June 2015.

National Institute for Occupational Safety and Health (NIOSH) (2008), *Exposure to Stress, Occupational Hazards in Hospitals* (Cincinnati, OH: Department of Health and Human Services).

National Institute for Occupational Safety and Health (NIOSH) (2012), *Health Concerns for Flight Attendants* (Cincinnati, OH: Department of Health and Human Services).

National Suicide Research Foundation (NSRF) (2013), 'Executive Summary', *National Registry of Deliberate Self-harm Ireland: Annual Report* (Cork: National Suicide Research Foundation).

National Union of Journalists (NUJ), *Code of Conduct*, http://www.nuj.org.uk/about/nuj-code/, accessed on 31 July 2014.

Naughton, G. (2015), 'Woman took her life on day she was due to be evicted', *The Irish Times*, 7 January 2015.

Nelson, R.E., Galas, J.C. (1994), *The Power to Prevent Suicide: A Guide for Teens Helping Teens* (Minneapolis: Free Spirit Publishing).

Norman, M. (2011) 'Embodying the Double-Bind of Masculinity: Young Men and Discourses of Normalcy, Health, Heterosexuality, and Individualism', *Men and Masculinities* 14(4):430–49.

O'Brien, C. (2012), 'Funds for suicide prevention diverted', *The Irish Times*, 29 December 2012.

O'Callaghan, Miriam, interview with Terence Casey, Coroner for Kerry South and East, *The John Murray Show*, RTÉ Radio 1 (5 May 2013), http://www.rte.ie/radio/utils/radioplayer/rteradioweb.html#!rii=9%3A10144917%3A4502%3A07%2D05%2D2013%3A.

Ó Cionnaith, F. (2013), 'Real suicide rate higher than official data: Charity', *The Irish Examiner*, 10 September 2013.

Oireachtas Library and Research Services (2012), *Spotlight: Well-Being: Promoting Mental Health in Schools*, 2 (Dublin).

O'Keefe, E. (2012), 'Congress votes to strike "lunatic" from federal laws', *The Washington Post*, 6 December 2012.

Olweus, D. (1978), *Aggression in the Schools: Bullies and Whipping Boys* (Washington DC: Hemisphere Publishing Corp).

Olweus, D. (1993a), *Bullying at School: What We Know and What We Can Do* (Oxford, UK: Blackwell).

Olweus, D., Limber, S., Mihalic, S. (1999), 'Bullying prevention program', D.S. Elliott (series ed.), *Fight Crime: Invest in Kids, Blueprints for violence prevention: Book Nine* (CO: Center for the Study and Prevention of Violence Boulder).

O'Moore, M., Stevens, P. (eds) (2013), *Bullying in Irish Education* (Cork: Cork University Press).

O'Neill, S., Corry, C. (2013), *Unique Characteristics of Suicide: Analysis of the Northern Ireland Suicide Database (2004–2011)* (Irish Association of Suicidology; Mental Health Sciences, University of Ulster; and Bamford Centre for Mental Health and Wellbeing).

Organisation for Economic Co-operation and Development (OECD) (2012), 'Health at a Glance: Europe 2012', OECD iLibrary, http://www.oecd-ilibrary.org/sites/9789264183896-en/01/07/index.html;jsessionid=97t37ei8gnkj.x-oecd-live-02?contentType=&itemId=/content/chapter/9789264183896-10-en&containerItemId=/content/serial/23056088&accessItemIds

=/content/book/9789264183896-en&mimeType=text/html, accessed 2 September 2014.

Organisation for Economic Co-operation and Development (OECD) (2013), 'Suicides', *Health: Key Tables from OECD*, No. 17.

O'Riordan, S. (2014), 'Recession Directly to Blame for up to 560 Suicides', *The Irish Examiner*, 7 March 2014.

Osgood, N.I., Brandt, B.A. (1988), *Suicidal Behaviour in Long-Term Care Facilities*, paper presented at the annual meeting of the American Association of Suicidology, Washington DC, 16 April 1988.

O'Sullivan, M., Rainsford, M., Sihera, N. (2011), *Suicide Prevention in the Community: A Practical Guide* (Ireland: Health Service Executive).

Orbach, S. (1993), *Hunger Strike* (London: Penguin).

Owens, D., Horrocks, J., House, A. (2002), 'Fatal and non-fatal repetition of self-harm: Systematic review', *British Journal of Psychiatry*, 181(3):193–9.

Patel, V., Araya, R., de Lima, M., Ludermir, A., Todd, C. (1999), 'Women, Poverty and Common Mental Disorders in Four Reconstructuring Societies', *Social Science and Medicine*, 49:1461–71.

Pestieau, P. (2006), *The Welfare State in the European Union: Economic and Social Perspectives* (New York: Oxford University Press).

Phelan, C., Link, B.G. (1998), 'The Growing belief that people with mental illness are violent: The role of the dangerousness criterion for civil commitment', *Psychiatry and Psychiatric Epidemiology*, 33:7–12.

Phillips, D. (1980), 'Airplane Accidents, Murder, and the Mass Media: Towards a Theory of Imitation and Suggestion', *Social Forces*, 58(4):1001–24.

Phillips, D., Lesyna, K., Paight, D.J. (1992), 'Suicides and the Media', in R.W. Maris, A.L. Berman, J.T. Maltsberger et al (eds), *Assessment and Prediction of Suicide* (New York: The Guildford Press), 499–519.

Phipps, W.E. (1985), 'Christian Perspectives on Suicide', *The Christian Century*, 30 October 1985, 970–2.

Pirkis, J., Blood, W., Beautrais, A., Burgess, P., Skehan, J. (2006), 'Media Guidelines on the Reporting of Suicide', *The Journal of Crisis Intervention and Suicide Prevention*, 27(2).

Polce-Lynch, M., Myers, B.J., Kilmartin, C.T., Forssmann-Falck, R., Kliewer, W. (1998), 'Gender and Age Patterns in Emotional Expression, Body Image, and Self-esteem: A Qualitative Analysis', *Sex Roles: A Journal of Research*, 38(11–12):1025–48.

Pompili, M., Mancinelli, I., Tatarelli, R. (2003), 'Stigma as a cause of Suicide', *The British Journal of Psychiatry*, 183:173–4: 10.1192/bjp.183.2.173-a.

Porter, S., Brinke, L., Gustaw, C. (2010), 'Dangerous decisions: the impact of first impressions of trustworthiness on the evaluation of legal evidence and defendant culpability', *Psychology, Crime & Law*, 16(6).

Press Association, 'Spanish couple in eviction suicide', 12 February 2013.

Princeton Survey Research Associates (1997), *Labour Day Survey: State of Workers* (Princeton, NJ: Princeton Survey Research Associates).

Prior, M. (ed.) (2010), *Asylums, Mental health Care and the Irish 1800–2010* (Dublin: The Irish Academic Press).

Ramstedt, M., Hope, A. (2003), *The Irish Drinking Culture: Drinking and Drinking-related Harm: A European Comparison* (Health Promotion Unit).

Reed, M. (1998), 'Predicting grief symptomatology among the suddenly bereaved', *Suicide and Life-Threatening Behaviour*, 28(3):285–300.

Reinherz, B.Z., Stewart-Berghauer, G., Pakiz, B., Frost, A.K., Moeykens, B.A., Holmes, W.M. (1989), 'The Relationship of early risk and current mediators to depressive symptomatology in adolescence', *American Academy of Childhood and Adolescent Psychiatry*, 28:942–7.

Ring, E. (2013), '62% of staff bullied or intimidated but "too scared to report"', *The Irish Examiner*, 20 June 2013.

Robertson, J.F., Simons, R.L. (1989), 'Family Factors, Self-esteem and Adolescent Depression', *Journal of Marriage and Family*, 51:125–8.

Rochefort, D.A. (1997), *From Poorhouses to Homelessness: Policy Analysis and Mental Health Care* (2nd edn, Westport, CT: Auburn House).

Roffman, A. (2010), *Gay, Lesbian and Bisexual Teens: Facing Challenges and Building Resilience* (NYU Child Study Center).

Rosen, M. (2012), *Dignity: Its History and Meaning* (Cambridge, MA: Harvard University Press).

Rosenberg, M. (1965), *Society and the Adolescent Self-Image* (Princeton, NJ: Princeton University Press).

Roy, A. (2003), 'Characteristics of drug addicts who attempt suicide', *Psychiatry Research*, 121:99–103.

SafeHorizon, 'Child Abuse Facts', SafeHorizon, http://www.safehorizon.org/page/child-abuse-facts-56.html, accessed 4 September 2014.

Safety, Health, and Welfare at Work (General Application) Regulations, 2007 (Dublin, Government Publications).

Salize, H.J., Hrebing, H., Peitz, M. (2002), *Compulsory Admission and Involuntary Treatment of Mentally Ill Patients: Legislation and Practice in EU-Member States* (Mannheim: European Commission).

Salmivalli, C., Kaukiainen, A., Kaistaniemi, L., Lagerspetz, K.M. (1999), 'Self-evaluated self-esteem, peer-evaluated self-esteem, and defensive egotism as predictors of adolescents' participation in bullying situations', *Personality and Social Psychology Bulletin*, 5:1268–78.

Salvatore, T. (2011), 'An Elder Suicide Primer: An Introduction to a Late Life Tragedy', Lifegard, http://lifegard.tripod.com/elder.html, 2 September 2014.

Saunders, W. (1995), 'Suicide: Gravity and Responsibility', *The Arlington Catholic Herald*, 6 July 1995.

Scheff, T. (2011), 'Emotions and Depression: Finding and Facing Intense Emotions', *Psychology Today*, 15 July 2011.

See Change Campaign, cited in Substance Abuse and Mental health Services Administration and Mental Health Services (SAMHSA), 2004.

Seguin, M.L. (1995a), 'Parental Bereavement after Suicide and Accident: A Comparative Study', *Suicide and Life-Threatening Behaviour*, 25(4):489–98.

Shields, S. (1987), 'The Media's impact on body image: Implications for prevention and treatment', *Eating Disorders: The Journal of Treatment and Prevention*, 3:115–23.

Siegel, B. (2002), 'Foreword', *How I Stayed Alive When My Brain Was Trying To Kill Me* (New York: William Morrow).

Silins, E., Horwood, L.J., Patton, G.C., Fergusson, D.M, Olsson, C.A., Hutchinson, D.M. (2014), 'Young adult sequelae of adolescent cannabis use: an integrative analysis', *The Lancet Psychiatry*, 1(4):286–93.

Sipe, A.W.R. (2004), *Living the Celibate Life: A Search for Models and Ministry* (Liguori, MI: Liguori Publications).

Skehan, P. (1989), *Individual Differences in Second-Language Learning* (London: Edward Arnold).

Skehan, P. (1994), 'Differenze Individuali e Autonomia di Apprendimento', Mariani L. (ed.), *L'Autonomia nell'Apprendimento Linguistico* (Firenze: La Nuova Italia/Quaderni del lend).

Slee, P.T. (1995), 'Bullying in the playground: the impact of inter-personal violence on Australian children's perceptions of their play environment', *Children's Environments*, 12(3):320–7.

Smolak, L., Stein, J.A. (2006), 'The Relationship of Drive for Muscularity to Sociocultural Factors, Self-esteem, Physical Attributes, Gender role, and Social Comparison in Middle School Boys', *Body Image*, 3:121–9.

Sorenson, S. (2007), 'Adolescent Romantic Relationships', *ACT Research Facts and Findings* (New York: Cornell University, University of Rochester, the New York State for School Safety, and Cornell Cooperative Extension of New York City).

Springer, S.H. (2012), 'Falling in Love is Like Smoking Crack Cocaine', Psychology Today (4 August 2012), https://www.psychologytoday.com/blog/the-joint-adventures-well-educated-couples/201208/falling-in-love-is-smoking-crack-cocaine.

Suls, J. (1989), 'Self-awareness and self-identity in adolescence', Worell, J., Danner, F. (eds), *The Adolescent Decision-Maker* (New York: Academic Press).

Suto, I., Arnaut, G.L.Y. (2010), 'Suicide in Prison: A Qualitative Study', *The Prison Journal*, 90(3):288–312.

Suzuki, L., Calzo, J.P. (2004), 'The Search for peer advice in Cyberspace: An examination of online teen bulletin boards about health and sexuality', *Applied Developmental Psychology*, 25:685–98.

Sweeney, L.T., Haney, C. (2006), 'The influence of race on sentencing: A meta-analytic review of experimental studies', *Behavioural Sciences and the Law*, 10(2):179–95.

Teicher, M.H. (2000), 'Wounds that won't heal: The neurobiology of child abuse', *Cerebrum*, 2(4):50–62.

Teicher, M.H. (2002), 'Scars that won't heal: The neurobiology of child abuse', *Scientific American*, 286(3):68–75.

Teicher, M.H., Andersen, S.L., Polcari, A., Anderson, C.M., Navalta, C.P. (2002), 'Developmental neurobiology of childhood stress and trauma', *The Psychiatric Clinics of North America*, 25(2):397–426.

Teicher, M.H., Samson, J.A., Polcari, A., McGreenery, C.E. (2006), 'Sticks, stones, and hurtful words: Relative effects of various forms of childhood maltreatment', *American Journal of Psychiatry*, 163(6):993–1000.

The American Institute of Stress (2002), *Newsletter*.

The Irish Association of Suicidology, 'Lifting the Stigma Associated with Suicide Championed by Local People', The Irish

Association of Suicidology, http://archive-ie.com/page/25780/2012-05-28/http://www.ias.ie/index.php?option=com_content&view=article&id=76%3Alifting-the-stigma-associated-with-suicide-championed-by-local-people&catid=2%3Anews&Itemid=25, accessed 2 September 2014.

The Irish Examiner (2013), 'Suicide Prevention Guidelines Announced for Schools', *The Irish Examiner*, 31 January 2013.

The Irish Examiner (2013), 'Third Suicide at School', 8 October 2013.

Murphy, Cormac (2013), 'Revealed: How the Government Plans to Tackle Alcohol Abuse', 24 October 2013.

The Irish Independent (2014), 'Children to learn "mindfulness"', 25 August 2014.

The Management Development Council (2010), *Management Development in Ireland: The Report of the Management Development Committee* (Dublin).

The National Archives, 'Education', The National Archives of Ireland, http://www.census.nationalarchives.ie/exhibition/dublin/education.html, accessed 2 September 2014.

The Pew Forum (2010), *Report 1: Religious Affiliation* (Washington DC)

Thomas, A., Pemberton. A. (2011), *Qualitative Research into Enhanced Jobseeker's Allowance Provision for +50*, Research Report no. 766, Department of Work and Pensions, United Kingdom.

Thomas, K., Gunnell, D. (2010), 'Suicide in England and Wales 1861–2007: a time-trends analysis', *International Journal of Epidemiology* (2010), doi:10.1093/ije/dyq094.

TNS Opinion & Social (2010), *EU Citizens' Attitudes Towards Alcohol*, Special Eurobarometer 331 (Brussels: European Commission).

Tolle, E. (1999), *The Power of Now: A Guide to Spiritual Enlightenment* (CA: New World Library).

Tsaousis, I., Nikolaou, I. (2005), 'Exploring the relationship of emotional intelligence with physical and psychological health functioning', *Stress Health*, 21:77–86.

Tucker, M.L, Sojka, J.Z. Barone, F.J., McCarthy, A.M. (2000), 'Training Tomorrow's Leaders: Enhancing the Emotional Intelligence of Business Graduates', *Journal of Education for Business*, 76(6):331–7.

Turner, F.J. (ed.) (1992), *Mental Health and the Elderly: A Social Work Perspective* (New York: The Free Press).

U.S. Bureau of Labour Statistics (2009), 'Suicides by Selected Occupations 2007–2008', *Census of Fatal Occupational Injuries and Occupational Suicides* (US Department of Labour, BLS).

Vijayakumar, Lakshmi (ed.) (2003), *Suicide Prevention: Meeting the Challenge Together* (Bangalore: Orient Longman).

Vock, R., et al (1999), 'Lethal child abuse through the use of physical force in the German Democratic Republic (1 January

1985 to 2 October 1990): results of a multicentre study', *Archiv für Kriminologie*, 204:75–87.

Walker, M.R. (2008), *Suicide Among the Irish Traveller Community 2000–2006* (Wicklow: Wicklow County Council).

Walsh, B.M., Walsh, D. (2011), 'Suicide in Ireland: the Influence of Alcohol and Unemployment', *Economic and Social Review*, 42(1):27–47

Wasserman, I.M. (1984), 'Imitation and Suicide: A Re-examination of the Werther effect', *American Sociological Review*, 52:401–12.

Watson, D., Parsons, S. (2005), *Domestic Abuse of Women and Men in Ireland: Report on the National Study of Domestic Abuse* (National Crime Council and the Economic and Social Research Institute).

Wilcox, H.C., Conner, K.R., Caine, E.D. (2004), 'Association of alcohol and drug use disorders and completed suicide: an empirical review of cohort studies', *Drug Alcohol Dependence*, 6 (suppl.), S11–S19.

Winnicott, D. (1964), *The Child, the Family and the Outside World* (Penguin Psychology).

Wolf, N. (1991), *The Beauty Myth* (London: Vintage).

Women's Aid (2012), *Women's Aid Annual Report, 2012*, http://www.womensaid.ie/download/pdf/womens_aid_annual_report_2012.pdf.

Women's Aid Website, www.womensaid.ie.

World Health Organisation (WHO) (2001a), *The World Health Report 2001: Mental Health: New Understanding, New Hope* (Geneva: World Health Organisation).

World Health Organisation (WHO) (2002), *World Health Organisation Facts: Child Abuse and Neglect* (Geneva: World Health Organisation).

World Health Organisation (WHO) (2003), *Mental Health in the WHO, European Region Fact Sheet Euro/03/03* (Geneva: World Health Organisation).

World Health Organisation (WHO) (2004), *Global Status Report on Alcohol* (Geneva: World Health Organisation).

World Health Organisation (WHO) (2014), *Global status report on alcohol and health 2014* (Geneva: World Health Organisation).

World Values Survey, Stockholm, Sweden, 2000.

Wyatt, D.A. (2002), *Gay/lesbian/bisexual television characters*, University of Manitoba, http://home.cc.umanitoba.ca/~wyatt/tv-characters.html, accessed 2 September 2014.

Wylie, C., Platt, S., Brownlie, J., Chandler, A., Connolly, S., Evans, R., Kennelly, B., Kirtley, O., Moore, G., O'Connor R., Scourfield, J. (2012), *Men, Suicide and Society: Why Disadvantaged Men in Mid-Life Die by Suicide* (United Kingdom: The Samaritans).

Wynne, R., Clarkin, N., Cox, T. (1995), *Guidance on the prevention of violence at work: Draft Report* (Work Research Centre).

Zechmeister, I., Kilian, R., McDaid, D. (2008), *Is it worth investing in mental health promotion and prevention of mental illness? A systematic review of the evidence from economic evaluations* (BMC Public Health).

Zehr, H. (2005), *Changing Lanes: A New Focus for Crime and Justice* (Scottsdale, PA: Herald Press).

A Vision for Change (2006), *Report of the Expert Group on Mental Health Policy* (Dublin: The Stationery Office).

Bunreacht Na hÉireann (The Irish Constitution), 1937.

Catechism of the Catholic Church (1993) (Vatican City: Libreria Editrice Vaticana).

Defamation Act (2009) (Dublin: Government Publications).

Prohibition of Incitement to hatred Act (1989), Government Publications, Dublin, Ireland.